Survival

GLOBAL POLITICS AND STRATEGY

Volume 63 Number 6 | December 2021–January 2022

T0333684

'Published excerpts from cables sent by US State Department officials after a visit to the Wuhan Institute of Virology suggested that there were safety problems at the laboratory. However, those cables were much less inflammatory when read in full than the published selections made them appear.'

Gigi Kwik Gronvall, The Contested Origin of SARS-CoV-2, p. 21.

'The US is at the centre of a complex web of security arrangements with some 70 states. By contrast, Russia and China are relatively friendless, with a few client states that are themselves quite weak. They have no one to work with on broad foreign-policy issues except each other.'

Lawrence Freedman, The Crisis of Liberalism and the Western Alliance, p. 41.

'Trust, especially among allies, is therefore paramount. The AUKUS affair may have the saving virtue of reminding us of the volatile and fragile nature of that quality, hard to build and easy to lose.'

François Heisbourg, Euro-Atlantic Security and the China Nexus, p. 58.

Survival

GLOBAL POLITICS AND STRATEGY

Volume 63 Number 6 | December 2021–January 2022

Contents

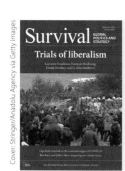

On the cover
Migrants who had
been encouraged by
Minsk to try to cross
the Belarus–Poland
border are held back
by Polish authorities
in November 2021.

On the web
Visit www.iiss.org/
publications/survival
for brief notices
on new books on
Counter-terrorism and
Intelligence, the United
States and Europe.

Survival **editors' blog**
For ideas and
commentary from
Survival editors and
contributors, visit
www.iiss.org/blogs/
survival-blog.

Cover: Stringer/Anadolu Agency via Getty Images

Survival

GLOBAL POLITICS AND STRATEGY

The International Institute for Strategic Studies

2121 K Street, NW | Suite 600 | Washington DC 20037 | USA
Tel +1 202 659 1490   Fax +1 202 659 1499   E-mail survival@iiss.org   Web www.iiss.org

Arundel House | 6 Temple Place | London | WC2R 2PG | UK
Tel +44 (0)20 7379 7676   Fax +44 (0)20 7836 3108   E-mail iiss@iiss.org

14th Floor, GBCorp Tower | Bahrain Financial Harbour | Manama | Kingdom of Bahrain
Tel +973 1718 1155   Fax +973 1710 0155   E-mail iiss-middleeast@iiss.org

9 Raffles Place | #49-01 Republic Plaza | Singapore 048619
Tel +65 6499 0055   Fax +65 6499 0059   E-mail iiss-asia@iiss.org

Pariser Platz 6A | 10117 Berlin | Germany
Tel +49 30 311 99 300   E-mail iiss-europe@iiss.org

Survival Online www.tandfonline.com/survival and www.iiss.org/publications/survival

Aims and Scope *Survival* is one of the world's leading forums for analysis and debate of international and strategic affairs. Shaped by its editors to be both timely and forward thinking, the journal encourages writers to challenge conventional wisdom and bring fresh, often controversial, perspectives to bear on the strategic issues of the moment. With a diverse range of authors, *Survival* aims to be scholarly in depth while vivid, well written and policy-relevant in approach. Through commentary, analytical articles, case studies, forums, review essays, reviews and letters to the editor, the journal promotes lively, critical debate on issues of international politics and strategy.

Editor **Dana Allin**
Managing Editor **Jonathan Stevenson**
Associate Editor **Carolyn West**
Assistant Editor **Jessica Watson**
Production and Cartography **Kelly Verity**

Contributing Editors

Målfrid Braut-Hegghammer	**Russell Crandall**	**Melissa K. Griffith**	**Jeffrey Mazo**	**Ray Takeyh**
Ian Bremmer	**Toby Dodge**	**John L. Harper**	**Teresita C. Schaffer**	**David C. Unger**
Rosa Brooks	**Bill Emmott**	**Matthew Harries**	**Steven Simon**	**Lanxin Xiang**
David P. Calleo	**Mark Fitzpatrick**	**Erik Jones**	**Karen Smith**	
	John A. Gans, Jr	**Hanns W. Maull**	**Angela Stent**	

Published for the IISS by
Routledge Journals, an imprint of Taylor & Francis, an Informa business.

Copyright © 2021 The International Institute for Strategic Studies. All rights reserved. No part of this publication may be reproduced, stored, transmitted or disseminated, in any form, or by any means, without prior written permission from Taylor & Francis, to whom all requests to reproduce copyright material should be directed, in writing.

About the IISS The IISS, a registered charity with offices in Washington, London, Manama, Singapore and Berlin, is the world's leading authority on political–military conflict. It is the primary independent source of accurate, objective information on international strategic issues. Publications include *The Military Balance*, an annual reference work on each nation's defence capabilities; *Strategic Survey*, an annual review of world affairs; *Survival*, a bimonthly journal on international affairs; *Strategic Comments*, an online analysis of topical issues in international affairs; and the *Adelphi* series of books on issues of international security.

Director-General and Chief Executive
John Chipman

Chair of the Trustees
Bill Emmott

Chair of the Council
Chung Min Lee

Trustees
Caroline Atkinson
Chris Jones
Kurt Lauk
Catherine Roe
Grace R. Skaugen
Matt Symonds
Matthew Symonds
Jens Tholstrup

IISS Advisory Council
Joanne de Asis
Caroline Atkinson
Shobhana Bhartia
Linden P. Blue
Garvin Brown
Alejandro Santo Domingo
Thomas Enders
Michael Fullilove
Yoichi Funabashi
Charles Guthrie
Alia Hatoug-Bouran
Badr Jafar
Bilahari Kausikan

Thomas Lembong
Eric Li
Peter Maurer
Moeletsi Mbeki
Charles Powell
George Robertson
Andrés Rozental
Mark Sedwill
Grace R. Skaugen
Debra Soon
Heizo Takenaka
Marcus Wallenberg
Amos Yadlin

SUBMISSIONS

To submit an article, authors are advised to follow these guidelines:

- *Survival* articles are around 4,000–10,000 words long including endnotes. A word count should be included with a draft.
- All text, including endnotes, should be double-spaced with wide margins.
- Any tables or artwork should be supplied in separate files, ideally not embedded in the document or linked to text around it.
- All *Survival* articles are expected to include endnote references. These should be complete and include first and last names of authors, titles of articles (even from newspapers), place of publication, publisher, exact publication dates, volume and issue number (if from a journal) and page numbers. Web sources should include complete URLs and DOIs if available.
- A summary of up to 150 words should be included with the article. The summary should state the main argument clearly and concisely, not simply say what the article is about.
- A short author's biography of one or two lines should also be included. This information will appear at the foot of the first page of the article.

Please note that *Survival* has a strict policy of listing multiple authors in alphabetical order.

Submissions should be made by email, in Microsoft Word format, to survival@iiss.org. Alternatively, hard copies may be sent to *Survival*, IISS–US, 2121 K Street NW, Suite 801, Washington, DC 20037, USA.

The editorial review process can take up to three months. *Survival*'s acceptance rate for unsolicited manuscripts is less than 20%. *Survival* does not normally provide referees' comments in the event of rejection. Authors are permitted to submit simultaneously elsewhere so long as this is consistent with the policy of the other publication and the Editors of *Survival* are informed of the dual submission.

Readers are encouraged to comment on articles from the previous issue. Letters should be concise, no longer than 750 words and relate directly to the argument or points made in the original article.

ADVERTISING AND PERMISSIONS

For advertising rates and schedules

USA/Canada: The Advertising Manager, Taylor & Francis Inc., 530 Walnut Street, Suite 850, Philadelphia, PA 19106, USA Tel +1 (800) 354 1420 Fax +1 (215) 207 0050.

UK/Europe/Rest of World: The Advertising Manager, Routledge Journals, Taylor & Francis, 4 Park Square, Milton Park, Abingdon, Oxfordshire OX14 4RN, UK Tel +44 (0) 207 017 6000 Fax +44 (0) 207 017 6336.

SUBSCRIPTIONS

Survival is published bimonthly in February, April, June, August, October and December by Routledge Journals, an imprint of Taylor & Francis, an Informa Business.

Annual Subscription 2021

	UK, RoI	US, Canada Mexico	Europe	Rest of world
Individual	£172	$290	€ 233	$290
Institution (print and online)	£620	$1,085	€ 909	$1,142
Institution (online only)	£527	$922	€ 773	$971

Taylor & Francis has a flexible approach to subscriptions, enabling us to match individual libraries' requirements. This journal is available via a traditional institutional subscription (either print with online access, or online only at a discount) or as part of our libraries, subject collections or archives. For more information on our sales packages please visit http://www.tandfonline.com/page/librarians.

All current institutional subscriptions include online access for any number of concurrent users across a local area network to the currently available backfile and articles posted online ahead of publication.

Subscriptions purchased at the personal rate are strictly for personal, non-commercial use only. The reselling of personal subscriptions is prohibited. Personal subscriptions must be purchased with a personal cheque or credit card. Proof of personal status may be requested.

Dollar rates apply to all subscribers outside Europe. Euro rates apply to all subscribers in Europe, except the UK and the Republic of Ireland where the pound sterling rate applies. If you are unsure which rate applies to you please contact Customer Services in the UK. All subscriptions are payable in advance and all rates include postage. Journals are sent by air to the USA, Canada, Mexico, India, Japan and Australasia. Subscriptions are entered on an annual basis, i.e. January to December. Payment may be made by sterling cheque, dollar cheque, euro cheque, international money order, National Giro or credit cards (Amex, Visa and Mastercard).

Survival (USPS 013095) is published bimonthly (in Feb, Apr, Jun, Aug, Oct and Dec) by Routledge Journals, Taylor & Francis, 4 Park Square, Milton Park, Abingdon, OX14 4RN, United Kingdom.

The US annual subscription price is $1,085. Airfreight and mailing in the USA by agent named WN Shipping USA, 156-15, 146th Avenue, 2nd Floor, Jamaica, NY 11434, USA. Periodicals postage paid at Jamaica NY 11431.

US Postmaster: Send address changes to Survival, C/O Air Business Ltd / 156-15 146th Avenue, Jamaica, New York, NY11434.

Subscription records are maintained at Taylor & Francis Group, 4 Park Square, Milton Park, Abingdon, OX14 4RN, United Kingdom.

ORDERING INFORMATION

Please contact your local Customer Service Department to take out a subscription to the Journal: **USA, Canada:** Taylor & Francis, Inc., 530 Walnut Street, Suite 850, Philadelphia, PA 19106, USA. Tel: +1 800 354 1420; Fax: +1 215 207 0050. **UK/ Europe/Rest of World:** T&F Customer Services, Informa UK Ltd, Sheepen Place, Colchester, Essex, CO3 3LP, United Kingdom. Tel: +44 (0) 20 7017 5544; Fax: +44 (0) 20 7017 5198; Email: subscriptions@tandf.co.uk.

Back issues: Taylor & Francis retains a two-year back issue stock of journals. Older volumes are held by our official stockists: Periodicals Service Company, 351 Fairview Ave., Suite 300, Hudson, New York 12534, USA to whom all orders and enquiries should be addressed. *Tel* +1 518 537 4700 *Fax* +1 518 537 5899 *e-mail* psc@periodicals.com *web* http://www.periodicals.com/tandf.html.

The International Institute for Strategic Studies (IISS) and our publisher Taylor & Francis make every effort to ensure the accuracy of all the information (the "Content") contained in our publications. However, the IISS and our publisher Taylor & Francis, our agents, and our licensors make no representations or warranties whatsoever as to the accuracy, completeness, or suitability for any purpose of the Content. Any opinions and views expressed in this publication are the opinions and views of the authors, and are not the views of or endorsed by the IISS and our publisher Taylor & Francis. The accuracy of the Content should not be relied upon and should be independently verified with primary sources of information. The IISS and our publisher Taylor & Francis shall not be liable for any losses, actions, claims, proceedings, demands, costs, expenses, damages, and other liabilities whatsoever or howsoever caused arising directly or indirectly in connection with, in relation to or arising out of the use of the Content. Terms & Conditions of access and use can be found at http://www.tandfonline.com/page/terms-and-conditions.

The issue date is December 2021–January 2022.

The print edition of this journal is printed on ANSI-conforming acid-free paper.

THE ADELPHI SERIES

ASIA'S NEW GEOPOLITICS

Military Power and Regional Order

Desmond Ball, Lucie Béraud-Sudreau, Tim Huxley,
C. Raja Mohan and Brendan Taylor

available at

amazon

OR

Routledge
Taylor & Francis Group

Adelphi 478–480; published
September 2021; 234x156; 236 pp;
Paperback: 978-1-032-18736-5

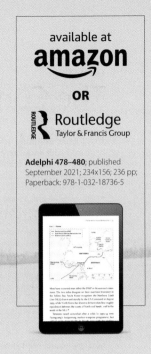

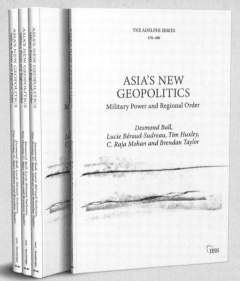

Intensifying geopolitical rivalries, rising defence spending and the proliferation of the latest military technology across Asia suggest that the region is set for a prolonged period of strategic contestation. None of the three competing visions for the future of Asian order – a US-led 'Free and Open Indo-Pacific', a Chinese-centred order or the ASEAN-inspired 'Indo-Pacific Outlook' – is likely to prevail in the short to medium term. In the absence of a new framework, the risk of open conflict is heightened, and along with it the need for effective mechanisms to maintain peace and stability.

As Asia's leaders seek to rebuild their economies and societies in the wake of COVID-19, they would do well to reflect upon the lessons offered by the pandemic and their applicability in the strategic realm. The societies that have navigated the crisis most effectively have been able to do so by putting in place stringent protective measures. Crisis-management and -avoidance mechanisms – and even, in the longer term, wider arms control – can be seen as the strategic equivalent of such measures, and as such they should be pursued with urgency in Asia to reduce the risks of an even greater calamity.

'Asia is one of the world's most complex regions and one whose impact is increasingly felt globally. No one can claim to understand geopolitics anywhere without some understanding of Asian geopolitics. This is an invaluable, clear and comprehensive guide to the past, present and possible futures of Asian geopolitics.'

Bilahari Kausikan, former permanent secretary of Singapore's Ministry of Foreign Affairs

IISS THE INTERNATIONAL INSTITUTE FOR STRATEGIC STUDIES   www.iiss.org/publications/adelphi

The Contested Origin of SARS-CoV-2

Gigi Kwik Gronvall

The COVID-19 pandemic is the worst pandemic in a century. The early response to the disease was inept and slow, particularly in the United States, which has suffered more deaths so far than any other country despite rapidly developed and deployed vaccines. It is not unusual for public-health authorities to be challenged when making decisions affecting lives and livelihoods – the job is inherently political. During the COVID-19 pandemic, however, public-health experts have been stymied by poor political leadership, institutional failures and geopolitically tinged decision-making that has often run counter to emerging science. There has also been a highly politicised, and thereby distorting, debate about how it all began. This politicisation is harmful because the question is important. Figuring out how the SARS-CoV-2 virus made its way from 'patient zero' to a chain of infections to a pandemic is the first step towards making sure that it does not happen again – or, if it does, that the world is better prepared to intervene before so many lives are lost.

Even in the best of circumstances, the search for the origin of an infectious-disease outbreak can be complicated, slow and full of uncertainties. It is more typical than not for a disease origin to not be conclusively determined, as in the cases of Ebola (which likely emerged from a virus circulating in

Gigi Kwik Gronvall, an immunologist by training, is a Senior Scholar at the Johns Hopkins Center for Health Security and an Associate Professor in the Department of Environmental Health and Engineering at the Johns Hopkins Bloomberg School of Public Health. She is the author of *Synthetic Biology: Safety, Security, and Promise* (Health Security Press, 2016).

Survival | vol. 63 no. 6 | December 2021–January 2022 | pp. 7–36   https://doi.org/10.1080/00396338.2021.2006442

bats), HIV/AIDS (which probably came from a virus circulating among non-human primates) and most years' influenzas (now known to originate in birds and pigs). Yet the scientific tools available for determining the origin of an outbreak are more powerful now than they were before. Single-base genetic changes in a virus can be detected, and chains of infection – who got what from whom – can be precisely determined provided samples are collected at the appropriate time. Information about the earliest cases of disease and transmission can be plentiful, even if the record remains incomplete.

The issue of the origin of SARS-CoV-2 has been controversial and attracted hyperbolic speculation. Theories abound. They include a natural pathway; a laboratory accident with a naturally harvested strain; a laboratory accident with a naturally harvested strain that has been modified in the laboratory; and a biological weapon. To lend calmness and clarity to the debate, this essay will attempt to delineate the relevant questions about the origin of the coronavirus, describe remaining gaps in knowledge and recommend what should be done next to address uncertainties about its origin, and to make all possible contributing causes of a pandemic less likely to produce one in the future.

A diplomatic search

A cluster of cases of pneumonia of unknown cause in Wuhan, China, was reported to the World Health Organization (WHO) on 31 December 2019. They were determined to be caused by a virus that was later named SARS-CoV-2.[1] The virus was likely circulating for some weeks earlier, triggering COVID-19 disease around mid-November.[2] As cases spread around the globe, the origin of SARS-CoV-2 – and blame for both the virus and how public health was managed – became a matter of rumours, misinformation and disinformation. A WHO investigation into its origins made some progress but is now at a standstill.

The WHO started the search after a World Health Assembly resolution in May 2020. By July, terms of reference for the study had been negotiated with China. Following online meetings, an on-the-ground investigation in Wuhan – the epicentre of the earliest known cases of COVID-19 – began on 14 January and ended on 10 February 2021. The investigative team comprised 17 Chinese experts and 17 experts from other countries, as well as medical professionals from international organisations including the WHO, the Global Outbreak Alert and Response Network and the World Organisation for Animal Health.

The team's work was intended to be an initial phase-one study. It resulted in a 120-page technical report that set forth what was known about the early epidemiology findings, test results for the virus at the animal markets with which initial cases were associated and possible subjects of future investigation, including stored blood samples, farmed animals that may have been present in the markets and samples taken from bats.[3] The report explored and evaluated four possible origins of SARS-CoV-2 and the team rated their likelihood based on the available evidence. A direct 'zoonotic spillover' – that is, a direct infection from a bat to a human – was considered possible to likely. Introduction of the virus through an intermediate animal, such as a raccoon dog or pangolin, was considered likely to very likely. Introduction through cold food-chain products such as whole, frozen and unprocessed animals was considered possible, as such types of infections had been documented before. Finally, the possibility that SARS-CoV-2 originated from a laboratory incident was considered 'extremely unlikely'.

Media preoccupation with the laboratory-accident possibility obscured the technical details of the WHO report. Critics claimed that the WHO team had too easily dismissed that possibility. Charges also arose of conflicts of interest among the members of the WHO team that discouraged serious consideration of the possibility.[4]

There had been speculation that a laboratory accident could be the source of SARS-CoV-2 since the beginning of the epidemic, some lodged in op-eds published in respectable media sources such as the *Washington Post*, the *Wall Street Journal* and the *Bulletin of the Atomic Scientists*. But it was an open letter signed by 17 well-known and respected scientists, including coronavirus researchers, to *Science*, a prestigious scientific journal, that gave the accidental-origin theory genuine weight. The letter stated that 'greater clarity about the origins of this pandemic is necessary and feasible to achieve' and called for 'dispassionate science-based discourse' to illuminate the issues, adding that 'a proper investigation should be transparent, objective, data-driven, inclusive of broad expertise, subject to independent oversight, and responsibly managed to minimize the impact of conflicts of interest'. The scientists called for open records from Chinese public-health agencies and research laboratories.[5]

Shortly after the letter was published in May 2021, US President Joe Biden ordered a 90-day review of the intelligence that supported either a natural or accidental origin. The review was inconclusive.[6] On 16 July, WHO Director-General Tedros Adhanom discussed a plan to resume an investigation into the origin of SARS-CoV-2, which included a variety of animal sampling and geographic studies, but also audits of 'relevant laboratories and research institutions operating in the area of the initial human cases identified in December 2019'.[7]

The Chinese government rejected the terms of the WHO follow-on investigation into the 'laboratory-leak theory', and there was no follow-on investigation to support any origin theory planned at the time this article was published.[8] The WHO has formed a new expert group, the Scientific Advisory Group for the Origins of Novel Pathogens (SAGO), which will advise on future disease-origin technical considerations, as well as provide guidance on next steps in understanding SARS-CoV-2 origins.[9]

Evidence for the origins

The natural emergence of a virus like SARS-CoV-2 is not without precedent. In 2002, at the same time of year that the COVID-19 pandemic began, the virus that causes severe acute respiratory syndrome (SARS) started spreading, producing infections for months before Chinese authorities finally alerted the WHO. It was soon determined that many of the people who worked in animal markets had gotten ill from SARS; that the virus was widespread in palm civets, a furry, cat-like creature sold for meat; and that the coronavirus that infected civets jumped to people. The virus originally came from horseshoe bats, though that wasn't conclusively determined until 2017.[10]

Such zoonotic events, in which animal diseases jump to people, have been estimated to be responsible for 75% of emerging diseases, including Nipah, Hendra, Zika and Ebola.[11] Zoonoses like these are also becoming more common, as people encroach on wildlife populations by pushing them out of their natural habitats, living closer to wildlife areas and eating wild animals – activities that provide more opportunities for viruses to spill over from animals to people. Bats are a frequent source of these viruses, likely because there are so many of them, they have a great deal of genetic diversity (comprising about 22% of all named mammalian species) and they often do not get sick when carrying viruses that can infect other animals.[12]

There are parallels between the emergence of SARS and that of SARS-CoV-2. Like SARS, the initial cases were associated with food markets. One Huanan market was associated with two out of the three earliest cases, and 28% of all cases in December 2019. Other markets appeared to have a connection to disease as well, as half the COVID-19 cases in December were associated with some market. In the districts hosting markets, people died at higher levels than in a typical year.[13]

Unlike with SARS, however, there were no opportunities to sample the markets to look for animals infected with SARS-CoV-2. Chinese authorities closed and cleared out the markets soon after the epidemic started, citing public-health concerns, and banned all wildlife trade on 26 January 2020. Eating and trading wild animals were permanently banned in February 2020. Samples at the market to test for SARS-CoV-2 were not taken until months later. The virus was found in the drains of the market, but there were no live animals to test. The WHO investigation report noted that

> market authorities have confirmed that all reported live and frozen animals sold in the Huanan market were from farms that were legally licensed for breeding and quarantine, and that no illegal trade in wildlife has been found. Although there is photographic evidence in a published paper that live mammals were sold at the Huanan market in the past (2014) … and unverified media reports in 2020, no verified reports of live mammals being sold around 2019 were found.[14]

The market authorities' assertion that there was no illegal activity in their markets – which would have been very profitable – was dubious. Although it was more difficult to refute after the animals were removed, evidence did arise of illegally held animals at the market, and the information given to the WHO investigation team about which animals were present in the market was proven to be inaccurate. A fortuitously timed study looking for animal carriers of tick-borne severe fever with thrombocytopenia syndrome (SFTS) documented many animals that were not supposed to be at the market and were not reported to the WHO, including 31 protected species sold between May 2017 and November 2019 in Wuhan's markets. Raccoon dogs, marmots, civets, mink, Siberian badgers and many other furry mammals that could have served as intermediate hosts for the SARS-CoV-2 virus were openly, illegally and profitably sold in the market. The wild and farmed animals were documented to be in poor health, and crowded together in their cages.[15] Raccoon dogs have been experimentally infected with SARS-CoV-2.[16] There have been outbreaks in mink that have then passed to people, demonstrating the possibility of an animal link for the disease.[17] SARS-CoV-2 is also classified as a 'generalist' virus in the sense that it is able to infect many types of animals.[18] An intermediate-animal origin for the virus could have been present in the markets, but as no samples were taken immediately, a conclusive determination may never be made about the role that animals in the markets played in sparking the pandemic.

The sale of wild animals without permits in China carries severe penalties involving steep fines and imprisonment. The tick study that documented the sale of illegal animals in the Huanan market observed, however, that the sellers were not too concerned about law enforcement, and that plainly illegal animals were openly sold. It is unclear whether any of the animal traders engaged in illegal wildlife commerce have been since found, fined or punished. The swift clear-out of the market may have been intended to protect them as well as the law-enforcement officers and local politicians who had looked the other way. But even though a great deal of information was thus lost, the fact that samples that were positive for SARS-CoV-2 were found in the gutters in the market area where the contraband animals were butchered reinforced the possibility of an animal-market SARS-CoV-2 link.[19]

The fact that the genetic sequence of the virus from the earliest known cases was not identical constitutes additional scientific evidence for a natural emergence. The viral samples taken from the cases associated with the markets had already genetically diverged into two lineages – A and B – and it was the B lineage that went on to spread around the globe. One explanation for this genetic diversity is that an ongoing outbreak of the disease in animals had multiple spillover events to people. While there were two markets in Wuhan associated with cases of COVID-19, they probably had similar animal supply chains, so a group of diseased animals from the same source could have been present at multiple markets, causing infections in other animals and susceptible humans.

An obvious next step in the investigation would be to sample animals from the farms that supplied the markets as well as the animal distributors, but this is perhaps not achievable: many months have passed since the outbreak started; and if the animal sales were illegal to begin with and the suppliers managed to escape punishment, those suppliers are unlikely to come forward now. Furthermore, the fact that SARS and SARS-CoV-2 started at about the same time of year suggests seasonality with respect to the coronavirus infections in animals, which would also hinder the hunt for the origin.

Even so, there is more that science can do to shed light on a potential natural origin. Bat populations could be sampled for similar viruses. If China is not interested in conducting or facilitating such studies, perhaps authorities in Indonesia and Cambodia, which also have the bat colonies, could be persuaded to do so. Close relatives of SARS-CoV-2 have also been identified in bats in Laos.[20] Blood banks that stored samples of blood from November and December 2019 could be examined for earlier, perhaps asymptomatic cases. This could provide information about locations of infections and about the genetic sequence of the virus. Testing routinely collected historical samples was one of the recommendations the WHO investigation team made, and this was planned for a second visit of the WHO team.

The non-natural-origin hypothesis

When the SARS-CoV-2 virus was first genetically sequenced, there were some features that alarmed some scientists, and the possibility that SARS-CoV-2 might have originated in a laboratory was considered.[21] One feature that seemed to support this hypothesis was the 'furin cleavage site', which allows the virus to enter the cells it infects. Another was the relative proportion of some ribonucleic acid (RNA) base pairs in the SARS-CoV-2 virus, which seemed atypical. By April 2020, however, a letter in *Nature Medicine* indicated that multiple coronaviruses had similar features, and that the virus in question was clearly 'not a laboratory construct or a purposefully manipulated virus'.[22] In the months since, there has been ample additional scientific support for the non-atypical nature of the virus's genetics.[23] The genetics of SARS-CoV-2 only seemed unusual because of the limited information about comparators known at the time.

Another factor that makes it difficult to support a non-natural virus theory is the serious limitations on the ability to predict function from genetic sequence. For example, current computational analysis would predict that SARS-CoV-2 would not bind to its host cellular target well, but there is empirical evidence to the contrary.[24] Introducing complex traits such as pathogenicity or transmissibility into a virus is generally not feasible except in very limited and well-characterised systems.

Pathogenicity is challenging to manipulate

Even for influenza viruses, which are far better studied than the coronavirus family that includes SARS-CoV-2, pathogenicity and transmissibility are still only partially understood and challenging to manipulate. While it may be established that a particular influenza sequence is likely to infect humans based on some genetic features, how pathogenic or transmissible a particular virus is in a whole organism, or how bad a pandemic would be if it were able to spread from person to person, is not easily predictable. These fundamental gaps in knowledge are why the 2018 National Academies of Sciences, Engineering, and Medicine report, *Biodefense in an Age of Synthetic Biology*, did not rank the novel design of viruses as one of the top biological-weapons threats: any novel pathogen design would require a daunting degree of research, development and testing to be successful. Instead, the committee identified the top biosecurity threats as those pathogens which can now be made from scratch in a laboratory and which have a known pathogenicity and transmissibility profile – for example, smallpox virus.[25] It is well known what the genetic programme of that virus could do to humans, so a booted-up version of 'known code' would be predictably devastating.

Designing a novel virus to be pathogenic and transmissible may be beyond current scientific capabilities. However, it is possible to use the natural process of viral evolution to select a virus that could become more transmissible in a particular animal, or replicate in cells taken from an animal. Typically, this kind of serial passage from one organism to cells in another results in attenuation in the original host. The yellow-fever vaccine was made in this manner, through serial passage in chicken and mouse cells in the 1930s.[26] There has been speculation in the press and from lawmakers about whether, instead of intentional virus design, the processes of serial passage of the virus from one animal to another, or so-called 'gain-of-function' experiments, could have produced the SARS-CoV-2 virus. There has also been speculation about whether such research was being performed in the Wuhan Institute of Virology, based upon the fact that US National Institutes of Health funding was awarded to the non-profit EcoHealth Alliance to work with the Wuhan Institute to examine the host range and emergence potential of viruses using 'reverse genetics, pseudovirus and receptor binding assays, and virus infection experiments across a range of cell cultures from different species and humanized mice'.[27] In such a theoretical scenario, a laboratory-created virus could have been developed and released either accidentally through an infected laboratory worker or deliberately. However, there is little support based on available information that such a thing occurred for SARS-CoV-2.

'Gain of function' is a term coined during policy debates about two scientific papers focused on the transmissibility of the H5N1 (avian) strain of influenza, in research ultimately published in 2012.[28] Reducing the number of variables that affect whether a function is gained or lost is part of the process for how scientists determine which individual genes, proteins or other biological components function in an organism. Originally, the term 'gain of function' was not focused on a host's acquisition of all functions of a virus, but rather on its acquisition of two especially important functions: transmissibility and pathogenicity.

In one of the most controversial H5N1 influenza experiments, ferrets were deliberately infected with a modified strain that had some mutations known to confer transmissibility in mammals. Through the passage of the virus from ferret to ferret, changes eventually evolved in the influenza virus that made transmission from ferret to ferret possible without deliberate intervention. This demonstrated that H5N1 was capable of evolving transmissibility between mammals, and that there were specific genetic mutations associated with that capability. H5N1 does not currently transmit between mammals but has a high mortality rate (about 60%) when humans contract H5N1 from an infected animal. Because the sequences associated with transmissibility in the laboratory have all been found in influenza strains in the wild, but not all together in one strain, this type of research signalled that H5N1 was an emergent threat and provided early warning of potentially dangerous strains that could be subject to public-health surveillance.

Gain-of-function research does have limitations. Genetic changes in a virus produced by selective pressure can lead to functional changes in transmissibility, as the gain-of-function H5N1 influenza research demonstrated. But the original strain for that research was genetically close to the strain that developed increased transmissibility. SARS-CoV-2 is not genetically close to any known laboratory sample of coronaviruses. Gain-of-function research would not be able to create SARS-CoV-2 from any known starting point. The fact that SARS-CoV-2 could not infect mice and rats, two commonly used laboratory animal models, also cuts against the virus having been handled in a laboratory setting.[29] If there are additional strains much closer to SARS-CoV-2 than those identified so far that were manipulated in Wuhan laboratories, the possibility of laboratory involvement in the origin of the COVID-19 pandemic could be considered.

The virus RaTG13, which is 96.2% identical to SARS-CoV-2 and has received considerable attention in the search for the latter's origin, was the subject of research at the Wuhan Institute of Virology.[30] While 96.2% identity seems very close in lay terms, the genetic distance between RaTG13 and SARS-CoV-2 is in fact much greater than that number suggests. The 3.8% dissimilarity is not one continuous chunk of genetic material that could be added in one piece, like a paragraph into a document. Instead, that 3.8% dissimilarity is sprinkled throughout the genome. As coronaviruses are relatively large, a 3.8% difference amounts to more than a thousand base-pair differences. Furthermore, many of those differences are 'silent' – that is, they do not involve alteration of the amino acids assembled using those genetic instructions to make proteins, which means that the mutations required a very long evolution.[31] To start with RaTG13 and end up with SARS-CoV-2 through gain of function or serial passage would require many years, possibly decades, of work, and more animals than a laboratory could assemble. Nature has a much bigger laboratory.

The accident hypothesis

Another possibility for the origin of the COVID-19 pandemic is that the SARS-CoV-2 virus was being studied in a laboratory where an accident occurred, causing a laboratory worker (or workers) to become infected. Based on available evidence, such an event is unlikely to have been the root cause of the COVID-19 pandemic. Relevant history tends to reinforce this conclusion. Accidents, of course, do happen. But when laboratory accidents have happened, they have typically affected only the laboratory worker and occasionally close contacts. Though it is theoretically possible, no prior epidemic or pandemic has originated in a bioresearch laboratory.

Some incidents have been mischaracterised in the media as lab-sourced outbreaks. The first is the 1977 flu, also called the 'Russian flu'. The seasonal flu that year was not an ordinary, predictable event because it was nearly identical to a strain that had not been circulating since the 1950s. Available evidence points to a massive vaccination campaign with a live and poorly attenuated vaccine involving thousands of people in China and possibly the Soviet Union. Although the details remain opaque, the cause of this aberrational flu epidemic was almost certainly not a single-source laboratory research accident, but rather a major public-health intervention that went awry.[32]

The second event occurred in 1979 in what was then called Sverdlovsk, in the former Soviet Union. The Soviet Union was violating the Biological Weapons Convention, which prohibits the development and stockpiling of biological weapons, by clandestinely producing a variety of biological weapons by the tonne, including anthrax and smallpox. Sverdlovsk was home to one of the plants producing them, and after an explosion or other accident, aerosolised anthrax spores were released into the air. At least 66 people died, and possibly far more. The Soviets insisted that the victims died from eating naturally caused anthrax-contaminated meat, and some American scientists gullibly believed their account.[33] Intelligence collected by the US made it clear early on that an accident at an illegal weapons-production facility had led to the release of a weaponised pathogen in a plume, and that this phenomenon had caused the anthrax deaths. Russian defectors confirmed this account in the 1990s.[34]

Another often-mentioned example of a laboratory accident involved the last incidences of smallpox in 1978 in Birmingham, United Kingdom, before all smallpox samples were moved to the two places in the world where smallpox is legally kept, in Russia and the United States (at the Centers for Disease Control and Prevention). Janet Parker, a medical photographer, contracted smallpox. The head of the laboratory, scientist Henry Bedson, died by suicide shortly after Parker was diagnosed. Parker died. Her mother was infected and recovered. How Parker was exposed in the first place was the subject of two major inquiries. Bedson, who was known to be strict about biosafety in his lab, was posthumously cleared of wrongdoing.[35] It is still not known exactly how Parker contracted the disease. She almost certainly visited the laboratory, possibly to sell film to scientists before the holidays. Both the visit and selling the film would have violated lab policy.

In addition, after the SARS outbreak there were three infection incidents in 2003–04 in laboratories in Singapore, Taiwan and China that were caused by a combination of poor training and improper procedures.[36] The accidents in Singapore and Taiwan affected only the laboratory workers exposed, but one of the two laboratory workers exposed in the Chinese laboratory went on to infect others, including a laboratory worker's mother, who died of the disease. Notably, once the infection was recognised, the Chinese laboratory was shut down, the WHO was invited to investigate and hundreds of people were quarantined.[37] The accidents led directly to the 2005 World Health Assembly Resolution 58.29 'Enhancement of Laboratory Biosafety', which called upon member states to examine their biosafety programmes, plans and training for biosafety and to ensure that funds were committed to compliance with WHO guidance.[38] The incidents also fuelled calls for SARS to be designated a regulated pathogen in the US, which controls access and requires training, reporting and specialised facilities. It was so designated in 2009.

Despite the lack of historical support for a pandemic stemming from a laboratory accident, hypotheses have emerged that the COVID-19 outbreak may be one. Wuhan is home to two research institutions at which coronavirus research was under way at the time the pandemic began – the Wuhan Institute of Virology and the Wuhan Center for Disease Control and Prevention public-health laboratory. To a significant degree, initial suspicions that a laboratory accident was responsible for the pandemic turned on the presence of those two laboratories in Wuhan and China's obfuscations concerning the beginning of the pandemic. Chinese authorities vastly underreported the number of early cases, and dangerously minimised the scale and seriousness of the virus.[39] They were behind rumours and conspiracy theories that the US was the source of the pandemic.[40] The markets were shut down immediately, without first sampling the animals there, impeding the proving or disproving of animal origin. Once it was resolved that the WHO would send a team

Chinese authorities minimised the scale of the virus

of experts to China to try to determine the origin, negotiations dragged on for months to determine the scope of the investigation. When the WHO investigation was under way, not all requested information was provided. The WHO team had asked for raw data on the 174 patients identified as being ill with COVID in December 2019, but was given summary data instead.[41] Compounding the problem was the dearth of human-intelligence collection in China, a long-standing problem for the US in particular.[42] There were steps taken to stiffen penalties for engaging in illegal wildlife trade in China, suggesting that this was the governmental theory of how the pandemic started, but biosecurity and biosafety legislation to tighten laboratory controls in China was also introduced.[43]

However, an accident scenario would be viable only if the SARS-CoV-2 virus (or something very similar) was in those laboratories. This has not yet been established for either laboratory. Without perfect knowledge of the early cases of SARS-CoV-2, it is impossible to completely rule out a laboratory accident origin of the virus. But particularly if it was a naturally evolved virus, certain additional pieces of information suggest that a laboratory accident is not a likely scenario. A single laboratory accident cannot explain evidence of genetic diversity in early samples of the virus. Furthermore, all laboratory personnel working with coronaviruses and bat samples were under regular medical surveillance, were stated to have had serology tests and were demonstrated not to have been exposed to SARS-CoV-2.[44] Reports that three lab workers sought hospital care in December 2019 are not terribly probative given that it was flu season, that in China it is compulsory to get a sick note to miss work and that care is routinely given in hospitals.[45] Also, an Australian researcher who worked at the Wuhan Institute of Virology through 2019 countered accusations about lax biosafety in the high-containment laboratories, noting that people were not getting sick at the lab at a time when the COVID-19 epidemic was starting.[46]

The balance of evidence indicates that the SARS-CoV-2 virus emerged naturally and spilled over to people at the animal markets. Early cases were associated with the markets; there were susceptible animals present; virus was detected in the drains where susceptible animals were butchered; and there was genetic diversity in the early cases that suggests a virus present in an animal population had been transmitted to people multiple times. Doubts will continue to linger because the trail to the intermediate host animal is now cold, searches for such hosts are not currently under way, and information that could definitively disprove a laboratory origin is impossible to develop no matter how invasive the investigation into a laboratory might be. In any case, China is unlikely to agree to such an investigation.

Some observers have inferred that China had something to hide, probably a laboratory connection to the pandemic. But it is important to avoid the hazards, familiar in intelligence and strategic analysis, of mirror-imaging – that is, of assuming that the actions of Chinese officials and others would be the same independent of social and political context.[47] A lack of data, compensated for by the observers' personal experience and preconceptions, has often led the intelligence community to reach incorrect and highly consequential conclusions on this basis – for instance, that Japan would not attack Pearl Harbor, that the Soviet Union was stable in the 1980s, that Saddam Hussein was hiding weapons of mass destruction and that the World Trade Center was not especially vulnerable.

Experts on China's cultural and political systems have pointed to contra-indicators of China's culpability in a theoretical laboratory accident. These should be considered, especially as there is no evidence to support laboratory involvement or accidental release. Early underreporting of COVID-19 cases could be the result of lower-level officials trying to manage the optics of the epidemic situation, as accurate numbers might not have made the officials look good.[48] Indeed, many junior officials were fired for their mismanagement of the epidemic. The fact that Wuhan Institute of Virology scientists were not fired may indicate that China does not believe that the laboratory is culpable.[49] Officials might have closed the market before samples could be taken because they had been turning a blind eye to the profitable wild-animal trade and refraining from enforcing the laws on the books. The Chinese illegal animal trade is estimated to be worth from $18 billion to over $75bn per year and is a boost to local economies.[50] Once it looked as if a disease that came from the market was spreading, sweeping illegal activity under the rug would be a priority to avoid blame and hold onto profits.

There is no evidence to support accidental release

Published excerpts from cables sent by US State Department officials after a visit to the Wuhan Institute of Virology suggested that there were safety problems at the laboratory.[51] However, those cables were much less inflammatory when read in full than the published selections made them appear. Rather than describing an unsafe work environment, the full cables explained how the laboratory was coming online to full productivity more slowly than was originally hoped, and that it was unable to initiate some research programmes due to insufficient numbers of trained staff.[52] Furthermore, according to seasoned China watchers, Chinese scientists have long importuned outside international experts to point out problems, including hiring, so that the government would commit funding.[53] And, as one China expert said, 'when it comes to the Chinese Communist Party, cover-up is business as usual'.[54] Though China is in many ways a surveillance state, it has many blind spots, particularly about things that are not important to the leadership, which is far more interested in controlling speech than the wildlife trade.[55] Furthermore, for the pandemic to have originated in China is embarrassing, as many of the preparations China undertook since the SARS outbreak in 2003 were apparently for naught. Although the wildlife trade was a known disease risk, and there were laws restricting it on the books, it wasn't stopped.

Despite these explainable uncertainties, some have called for reparations from China to the countries most affected by COVID-19.[56] Donald Trump repeatedly referred to COVID-19 as 'Chinese flu' or 'kung flu', and the Trump administration examined limiting sovereign immunity, allowing people to sue China, or cancelling interest on US debt held by China, even though legal scholars consider such moves ineffective, illegal, or legally and diplomatically imprudent.[57]

The *Science* letter, Biden's ordering a 'deep dive' by the US intelligence community, WHO calls for a full laboratory investigation, and inflammatory rhetoric and threats have annoyed and embittered China. The WHO investigation was supposed to have a second part, but that is not going forward due to lack of support from China. The potential for long-term progress – such as worldwide vaccination, investigations to find an intermediate animal host for SARS-CoV-2, curtailing the wild-animal trade or influencing laboratory-safety governance – appears to be in doubt.

Living with uncertainty

Knowing how SARS-CoV-2 came to afflict humans would undoubtedly inform efforts to prevent future pandemics. But it may take years to determine what the virus's pathway was. In the meantime, the human population has no choice but to live with uncertainty and to do its best to mitigate risks.

Security by scientific achievement

Among the most important steps is to sustain robust engagement among scientists, including Chinese ones. Within weeks of the announcement that a respiratory disease was spreading in Wuhan, the genetic sequence of the virus was available, and nearly every scientist who could contribute set to work in a global response. Particularly in comparison to the scientific response during SARS in 2003, the energised early response to COVID-19 was fuelled by years of fruitful interaction among scientists from around the world.[58] Another factor was China's remarkable and enduring financial investments in its scientific research institutions.[59]

The successful collaborations among scientists that fuelled the scientific response to the pandemic came against a backdrop of US concerns about scientific and technological competition with China. Even before the pandemic, there was justifiable concern that China gained from the open research environment of Western countries, and that the US gave away too much, including medical genetic information and biotechnologies. Though it may be tempting to block access, the US and other Western countries should recognise that even though openness in research fuels competition, it directly leads to greater and wider long-term benefits, including job creation as well as scientific, technological, medical and agricultural advances. Steps can be taken to protect some technologies, and there has been progress in increasing the biological expertise in the Committee on Foreign Investment in the United States. Instead of limiting access, the US might focus on making its own research environment more appealing.

The dilemma of scientific openness was also debated during the Cold War, though the focus was more on physics and engineering than biology. There were substantiated concerns that the Soviets were advancing their nuclear-weapons programmes by virtue of basic physics research published openly in Western journals, and some called for more basic scientific information to be classified. Opponents pointed out that classification generally stultified science by foreclosing inquiry and cross-pollination among experts. An influential report on the issue composed by a National Academies committee – known as the 'Corson Report' after the committee's chair, Cornell University nuclear physicist and former president Dale R. Corson – concluded that the benefits of research openness to scientific progress far outweighed the risks. The committee advised that the US concentrate on 'security by achievement', not by classification.[60] This became US policy under Ronald Reagan by way of National Security Decision Directive 189, which was reaffirmed by George W. Bush in the aftermath of the 9/11 attacks and is in effect to this day.[61]

For the US vis-à-vis China, security by achievement means redoubling efforts to make the US a biological-research powerhouse, and fixing long-standing problems that hinder competitiveness. More can be done to create an environment in which research can flourish, biotechnology companies can be formed, opinions can be expressed freely and scientific dogma can be questioned. The playbook is familiar: funding basic research with minimal fluctuations year-to-year; funding science, technology, engineering and mathematics (STEM) education; incentivising biotechnology companies not to locate offshore; developing workforce needs through training programmes; targeting female advancement in STEM fields; and encouraging foreign students who receive their PhDs in the United States to stay there by issuing them green cards.[62]

Countering disinformation and misinformation

A great deal of misinformation (which is simply false) and disinformation (which is deliberately false) has been spread about the origin of the pandemic, making legitimate scientific investigation all the more difficult. The scientific community should address the problem. One example of disinformation was the 'Yan Report', posted on a preprint server, which alleged that the Chinese government had deliberately created SARS-CoV-2 and released it as an 'unrestricted bioweapon'.[63] The work was funded by Steve Bannon and Guo Wengui, a Chinese expatriate billionaire. Li-Meng Yan, another Chinese expatriate and lead author of the Yan Report and other reports, has appeared multiple times on the conservative Fox News talk show *Tucker Carlson Today*, and has over 100,000 Twitter followers. Her reports have been downloaded from a preprint server thousands of times. Although Yan has an ostensibly impressive scientific background, and the reports include a great deal of scientific terminology, they are scientifically nonsensical. Despite the publication of a well-received point-by-point critical review that repudiated the original report, Yan has continued to publish baseless assessments and to appear on Carlson's show.[64]

In Yan's case, the falsehood appeared to be deliberate. But other merely inaccurate and slipshod preprints regarding the origin of SARS-CoV-2 that did not meet scientific standards for publication have also drawn considerable attention. For example, a paper was posted on the preprint server bioRXiv theorising that the SARS-CoV-2 virus was already 'pre-adapted' for human transmission – that is, manipulated in a laboratory and then accidentally or deliberately released.[65] The paper was never published in a scientific journal, which an author of the preprint believed was due to censorship but others maintain was because the analysis was incorrect.[66] Especially given that the emergence of SARS-CoV-2 variants shows that the virus is continuing to adapt to humans, the prior unsupported claim that it was intentionally pre-adapted has only become more incendiary and exacerbated public confusion about, and mistrust of, science.[67]

Dealing with bad information in science and how it is interpreted is an urgent priority for scientists and scientific institutions. The problem is daunting: people, institutions and nations have their own motivations, and complex technical details are ripe for misinterpretation. News often focuses on the personalities involved at the expense of verifiable facts.[68] Jevin West and Carl Bergstrom have underscored the urgency of this issue, as 'science relies on public trust for its funding and opportunities to interface with the world. Misinformation in and about science could easily undermine this trust.'[69] There may need to be more programmes like the American Association for the Advancement of Science's Science and Technology Policy Fellowships programme, which has been placing PhD holders in US congressional and executive-branch offices for year-long fellowships since 1973, but now for journalists.

Implementing 'One Health'

Another outcome of the COVID-19 pandemic should be the full implementation of the 'One Health' concept. One Health is an approach to health that recognises the 'interconnection between people, animals, plants, and their shared environment'.[70] While One Health has many intellectual adherents and enjoys broad international agreement, an approach that deliberately breaks down institutional silos and requires cooperation among agencies that have existed separately and operated in a largely stovepiped fashion for generations has been exceedingly difficult to put into practice. This is especially the case when health and economic interests operate at cross purposes, as they often do with respect to wild-animal farming, land development and use, and agricultural practices. A 2005 call to action forewarned that 'zoonotic pathogens do not respect national borders, so it is in the best interests of wealthy nations to invest in improved animal surveillance programs in all parts of the world'.[71] COVID-19 should provide ample impetus to exponentially boost knowledge and surveillance of what happens at the animal, plant, human and environmental interface, including but not limited to bats and coronaviruses.

The SARS-CoV-2 virus is the ninth coronavirus identified that infects humans, and it likely has its evolutionary roots in a bat virus. Ebola, Marburg, Nipah, Hendra, SARS and Middle East respiratory syndrome (MERS) also have links to viruses circulating in bat populations. While knowledge of bats and their role in human disease has increased substantially since Trinidadian scientist Joseph Pawan discovered that vampire bats spread rabies virus to people in the 1930s, there is still much to learn about both bats and the diseases they may carry. A recent review of the state of bat research warned that 'there is a growing anxiety in the field that merely identifying all the novel animal-derived viruses will do little to prevent the next outbreak'.[72] Deforestation and the establishment of human habitats closer to bat populations are demonstrated factors in viral spillover events, but a better understanding of disease ecology is needed, and it will require using new tools including the Global Positioning System and artificial intelligence as well as forging better ties between disease experts and bat conservationists.[73] There is also more to learn about the complicated evolutionary path some coronaviruses may take and how they circulate and transmit among bat families.[74]

Some steps have been taken to strengthen One Health since the emergence of SARS-CoV-2. The WHO, the Food and Agriculture Organization, the World Organisation for Animal Health and the United Nations Environment Programme issued guidance about how to keep mammalian traditional-food markets safe in April 2021.[75] But more work needs to be done to monitor and regulate the sale of farmed wild mammals; stem illegal wildlife sales and the introduction of wildlife into farmed populations; increase biosecurity measures in food markets (for example, by separating slaughter and butchering areas from those where animals are dressed for sale, so that blood and faeces from the animals does not contaminate the products); and establish surveillance that spans human and animal health. And for a generalist virus such as SARS-CoV-2 and potentially other coronaviruses, it is not just the animals of economic importance that need to be monitored. Other wildlife and even companion animals such as dogs and cats can get COVID-19. Surveillance of hospitalised children in Malaysia revealed that a different coronavirus in dogs has made the jump to people.[76]

Reining in the wildlife trade

The wildlife trade is a prime potential source of future disease outbreaks. China took some useful steps in response to COVID-19 that it had not taken in response to SARS.[77] A ban publicly endorsed by Xi Jinping was instituted on the consumption of almost all wild animals. All 31 provinces have imposed similar bans, wildlife farms have been shut down and online sources for purchasing wildlife have been taken down. In response to SARS, there had been a short-term suspension on trading and consuming palm civets. There are risks, however, that the economic pressures these actions place on wildlife farmers and traders will drive the lucrative business farther underground, or induce local officials, eager to spur economic recovery or susceptible to bribery, to tolerate it, as occurred in the wake of SARS.[78] Arrests are up for commercial wildlife crimes in China, and public support for a ban on consumption of wildlife appears to be growing, especially among the more urban and young people.[79] Outside experts, however, question how well the bans are being enforced, and believe they do not go far enough, as demand is still fuelling a transboundary wildlife supply chain in neighbouring countries.[80]

*   *   *

Though a great deal more scientific evidence supports a natural spillover cause for SARS-CoV-2 than any other explanation, there are lingering questions. For some, the preponderance of evidence will not seem sufficient. But it's not possible to turn back the clock to get the samples that would conclusively determine who got what when, and how they got it. Furthermore, it is undeniable that diseases like SARS-CoV-2 will continue to emerge.

We are encroaching on the territory of wild animals with which we share many immunological weaknesses. Viruses and bacteria will evolve to exploit those weaknesses and adapt to human hosts. While the biological future is full of scientific unknowns, and those left by the COVID-19 pandemic remain vexing, that crisis has at least illuminated the need for scientific work to be conducted safely and, to the extent possible, globally coordinated – including with China.

Just over 100 years ago, in 1918, a devastating influenza pandemic killed at least 50 million people worldwide. Brilliant scientists worked to understand that disease as they had come to understand bacterial diseases such as anthrax, tetanus and syphilis. But with the scientific tools available, viruses like influenza were an undetectable blind spot. Even before 1918, Joseph E. Ransdell, a senator from Louisiana, saw how similarly inscrutable diseases such as yellow fever and malaria had sickened and killed the workers building the Panama Canal, leading him to believe that public heath should be a priority and a federal responsibility as 'disease has absolutely no regard for state lines'.[81] The 1918 flu pandemic proved his point. Yet lawmakers did nothing. It wasn't until 1930 that the Ransdell Act, creating the National Institutes of Health, had enough congressional support to pass. What caused the legislators to finally act was the influenza epidemic of 1929. The flu was comparatively mild that year, but the experience reminded the lawmakers just how bad the 1918 influenza pandemic had been.[82]

The COVID-19 pandemic and its consequences should galvanise world leaders to invest in pandemic preparedness, studying major environmental changes and their effect on viral spillovers, virology, immunology, surveillance and treatments, as well as in understanding and determining the origins of new diseases. If they don't take these steps now, they will be painfully reminded of their failures in the future.

Notes

1   See WHO, 'Listings of WHO's Response to COVID-19', 29 June 2020 [updated 29 January 2021], https://www.who.int/news/ item/29-06-2020-covidtimeline.

2   See David L. Roberts, Jeremy S. Rossman and Ivan Jarić, 'Dating First Cases of COVID-19', *PLOS Pathogens*,

24 June 2021, https://journals.plos.
org/plospathogens/article?id=10.1371/
journal.ppat.1009620.

3   See WHO, 'WHO-convened Global
Study of Origins of SARS-CoV-2:
China Part', Joint WHO–China
Study, 6 April 2021, https://www.
who.int/publications-detail-redirect/
who-convened-global-study-of-
origins-of-sars-cov-2-china-part.

4   See Editors of the Lancet,
'Addendum: Competing Interests
and the Origins of SARS-CoV-2',
Lancet, 21 June 2021, https://www.
thelancet.com/action/showPdf?pi
i=S0140-6736%2821%2901377-5.

5   Jesse D. Bloom et al., 'Investigate
the Origins of COVID-19', Letter
to the Editor, *Science*, vol. 372,
no. 6,543, 14 May 2021, p. 694,
https://science.sciencemag.org/
content/372/6543/694.1.

6   See Office of the Director of National
Intelligence, 'Unclassified Summary
of Assessment on COVID-19 Origins',
27 August 2021, https://www.dni.gov/
files/ODNI/documents/assessments/
Unclassified-Summary-of-Assessment-
on-COVID-19-Origins.pdf.

7   'WHO Director-General's Opening
Remarks at the Member State
Information Session on Origins',
16 July 2021, https://www.who.int/
director-general/speeches/detail/
who-director-general-s-opening-
remarks-at-the-member-state-
information-session-on-origins.

8   See Eva Dou and Emily Rauhala,
'China Sets Back Search for
Covid Origins with Rejection of
WHO Investigation Proposal',
Washington Post, 22 July 2021,
https://www.washingtonpost.

com/world/2021/07/22/
china-covid-who-wuhan/.

9   See WHO, 'Call for Experts to
Join Scientific Advisory Group for
the Origins of Novel Pathogens',
news release, 8 September 2021,
https://www.who.int/news/
item/20-08-2021-call-for-experts-to-
join-scientific-advisory-group-for-the-
origins-of-novel-pathogens.

10 See Ben Hu et al., 'Discovery of a
Rich Gene Pool of Bat SARS-related
Coronaviruses Provides New
Insights into the Origin of SARS
Coronavirus', *PLOS Pathogens*, 30
November 2017, https://journals.plos.
org/plospathogens/article?id=10.1371/
journal.ppat.1006698.

11 See Louise H. Taylor, Sophia M.
Latham and Mark E.J. Woolhouse,
'Risk Factors for Human Disease
Emergence', *Philosophical Transactions
of the Royal Society B*, vol. 356,
no. 1,411, 29 July 2001, https://
royalsocietypublishing.org/
doi/10.1098/rstb.2001.0888.

12 See Michael Letko et al., 'Bat-
borne Virus Diversity, Spillover
and Emergence', *Nature Reviews
Microbiology*, vol. 18, no. 8, August
2020, pp. 461–71, https://www.nature.
com/articles/s41579-020-0394-z.pdf.

13 See Ben Jackson et al., 'Generation
and Transmission of Interlineage
Recombinants in the SARS-
CoV-2 Pandemic', *Cell*, no. 184,
30 September 2021, https://www.
cell.com/action/showPdf?pi
i=S0092-8674%2821%2900984-3.

14 WHO, 'WHO-convened Global Study
of Origins of SARS-CoV-2: China
Part', p. 98.

15 See Xiao Xiao et al., 'Animal Sales from

Wuhan Wet Markets Immediately Prior to the COVID-19 Pandemic', *Scientific Reports*, no. 11, art. 11,898, 7 June 2021, https://www.nature.com/articles/s41598-021-91470-2.pdf.

16 See Conrad M. Freuling et al., 'Susceptibility of Raccoon Dogs for Experimental SARS-CoV-2 Infection', *Emerging Infectious Diseases*, vol. 26, no. 12, December, pp. 2,982–5, https://www.ncbi.nlm.nih.gov/pmc/articles/PMC7706974/pdf/20-3733.pdf.

17 See Nadia Oreshkova et al., 'SARS-CoV-2 Infection in Farmed Minks, the Netherlands, April and May 2020', *Eurosurveillance*, vol. 25, no. 23, 11 June 2020, https://www.eurosurveillance.org/content/10.2807/1560-7917.ES.2020.25.23.2001005.

18 See Oscar A. MacLean et al., 'Natural Selection in the Evolution of SARS-Cov-2 in Bats Created a Generalist Virus and Highly Capable Human Pathogen', *PLOS Biology*, 12 March 2021, https://journals.plos.org/plosbiology/article?id=10.1371/journal.pbio.3001115.

19 See WHO, 'WHO-convened Global Study of Origins of SARS-CoV-2: China Part', p. 95.

20 See Sarah Temmam et al., 'Coronaviruses with a SARS-Cov-2-like Receptor-binding Domain Allowing ACE2-Mediated Entry into Human Cells Isolated from Bats of Indochinese Peninsula' [under review], *Nature Portfolio*, 17 September 2021, https://www.researchsquare.com/article/rs-871965/v1.

21 See James Gorman and Carl Zimmer, 'Scientist Opens Up About His Early Email to Fauci on Virus Origins', *New York Times*, 14 June 2021 [updated 20 June 2021], https://www.nytimes.com/2021/06/14/science/covid-lab-leak-fauci-kristian-andersen.html.

22 Kristian G. Andersen et al., 'The Proximal Origin of SARS-CoV-2', Correspondence, *Nature Medicine*, vol. 26, no. 4, April 2020, p. 450, https://www.nature.com/articles/s41591-020-0820-9.pdf.

23 See Jackson et al., 'Generation and Transmission of Interlineage Recombinants in the SARS-CoV-2 Pandemic'.

24 See Andersen et al., 'The Proximal Origin of SARS-CoV-2'; and Yushun Wan et al., 'Receptor Recognition by the Novel Coronavirus from Wuhan: An Analysis Based on Decade-long Structural Studies of SARS Coronavirus', *Journal of Virology*, vol. 94, no. 7, 17 March 2020, https://journals.asm.org/doi/epub/10.1128/JVI.00127-20.

25 See National Academies of Sciences, Engineering, and Medicine, *Biodefense in the Age of Synthetic Biology* (Washington DC: National Academies Press, 2018).

26 See Natalie D. Collins and Alan D.T. Barrett, 'Live Attenuated Yellow Fever 17D Vaccine: A Legacy Vaccine Still Controlling Outbreaks in Modern Day', *Current Infectious Disease Reports*, vol. 19, no. 3, March 2017, https://www.ncbi.nlm.nih.gov/pmc/articles/PMC6008154/pdf/nihms970490.pdf.

27 See EcoHealth Alliance Inc., FY2014, 'Project Details', NIH Reporter, https://reporter.nih.gov/search/xQW6UJmWfUuOV01ntGvLwQ/project-details/8674931#details.

28 See Gigi Kwik Gronvall, 'H5N1: A Case Study for Dual-use Research', Working Paper, Council

on Foreign Relations, July 2013, https://cdn.cfr.org/sites/default/files/pdf/2013/05/WP_Dual_Use_Research.pdf?_ga=2.47606244.2142736497.1575382530-1043326905.1575382530.

29 See Wan et al., 'Receptor Recognition by the Novel Coronavirus from Wuhan'.

30 See Peng Zhou et al., 'Addendum: A Pneumonia Outbreak Associated with a New Coronavirus of Probable Bat Origin', Corrections & Amendments, *Nature*, vol. 588, 5 December 2020, p. E6, https://www.nature.com/articles/s41586-020-2951-z.pdf.

31 See Maciej F. Boni et al., 'Evolutionary Origins of the SARS-Cov-2 Sarbecovirus Lineage Responsible for the COVID-19 Pandemic', *Nature Microbiology*, vol. 5, November 2020, pp. 1,408–17, https://www.nature.com/articles/s41564-020-0771-4.pdf.

32 See Michelle Rozo and Gigi Kwik Gronvall, 'The Reemergent 1977 H1N1 Strain and the Gain-of-function Debate', *mBio*, vol. 6, no. 4, July–August 2015, pp. 1–6, https://journals.asm.org/doi/pdf/10.1128/mBio.01013-15.

33 See Sarah Zhang, 'How DNA Evidence Confirmed a Soviet Cover-up of an Anthrax Accident', *Atlantic*, 22 November 2016, https://www.theatlantic.com/health/archive/2016/11/sverdlovsk-russia-anthrax/508139/.

34 See Robert A. Wampler and Thomas S. Blanton (eds), 'Volume V: Anthrax at Sverdlovsk, 1979 – U.S. Intelligence on the Deadliest Modern Outbreak', National Security Archive Electronic Briefing Book No. 61, 15 November 2001, https://nsarchive2.gwu.edu/NSAEBB/NSAEBB61/.

35 See Mark Pallen, *The Last Days of Smallpox: Tragedy in Birmingham* (Independently published, 2018).

36 See Dennis Normile, 'Mounting Lab Accidents Raise SARS Fears', *Science*, 30 April 2004, https://science.sciencemag.org/content/304/5671/659; Dennis Normile, 'Second Lab Accident Fuels Fears About SARS', *Science*, 2 January 2004, https://science.sciencemag.org/content/303/5654/26; and Kathryn Senior, 'Recent Singapore SARS Case a Laboratory Accident', *Lancet Infectious Diseases*, vol. 3, no. 11, 1 November 2003, p. 679, https://www.thelancet.com/journals/laninf/article/PIIS1473-3099(03)00815-6/abstract.

37 See Normile, 'Mounting Lab Accidents Raise SARS Fears'.

38 See Gigi Kwik Gronvall and Michelle Rozo, 'Synopsis of Biological Safety and Security Arrangements', UPMC Center for Health Security, July 2015, https://www.centerforhealthsecurity.org/our-work/pubs_archive/pubs-pdfs/2015/SynopsisofBiologicalSafetyandSecurityArrangements-112915.pdf.

39 See Annie Sparrow, 'The Chinese Government's Cover-up Killed Health Care Workers Worldwide', *Foreign Policy*, 18 March 2021, https://foreignpolicy.com/2021/03/18/china-covid-19-killed-health-care-workers-worldwide/.

40 See Erika Kinetz, 'Anatomy of a Conspiracy: With COVID, China Took Leading Role', AP News, 15 February 2021, https://apnews.com/article/pandemics-beijing-only-on-ap-epidemics-media-122b73e134b780919cc1808f3f6f16e8.

41 See 'Covid-19 Pandemic: China "Refused to Give Data" to WHO Team', BBC News, 14 February 2021, https://www.bbc.com/news/world-asia-china-56054468.

42 See Josh Meyer, 'The Real Issue with the COVID-19 Lab Leak Theory? The US Isn't Spying on China Like It Used To', *USA Today*, 4 June 2021, https://www.usatoday.com/in-depth/news/world/2021/06/04/wuhan-lab-leak-theory-murky-due-us-lack-human-intel-china/7492291002/.

43 See 'China Passes Biosecurity Law to Prevent Infectious Diseases', Reuters, 18 October 2020, https://www.reuters.com/article/us-china-parliament-biosecurity-idUSKBN273064.

44 See Jon Cohen, 'Wuhan Coronavirus Hunter Shi Zhengli Speaks Out', *Science*, vol. 369, no. 6,503, 31 July 2020, pp. 487–8, https://science.sciencemag.org/content/369/6503/487.

45 See Justin Ling, 'The Lab Leak Theory Doesn't Hold Up', *Foreign Policy*, 15 June 2021, https://foreignpolicy.com/2021/06/15/lab-leak-theory-doesnt-hold-up-covid-china/.

46 See Michelle Cortez, 'Australian Scientist, the Sole Foreign Researcher at the Wuhan Lab, Speaks Out', *Sydney Morning Herald*, 28 June 2021, https://www.smh.com.au/world/asia/australian-scientist-the-sole-foreign-researcher-at-the-wuhan-lab-speaks-out-20210628-p584sv.html.

47 See, for example, Lauren Witlin, 'Of Note: Mirror-imaging and Its Dangers', *SAIS Review of International Affairs*, vol. 28, no. 1, Winter–Spring 2008, pp. 89–90.

48 See Julian E. Barnes, 'C.I.A. Hunts for Authentic Virus Totals in China, Dismissing Government Tallies', *New York Times*, 2 April 2020 [updated 16 April 2020], https://www.nytimes.com/2020/04/02/us/politics/cia-coronavirus-china.html.

49 See Kaiser Kuo, 'Sinica Podcast: COVID-19 Origins Revisited, with Deborah Seligsohn', SupChina, 17 June 2021, https://supchina.com/podcast/covid-19-origins-revisited-with-deborah-seligsohn/.

50 See Echo Xie, 'China Bans Trade, Eating of Wild Animals in Battle Against Coronavirus', *South China Morning Post,* 24 February 2020, https://www.scmp.com/news/china/article/3052151/china-bans-trade-eating-wild-animals-battle-against-coronavirus; and Wilson Center, 'Wild Laws: China and Its Role in Illicit Wildlife Trade', 2 June 2016, https://www.wilsoncenter.org/event/wild-laws-china-and-its-role-illicit-wildlife-trade. On the monetary scale of the illegal wildlife trade, see Leo Lin, 'The Illicit Wildlife Trade in China and the State Response Following the Coronavirus Outbreak', Jamestown Foundation, *China Brief*, vol. 20, no. 5, https://jamestown.org/program/the-illicit-wildlife-trade-in-china-and-the-state-response-following-the-coronavirus-outbreak/.

51 See Josh Rogin, *Chaos Under Heaven: Trump, Xi, and the Battle for the Twenty-first Century* (Boston, MA, and New York: Houghton Mifflin Harcourt, 2021); and Josh Rogin, 'Opinion: State Department Cables Warned of Safety Issues at Wuhan Lab Studying Bat Coronaviruses', *Washington Post*, 14 April 2020, https://www.washingtonpost.com/

opinions/2020/04/14/state-department-cables-warned-safety-issues-wuhan-lab-studying-bat-coronaviruses/.

52 See Zichin Wang, 'Josh Rogin's WashPo Column & Book Misrepresented a U.S. Diplomatic Cable from Wuhan', Pekingology, 2 April 2021, https://pekingnology.substack.com/p/josh-rogins-washpo-column-and-book.

53 See Kuo, 'Sinica Podcast'.

54 Ling, 'The Lab Leak Theory Doesn't Hold Up'.

55 See James Palmer, 'Why Beijing Will Never Cooperate with a COVID-19 Investigation', Foreign Policy, 9 June 2021, https://foreignpolicy.com/2021/06/09/china-cooperate-covid-19-origins-investigation-wuhan/.

56 See, for example, Obiageli Ezekwesili, 'China Must Pay Reparations to Africa for Its Coronavirus Failures', Washington Post, 16 April 2020, https://www.washingtonpost.com/opinions/2020/04/16/china-must-pay-reparations-africa-its-coronavirus-failures/.

57 On Trump officials' urging of legal action, see 'Sen. Marsha Blackburn (R-TN) on Ways to Hold China Accountable for Missteps Handling COVID-19: We Need to Raise the Question of "The Interest on the Debt Payments that They Hold"', FOX News Radio, 28 April 2020, https://radio.foxnews.com/2020/04/28/sen-marsha-blackburn-r-tn-on-ways-to-hold-china-accountable-for-missteps-handling-covid-19-we-need-to-raise-the-question-of-the-interest-on-the-debt-payments-that-they-hold/; and Jeff Stein et al., 'U.S. Officials Crafting Retaliatory Actions Against China over Coronavirus as President Trump Fumes', Washington Post, 20 August 2020, https://www.washingtonpost.com/business/2020/04/30/trump-china-coronavirus-retaliation/. On the pitfalls of legal action, see Rachel Esplin Odell, 'Why Retribution Against China for Coronavirus Would Harm America and the World', War on the Rocks, 9 April 2020, https://warontherocks.com/2020/04/why-retribution-against-china-for-coronavirus-would-harm-america-and-the-world/; and Jessica Chen Weiss, 'Can the U.S. Sue China for Covid-19 Damages? Not Really', Washington Post, 29 April 2020, https://www.washingtonpost.com/politics/2020/04/29/can-us-sue-china-covid-19-damages-not-really-this-could-quickly-backfire/. In the nuclear disaster at Fukushima, the Japanese government and the plant operator were ordered to pay damages to survivors, but that did not extend to other nations. See Makiko Inoue and Mike Ives, 'Japanese Government Is Ordered to Pay Damages over Fukushima Disaster', New York Times, 3 September 2020 [updated 13 April 2021], https://www.nytimes.com/2020/09/30/world/asia/japan-fukushima-tokyo-electric.html. But when the US Department of Defense accidentally sent insufficiently irradiated samples of Bacillus anthracis, the causative agent of anthrax disease, to many states and several countries, no representatives of other countries were present for the investigation and no compensation was offered.

58 See Gigi Kwik Gronvall, 'The Scientific Response to COVID-19 and Lessons for Security', *Survival*, vol. 62, no. 3, June–July 2020, pp. 72–92.

59 See David Cyranoski, 'The Pandemic Is Challenging China's Breakneck Race to the Top of Science', *Nature*, no. 582, 3 June 2020, pp. 170–1, https://www.nature.com/articles/d41586-020-01522-2.

60 See National Academies of Science, Engineering, and Medicine, *Scientific Communication and National Security* (Washington DC: National Academies Press, 1982).

61 See 'National Policy on the Transfer of Scientific, Technical and Engineering Information', National Security Decision Directive 189, 21 September 1985, https://fas.org/irp/offdocs/nsdd/nsdd-189.htm.

62 See Gigi Kwik Gronvall, 'Maintaining US Leadership in Emerging Biotechnologies to Grow the Economy of the Future', *Health Security*, vol. 15, no. 1, February 2017, pp. 31–2, http://www.liebertpub.com/doi/10.1089/hs.2016.0099.

63 See, for example, Rob Kuznia et al., 'Weird Science: How a "Shoddy" Bannon-backed Paper on Coronavirus Origins Made Its Way to an Audience of Millions', CNN, 19 October 2020 [updated 21 October 2020], https://lite.cnn.com/en/article/h_6d1f4f887138f8854cb1fd6a29f5a879.

64 I was a co-author of the review. See Kelsey Lane Warmbrod et al., 'In Response: Yan et al Preprint Examinations of Origin of SARS-CoV-2', Johns Hopkins Center for Health Security, 21 September 2020, https://www.centerforhealthsecurity.org/our-work/pubs_archive/pubs-pdfs/2020/200921-in-response-yan.pdf.

65 Shing Hei Zhan, Benjamin E. Deverman and Yujia Alina Chan, 'SARS-CoV-2 Is Well Adapted for Humans. What Does This Mean for Re-emergence?', *bioRxiv*, 2 May 2020, https://www.biorxiv.org/content/10.1101/2020.05.01.073262v1.

66 See Antonio Regalado, 'They Called It a Conspiracy Theory. But Alina Chan Tweeted Life into the Idea that the Virus Came from a Lab', *MIT Technology Review*, 25 June 2021, https://www.technologyreview.com/2021/06/25/1027140/lab-leak-alina-chan/.

67 See Tara Kirk Sell et al., 'National Priorities to Combat Misinformation and Disinformation for COVID-19 and Future Public Health Threats: A Call for a National Strategy', Johns Hopkins Center for Health Security, March 2021, https://www.centerforhealthsecurity.org/our-work/pubs_archive/pubs-pdfs/2021/210322-misinformation.pdf.

68 See Nicholas Wade, 'The Origin of COVID: Did People or Nature Open Pandora's Box at Wuhan?', *Bulletin of the Atomic Scientists*, 5 May 2021, https://thebulletin.org/2021/05/the-origin-of-covid-did-people-or-nature-open-pandoras-box-at-wuhan/.

69 Jevin D. West and Carl T. Bergstrom, 'Misinformation in and About Science', *Proceedings of the National Academy of Sciences*, vol. 118, no. 15, 13 April 2021, p. 6, https://www.pnas.org/content/pnas/118/15/e1912444117.full.pdf.

70 Centers for Disease Control and Prevention, 'One Health Basics',

https://www.cdc.gov/onehealth/basics/index.html.

71 T. Kuiken et al., 'Pathogen Surveillance in Animals', *Science*, vol. 309, no. 5,741, 9 September 2005, pp. 1,680–1, https://science.sciencemag.org/content/309/5741/1680.

72 Letko et al., 'Bat-borne Virus Diversity, Spillover and Emergence'.

73 See Kendra L. Phelps et al., 'Bat Research Networks and Viral Surveillance: Gaps and Opportunities in Western Asia', *Viruses*, vol. 11, no. 3, March 2019, p. 240, https://www.ncbi.nlm.nih.gov/pmc/articles/PMC6466127/pdf/viruses-11-00240.pdf.

74 See Alice Latinne et al., 'Origin and Cross-species Transmission of Bat Coronaviruses in China', *Nature Communications*, vol. 11, no. 1, 25 August 2020, art. 4,235, https://www.nature.com/articles/s41467-020-17687-3.pdf.

75 See World Organisation for Animal Health, World Health Organization and UN Environment Programme, 'Reducing Public Health Risks Associated with the Sale of Live Wild Animals of Mammalian Species in Traditional Food Markets: Interim Guidance', 12 April 2021, https://cdn.who.int/media/docs/default-source/food-safety/ig--121-1-food-safety-and-covid-19-guidance-for-traditional-food-markets-2021-04-12-en.pdf?sfvrsn=921ec66d_1&download=true.

76 See Michaeleen Doucleff, 'New Coronavirus Detected in Patients at Malaysian Hospital; the Source May Be Dogs', NPR, 20 May 2021, https://www.npr.org/sections/goatsandsoda/2021/05/20/996515792/a-newly-identified-coronavirus-is-making-people-sick-and-it-s-coming-from-dogs; and Anastasia N. Vlasova et al., 'Novel Canine Coronavirus Isolated from a Hospitalized Pneumonia Patient, East Malaysia', *Clinical Infectious Diseases*, 20 May 2021, https://doi.org/10.1093/cid/ciab456.

77 See Lian Pin Koh, Yuhan Li and Janice Ser Huay Lee, 'The Value of China's Ban on Wildlife Trade and Consumption', *Nature Sustainability*, vol. 4, no. 1, January 2021, pp. 2–4, https://www.nature.com/articles/s41893-020-00677-0.pdf.

78 *Ibid*.

79 See Emily Harwitz, 'In China, Public Support Grows to Rein in the Wildlife Trade in the Wake of the Pandemic', *Mongabay*, 9 December 2020, https://news.mongabay.com/2020/12/in-china-public-support-grows-to-rein-in-the-wildlife-trade-in-the-wake-of-the-pandemic/; and Xiangying Shi et al., 'Public Perception of Wildlife Consumption and Trade During the COVID-19 Outbreak', *Biodiversity Science*, vol. 28, no. 5, 20 May 2020, pp. 630–43.

80 See David Stanway, 'As WHO Highlights COVID Animal Origins, China Wildlife Crackdown Needs More Teeth – Experts', Reuters, 1 April 2021, https://www.reuters.com/article/us-health-coronavirus-china-wildlife-idUSKBN2BO6Y3.

81 Quoted in, for example, Greg Hilburn, 'Louisiana Senator Founded National Institutes of Health in 1930, Now Leading COVID-19 Fight', *Monroe News-Star*, 28 May 2020, https://eu.thenewsstar.com/story/news/2020/05/28/

louisiana-senator-founded-national-institutes-of-health-in-1930-fueled-spanish-flu-pandemic/5274543002/.

82 See John M. Barry, *The Great Influenza: The Epic Story of the Deadliest Plague in History* (New York: Viking, 2004).

Copyright © 2021 The International Institute for Strategic Studies

The Crisis of Liberalism and the Western Alliance

Lawrence Freedman

Liberalism is the surviving ideology of the post-Enlightenment era and is embraced, in a variety of forms, by the members of the Western alliance. The essence of liberalism is to distrust arbitrary and unaccountable power, focus on the individual over the collective and respect science over dogma. Beyond those core precepts, it often lacks coherence because it includes many competing strands. It describes partisan positions as much as an underlying ideology, which is why not all those who accept those precepts identify as liberals. During the course of this century, it has not performed well in the face of a series of challenges and is now in crisis.

The promise of liberalism

At the turn of this century liberalism appeared to be ascendant, having triumphed over Nazism in the Second World War and then communism in the Cold War. There was even talk of a 'liberal international order', offering the promise of a more harmonious system based on shared values, open trade and multilateral endeavours. Liberalism's sphere of influence grew as its perspectives permeated international institutions, which acquired more members and power. NATO and the European Union expanded, obliging new members, often former adversaries, to embrace the rule of law and honour human rights. Globalisation raised hopes that countries would follow common standards and uphold shared values, thereby reducing

Lawrence Freedman is Emeritus Professor of War Studies at King's College London. This essay is adapted from remarks delivered to an IISS–Europe conference on the future of alliances.

Survival | vol. 63 no. 6 | December 2021–January 2022 | pp. 37–44   https://doi.org/10.1080/00396338.2021.2006450

the risk of conflict and facilitating trade and free movement. There would be a virtuous circle as the political and economic reinforced each other. As people, commerce and finance moved freely around the world, so would ideas. Conflicts would lose their rougher edges and we would all become more prosperous.

Apartheid ended in South Africa and there were bold moves to address the Israeli occupation of Palestine. When there were conflicts, as in the Gulf after the Iraqi invasion of Kuwait, and then in the Balkans as the former Yugoslavia fell apart, the United Nations Security Council began to work as its founders intended. There was a consensus that shared problems required collective action, whether development, climate change or even the humanitarian distress caused by wars. The previous assumption that there should never be interference in internal affairs, which protected the rights of illiberal states, began to be put aside in a series of humanitarian interventions.

This all now seems a long time ago.

The optimism of that first post-Cold War decade seems naive, while the routines of multilateralism have become tired and ineffectual. Liberalism is in retreat, reflected in a decline in the number of governments that respect basic freedoms. The system is being reshaped by the leading illiberal states, notably China and Russia. Brutal regimes act with impunity, and there is little appetite or capacity to stop them. There is no global order, liberal or otherwise. This would require either a hegemon or a durable balance of power, and there is neither. There is still, for good reason, fear of a calamitous major war among the great powers. Nonetheless, the extent to which this will continue to act as a source of restraint into the future is uncertain. The question for members of the Western alliance is not whether they can design and implement a better global order but whether the current self-doubting liberalism is sufficient to bind them together. Even the term 'Western alliance' is now contested because of its geographical bias.

The crisis in liberalism reflects the tensions among its different strands. One tension is between the desire to strengthen international law and institutions to prevent recourse to war as a way of resolving disputes, on the one hand, and the belief that forceful action is at times necessary to protect all people from the ravages of illiberalism, on the other. A second tension is between a belief in free markets and competition as a source of productive efficiency and prosperity, and the need to intervene in markets to prevent corporations acquiring monopoly power, guard against socially inflammatory inequalities and ensure that collective needs are met.

The decline of liberalism

Coming into this century, the more ambitious strands – interventionism and free markets – were to the fore. In both cases these strands were discredited because of hubris and excessive ambition. Money was bundled into ever more esoteric financial instruments that became progressively detached from real, productive economic activity. The legacy was a black mark against modern capitalist practices, as ordinary people were left suffering the consequences, losing confidence in the political establishment and becoming attracted to new populist movements, sometimes on the left but largely on the right. Established institutions and values came to be challenged by political forces that disdained them and treated them with contempt. The COVID-19 pandemic then threw into sharp relief the problems caused by globalisation not only in the spread of disease but also in the dependence on supply chains, which became badly disrupted.

Even though the American-led occupations of Afghanistan and Iraq were prompted by counter-terrorism and counter-proliferation, they were recast as liberal projects. This was not only because they took on such illiberal figures as Osama bin Laden and Saddam Hussein, but also because of the effort to turn those countries into functioning liberal democracies. Occupations, however, are inherently illiberal activities, especially when they must be sustained against hostile and well-supported local political movements. The Taliban's return to power in Afghanistan in summer 2021, which had been on the cards for some time, was taken to mark the end of this project and even a stage in Western grand strategy. Governments might still be ready to take on Islamist terrorism directly, especially if their activists could be targeted using drones, but there was no longer any interest in immersing ground forces into long and indecisive counter-insurgency campaigns.

The awkward dependencies created by unrestricted globalisation and the pain caused by ill-conceived interventions led to retrenchment. Instead of addressing the issues raised by problems of fragile and vulnerable states, foreign policy came to be dominated by the question of how to address the harsher stances taken by Russia and China. A return to great-power competition is now described as a defining feature of the 2020s.

Liberalism and strategic affairs

With such competition comes unavoidable questions about the role of the United States as the source of security guarantees to the liberal democracies. As strategists assess potential responses to a Russian move into a Baltic state or a Chinese assault on Taiwan, they soon come to the big 'realist' questions: will the US really bring its military power to bear in these scenarios? Why should a state that is not directly at risk from aggression throw itself into a dangerous conflict which might be concluded with nuclear exchanges?

This is not a new question, and the alliance has coped for many years simply by avoiding a definitive answer. The credibility of extended nuclear deterrence became an issue as soon as a 'balance of terror' was first identified in the 1950s. Deterrence worked not because of the certainty of a nuclear riposte to any aggression but because nuclear escalation could never be ruled out entirely should a major war begin. If anything, uncertainties about how a conventional war would play out between 'peer competitors' with multi-domain capabilities have added a new layer of deterrence. Meanwhile, the shared wariness about a full-scale war has led to a focus on economic measures, cyber and information campaigns as means of pursuing grievances and highlighting disputes. These may be less dangerous, but they add irritants and grit to the system without leading to the resolution of any underlying conflict.

The question of the value of security guarantees when they need to be cashed in will therefore not go away, even though for the moment it can be ducked. At some point a supreme test might demand an answer. At such a time, risk-taking will depend not only on geopolitical considerations but also on the severity of the threat to core values and a way of life. This is why the crisis in liberalism matters. If the alliances do not appear to be in good order, and harbour mutual suspicions and stark policy differences, more queries will arise about the reliability of solemn obligations and rhetorical commitments undertaken in happier times. Long before the most testing moments, these queries could erode cohesion even more. Hence the anxiety behind much of the current commentary on the durability of the alliance – that the ties of interest and ideology will not be sufficient to hold it together as they come under pressure, to the point where it all might begin to unravel.

Against this gloomy prognosis there are three counters. The first is that in practice alliance activity has if anything been intensified in recent years. The heightened competition has reinforced rather than undermined the Western alliance. Russia's hostile stance towards Ukraine, including the annexation of Crimea in 2014, reminded NATO of its original purpose at a time when the Afghan experience had sown doubts about a more expansive role. Meanwhile, China's assertiveness, taken to a new level by President Xi Jinping, has led to a reaction among countries in the Indo-Pacific region, with new life being injected into the Quadrilateral Security Dialogue (consisting of Australia, India, Japan and the US) and the unexpected development of a high-technology partnership among Australia, the United Kingdom and the United States – known as AUKUS – with an initial focus on nuclear submarines.

All this has taken shape despite doubts about whether the United States is ready and willing to sustain its established alliances. Donald Trump was sceptical of their value, as well as free trade. President Joe Biden has taken a more traditional stance, although the abrupt departure from Afghanistan and the secrecy surrounding the AUKUS arrangement before its roll-out have led to concern about his readiness to consult allies before making major moves. Over the longer term, questions will arise about the implications of a possible Trump victory in the 2024 US presidential election and indeed about whether, with its persistent internal polarisation, the US can remain a liberal state.

The second counter follows Winston Churchill's observation that 'there is only one thing worse than fighting with allies, and that is fighting without them'. The US is at the centre of a complex web of security arrangements with some 70 states. By contrast, Russia and China are relatively friendless, with a few client states that are themselves quite weak. They have no one to work with on broad foreign-policy issues except each other. This has led to a tentative alliance of convenience between the two, as they both seek to undermine the US position, but it is asymmetrical and not based on any natural affinity other than shared illiberalism. Russia is stuck in eastern Ukraine, and while it can claim success in keeping Bashar al-Assad in power in Syria it lacks the resources to support recovery. China's Belt and Road Initiative has yielded far less than anticipated because of poorly designed infrastructure projects and issues with debt. 'Wolf-warrior diplomacy' and efforts to intimidate states that question Chinese policies, including, for example, Beijing's initial mismanagement of the COVID-19 pandemic, have not led them to fall into line.

Thirdly, illiberalism does not produce better or more efficient government than liberalism, or at least it offers its own dysfunctions. Illiberalism is presented as a critique of Western decadence and incoherence. Authoritarianism promises incisive and firm decision-making, without needing to take account of any opposition or bother with complex legal processes. China's remarkable economic progress over the past three decades has been taken to show that authoritarianism does not preclude growth and prosperity, although much of this took place while the country was more open than it is now and was not caught up in a cult of personality. As Xi has sought to extend control, the developing problems with the Chinese model have become more apparent, including a rapidly ageing population, environmental degradation and an economy distorted by a rush for growth. Moreover, illiberalism generates its own perverse, paranoid logic. If no diversity of opinion can be tolerated, then as each boundary is reached control must be extended and dissent squashed. Anything that cannot be controlled becomes potentially threatening. If individuals and groups lack outlets for their grievances and disaffection, and elite discourse becomes sycophantic to a supreme leader, then it becomes harder to identify emerging problems and make the case for policy shifts.

This is not to argue that China is on the verge of collapse, but it is entering a period when its system will face some severe challenges, which may be aggravated because of its inflexible and coercive character. The Chinese model is not one that others could readily emulate even if they wanted to – for example, in its high-technology social control. Accordingly, should

China's reputation for effortless progress be further dented, it will be even less likely to form a counter-alliance to the West. Illiberalism therefore has its own crises. Russia and China face serious policy dilemmas, and their systems, including their entrenched leaderships, do not always lead them to choose wisely.

*   *   *

The corollary is that liberalism should be better than authoritarianism at adapting to new circumstances, acknowledging the problems with existing policies, and gathering diverse views and evidence on alternatives. Liberalism remains in a defensive position after a series of missteps over the past few decades. There are major economic and social problems to be addressed, exacerbated by the pandemic. Illiberal political movements are strong in some Western states, including in the US. Addressing these issues would still leave the standard concerns of alliances: clarifying interests, identifying threats, maintaining trust, building strength and coping with unexpected events. Recovery from the crisis in liberalism will not be straightforward and cannot be guaranteed. For that to happen, the liberal states will need to draw on the qualities that have served them well in the past – honesty about failings, openness to new ideas, pragmatism and flexibility in policymaking, and confidence in core liberal values as essential to a well-ordered, tolerant and humane society.

Copyright © 2021 The International Institute for Strategic Studies

Euro-Atlantic Security and the China Nexus

François Heisbourg

Since the world financial crisis of 2007–09, China has emerged as a global power, and as a peer, or near-peer, competitor of the United States. Symbolically, Barack Obama's 'pivot to Asia' speech in Canberra in 2011 marked the rise of China as America's strategic priority.[1] During the ensuing decade, three American presidents have attempted to put an end to the 'forever wars' in Afghanistan and Iraq, a goal eventually achieved by President Joe Biden in Afghanistan, albeit rather messily, while Iraq remains in a strategic twilight zone. The three presidents have demonstrated great reluctance to engage in new conflicts in the Middle East, as demonstrated by America's 'leading from behind' in Libya, its forbearance after the Syrian regime crossed the chemical-weapons red line and Donald Trump's empty bombast vis-à-vis Iran. It took the explosive eruption of the Islamic State to prompt a return of US forces to the Middle East in 2014.

Even in Europe, US military engagement was kept within narrow limits when Russia invaded Ukrainian territory, with a battalion-sized US force deployed to the Baltics. In political terms, Obama handed the baton to France and Germany in the 'Normandy format' within weeks after armed conflict broke out in Donbas.[2] These and other examples of strategic prudence, to use Obama's term, may sometimes be justified. But they are also the corollary of America's tilt – the United Kingdom's current expression

François Heisbourg is IISS Senior Adviser for Europe and Special Adviser to the Fondation pour la Recherche Stratégique. This essay is adapted from remarks delivered to an IISS–Europe conference on the future of alliances.

Survival | vol. 63 no. 6 | December 2021–January 2022 | pp. 45–62   https://doi.org/10.1080/00396338.2021.2006453

– towards China and the Indo-Pacific.[3] As China's power in all its dimensions increases, the incentive grows for the US to limit its engagement in areas and for causes which are seen, rightly or wrongly, as being of limited relevance to the contest with Beijing.

China has further developed the material base of its power, with about a 6% annual GDP growth. It has made especially great strides in its technological capabilities, possibly achieving parity with the United States in areas such as quantum computing and artificial intelligence. China has also modernised and expanded its military. By 2020, the People's Liberation Army Navy was fielding as many major combatants as the US Navy, though with less tonnage and experience. At the same time, Chinese officials emphasised the leading role of the Chinese Communist Party (CCP) both in its visible expression of power and in its framing of a 'Chinese dream'. While forbidding foreign operators online freedom of action, China marshals its peerless data resources in the service of a kind of 'cyber dictatorship'. Beijing's assertiveness abroad has increased with the rise of 'wolf warrior' diplomats whose career success depends on their aggressive voicing of the party line rather than their ability to improve relations with other countries.

The COVID-19 pandemic has accelerated these developments. Given the threat of the disease at home, the CCP's leadership could not afford to be seen as failing. Accordingly, it comprehensively mobilised Chinese society, attaining impressive results in containing the spread of the pandemic outside Hubei province and eventually rolling it back as early as April 2020 there and in the Wuhan area. It has also resisted undertaking or assisting in any full-scale investigation into the origin of the novel coronavirus, punishing those countries, such as Australia, that have pressed the issue.[4] Progress in the fight against COVID has been recycled into a narrative of communist triumph, while all that goes wrong, such as the birth of the virus, is deemed the fault of the party's enemies.[5] The party's shrillness and China's sense of besiegement have grown more extreme as China's effort to achieve zero-COVID has flagged, with Beijing cancelling spectator attendance at the Beijing Winter Olympics and quarter-to-quarter economic growth in China dropping nearly to zero.[6] China's leadership has no incentive to acknowledge its shortcomings or to show weakness by lowering its foreign-policy profile.

The pandemic has also had the broader effect of demonstrating that even in the face of a truly global threat, the 'international community' is little more than an empty concept. Chinese President Xi Jinping's government and the Trump administration both instrumentalised the World Health Organization (WHO) to their own ends. The US imposed a strict embargo on the export of its vaccines and vaccine-related ingredients, which stretched into the first months of the Biden administration. The global north generally displayed reckless disregard for the needs of countries that could not produce or purchase effective vaccines in sufficient quantities.[7] This morally dubious conduct was perilous in global public-health terms, affording the virus unlimited opportunities to circulate and mutate. The pattern of national egotism and shortsightedness may well extend to the larger, longer and more lethal threat of global climate change.

Five scenarios

During the global financial crisis, China played a major role in avoiding a reprise of the Great Depression. Its stimulus plan was the largest in the world by any measure, and it was a constructive partner in upgrading the G20. Indeed, it came closer than ever to being the 'responsible stakeholder' many in the West believed it should and could be.[8] Several scenarios then seemed possible: a world run as a G2, with the US and China at the helm, as prominently voiced by Zbigniew Brzezinski;[9] a G20 – that had just worked rather well; or, *horresco referens,* a chaotic G-Zero.

The range of scenarios is now somewhat different.

Since Biden's policy recommendations are close to those of the intellectual father of containment, the George Kennan scenario comes first: the US takes a global approach to its relationship with its peer competitor and lies at the centre of an alliance system. Its aim is to preserve and protect the 'Free World', which includes both bona fide democracies and friendly dictatorships of the 'he may be a bastard but he's our bastard' variety.[10] Liberal principles and the existence of a liberal order are underscored, as America's peer competitor wages its Leninist ideological battle against decadent democracies. It is assumed that nuclear powers and those aligned with them avoid descending into direct conflict with one another. The peer competitor collapses peacefully some four decades later.

However, it takes two to tango, and the same applies to keeping war cold. China currently appears to be uninterested in developing an alliance system to balance against the United States in an orderly way. It does not display any interest in notions such as nuclear stability or crisis management. Beyond its national inclinations, the international battlefields have changed: economic power, technological prowess and digital dominance are now strategically crucial and call for different organisational approaches than those of the Soviet era.

As for the second scenario, Thucydides has been elevated in public debate, even in some of the Chinese debates, thanks to Graham Allison's recent book.[11] Like the incumbent Athenians facing an ascendant Sparta, the US feels threatened by the rise of China. Each contender adopts a worst-case reading of the actions of the other, thus falling into a Thucydides Trap, and war to the finish ensues. The US – Athens' stand-in – is defeated on the battlefield and loses the war.

China appears uninterested in an alliance system

There is nothing good to say of this catastrophic scenario. But it could indeed happen, and would best be avoided.

The third scenario is based on Charles Kindleberger's argument that the comparatively unremarkable Wall Street crash of late 1929 became the global Great Depression and eventually spawned a world war.[12] He concluded that the British Empire, the financial hegemon of the day, could not take the lead in helping prevent contagion from the New York Stock Exchange to the outside world, and that the rising US, with the world's largest GDP, could not or would not exercise leadership with respect to what became a global problem. From the ensuing disorder, other distinctly non-financial would-be hegemons arose in Tokyo and Berlin. What has been unfolding during the pandemic is all too reminiscent of the abdication of responsibility described by Kindleberger. It may happen again with respect to global climate change, with the US under a new administration showing too much strategic restraint and China acting in an increasingly coercive, predatory and unconstructive manner.

Of course, in January 1933, nobody knew what would follow. A new global system emerged from the rubble, but only a dozen years and some

60 million deaths later. Badly mismanaged climate change could also lead to a calamitous reordering.[13]

The Yugoslav leader Tito (Josip Broz) may make for a surprising fourth scenario, but also one that may tempt many, possibly even most, countries. Flanked by Gamal Abdel Nasser of Egypt and Jawaharlal Nehru of India, he was the leader of the Non-Aligned Movement, established in Belgrade in 1961. As its name suggests, the movement's stated purpose was to avoid taking sides or being caught up in the confrontation between the Soviet bloc and the Western alliances. In practice, it tended to lean eastward: Fidel Castro, not exactly a Cold War neutral, chaired the Non-Aligned Movement from 1979 to 1983 and again in 2006–08, after the collapse of the Soviet Union. However, the general concept of non-alignment proved to be highly attractive. By the mid-1980s, it counted close to 100 members, including all of the newly independent African states.

As the confrontation between the US and China intensifies, the desire to stand away from the fray will grow. Many European countries, including France – notwithstanding its repeated military excursions into the South China Sea and the Taiwan Strait, and its adoption of an Indo-Pacific strategy in 2018 – may tilt in this direction. In September 2021, Bruno Le Maire, the French finance minister and a major political figure, stressed France's quest for independence vis-à-vis America's China strategy.[14] His stridency no doubt owed something to French unhappiness at its cavalier and humiliating treatment at the hands of Australia, the United Kingdom and the US when these countries created the trilateral security arrangement known as AUKUS and deprived France of a €50 billion submarine deal.

The problem with Tito's approach is both historical and practical. The Cold War was not very cold at all for many non-aligned countries that eschewed membership of well-developed alliance systems. Several Middle Eastern states, the Democratic Republic of the Congo/Zaire and the Indian subcontinent demonstrated the cruel fate of some putative bystanders. In practical terms, for Europe to seek equidistance between China and the US would probably mean eventually getting into trouble with both rather than neither.

Finally, finding Jesus would be a highly desirable scenario. The lion and the lamb would lie in peace: China and the US would work together in a multilateral system to meet the huge challenge of global climate change. There were some hopes that this would happen when the Paris climate agreement was signed in 2016. But that was in the days when climate-change policies belonged to the realm of unenforced generalities. It is much more difficult to work together on hard choices entailing economically and socially painful and disruptive commitments. When France hits diesel fuel with a green tax, the *gilets jaunes* pick up the pitchforks. Each country has or will have similar or bigger problems of this sort, especially the two largest emitters of greenhouse gases if locked in superpower rivalry.[15]

Organising for uncertainty in Europe

Europe's first and obvious task will be to organise itself for the uncertainty that this broad array of possible outcomes presents. Amplifying that uncertainty is the current political opacity of the US, in which the two houses of Congress are narrowly divided, an unprecedentedly old president and an untried vice-president govern, and the previous president refuses to recognise the outcome of the 2016 election. Meanwhile, US policy on Europe has become dependent on the exigencies of its China policy. Thus, Washington suspended sanctions against Germany for proceeding with the Nord Stream 2 pipeline with Russia, yet successfully pressured the British government to cancel its prospective 5G deal with China's Huawei.

Accordingly, Europeans appear compelled to hedge at least as much as they did during the volatile Trump administration. They must assume that the US under this and the next administration will act negatively, even punitively, if Europe is seen as running counter to America's policy in the Indo-Pacific. A rational Europe would want to build resilience into its policies, planning for sudden and extreme shifts in US decision-making. Transatlantic burden-sharing, European strategic autonomy, Indo-Pacific risk-sharing, forgoing lucrative business with China as part of European Union and NATO cooperation with Washington against Beijing's predatory technological and commercial practices: each comes with substantial costs that could become unbearable for debt-ridden post-pandemic governments, making the Tito option seem tempting.

Irrespective of the preferred outcome, Europe, and especially the EU, must think globally about European China policy and how it will interact with US interests. It does not appear easy for the United States to reciprocate. By handling the AUKUS deal in deepest secrecy and in a purely regional context instead of doing so openly in a global context, the US did unnecessary damage to transatlantic relations. Arguably, European countries with imperial pasts, but without the weight of a hamstrung empire, are better equipped to manage their alliance relations.

As an increasingly hard-pressed US focuses increasingly on China, the EU and its governments need to answer several important questions. What should be Europe's key strategic objective? Who should lead policy coordination on China with the US? How should Europe balance its regional and Indo-Pacific security and defence policies?

Europe's overarching aims should be defending itself against a revisionist Russia, insulating Europe against direct Chinese coercion, helping like-minded countries – in particular, the US – to prevent China from overwhelming the rules-based international order and avoiding the catastrophe of a major war between nuclear powers. These priorities discourage virtue signalling with respect to the Tibetans or the Uighurs, without excluding support for their causes if they serve Europe's strategic ends. This framework is incompatible with strategic equipoise between the US and China. It calls for a new understanding between the US and Europe, and new institutions and processes enabling transatlantic cooperation.

No new cold war

The current strategic situation is not a new version of the Cold War, in which old building blocks, such as a merely refurbished NATO, can successfully apply the same military-centric policy prescriptions and use the same metrics, such as the totemic correlation of forces. That approach worked to a large extent because the world's technological, economic and financial order formed an essentially Western hinterland, which the Soviet Union sorely lacked. Today, the hinterland is no longer predominantly Western.

Furthermore, areas such as monetary affairs that are still US-centric will come under increasing attack, and not only from China. The strategic importance of Australia's putative nuclear-submarine fleet pales in comparison to that of the US and the EU working together to contain China's digital empire and technological ambitions. That contest is global. American tech titans have learned to respect Europe's global normative power, which is well worth directing against China.

Such considerations lead to a different institutional set-up than the old one. For broad-gauged technological and normative cooperation vis-à-vis China, the logical players are the West's two trading and regulatory superpowers, the US and the EU – in particular, the European Commission, which possesses the necessary institutional culture and the delegated enabling powers. The EU is expanding those powers, notably in the areas of technology and investment control with respect to China. The seminal moment occurred on 29 September 2021, when the EU–US Trade and Technology Council held its first meeting in Pittsburgh. Possibly not by accident, the decision to hold it was confirmed shortly after Biden and French President Emmanuel Macron had their first post-AUKUS phone conversation, abundant and perhaps deliberate leaks having suggested that the meeting could be delayed.[16]

NATO's focus should remain Russia

NATO has decided to draft a new Strategic Concept in which China will presumably figure prominently, whereas it was absent in the 2010 Strategic Concept. Macron's provocation that NATO was 'brain-dead' in November 2019 may have nudged the organisation in this direction.[17] In December 2019, the member-states meeting in London decided to launch a reflection study, 'NATO 2030'. By virtue of its mutual defence guarantee (Article V of the Washington Treaty) and as a consequence of Russia's revisionist ambitions and military capabilities, NATO's focus should remain Russia. Given its collective-security responsibility, however, it could also build up NATO's generic role in providing protection in the cyber and space domains, and by serving as the institutional anchor of a mechanism akin to the post-war Coordinating Committee for Multilateral Export Controls (COCOM) limiting the transfer of critical technologies to China.[18]

NATO's collective-security role also affords the organisation responsibility for providing data and analysis concerning China.[19] Indeed, in the last three years, NATO has been recruiting Chinese-speaking personnel.

The question of a specific military role for the EU as such, often summarised by the originally French term 'strategic autonomy', has been a touchy issue for a broad range of European countries. They include those that are unwilling to shoulder the costs of defence, whether in a NATO or a European context, and those that are afraid of scaring off the Americans at the risk of facing Russia on their own. Many belong to both groups. These fears understandably peaked during the Trump administration. The Biden administration appears ready to work with rather than against a greater strategic role for the Europeans provided that capacity-building is part of the process.[20] This may not satisfy the spending-shy cohort, but strategic autonomy will be more difficult to resist if the US plays along.

The harder issue may involve what are sometimes called 'minilaterals' – that is, de facto or *de jure* agreements between small groups of states. AUKUS, which tightens defence ties among Australia, the UK and the US, is one conspicuous example. The Quadrilateral Security Dialogue established in 2017 among Australia, India, Japan and the US is another. In September 2021, France and Greece signed a mutual defence treaty whereby one NATO member (France) extended a security guarantee to another NATO member (Greece) that was threatened by yet another NATO member (Turkey) in a region where the US no longer plays the same prominent leadership role that it did during the 1974 Turkish invasion of Cyprus. But NATO as an organisation remains unable to settle disputes between certain of its members: when the fire-control system of a Turkish frigate on a national mission 'painted' a French frigate participating in a NATO operation off the Libyan coast, NATO declined any substantial involvement in clearing up the matter.[21] A broadening of the French–Greek treaty to the EU as a whole could be a subsequent step, and a means of applying European strategic autonomy to contingencies in which NATO is unable or unwilling to act.

AUKUS, which derives from the post-Second World War intelligence pact among English-speaking allies known as Five Eyes, poses a different challenge. It could lead to a West divided into a muscular China-oriented Anglosphere and a continental Europe compelled to deal, maybe increasingly alone, with Russian and Mediterranean contingencies. Such an evolution has several superficial attractions. Firstly, it looks rational in terms of allocation of scarce resources: the US and its maritime linguistic kin would 'do China' while the continental Europeans handle Russia. Secondly, the idea may appeal to countries that are worried about insufficient focus on Russia's threat to its neighbours and to countries – pointedly, the UK – that are detaching themselves from the EU. Thirdly, it provides a convenient handle for the European quid of more burden-sharing for the American quo of endorsing European defence. Fourthly, the notion sits well with the United States' configuration of geographic combatant commands. It is not altogether surprising that during his recent Southeast Asian tour, US Secretary of Defense Lloyd Austin III expressed little enthusiasm for European military deployments in the Indo-Pacific region.[22]

Such a stark geographical and functional division of labour would be a mistake, however. Russia remains a nuclear superpower. Even as its GDP has shrunk to an eighth of China's, it has the military capabilities and the political will to push its often-repeated revisionist agenda in Europe, and the ability to project military nuisance value beyond the regional level, directly or through its mercenaries in the Wagner Group. That is reason enough for Europe and NATO to make Russia the dimensioning factor in their military planning.[23] It is also reason enough for the US to remain engaged in Europe at its current level, using NATO for deterrence and defence and US bases in Europe as a platform for global force projection.

An element of risk-sharing in the form of European deployments in the Indo-Pacific should be sustained. This would not be a novel innovation. Since 2015, France has been sending warships into the South China Sea, most recently a nuclear attack submarine and a submarine tender, and has deployed the *Dupuy de Lôme*, a substantial missile-telemetry and signals-intelligence-gathering vessel, in the Taiwan Strait under its legal navigation rights.[24] In 2021, Britain sent its new aircraft carrier, HMS *Queen Elizabeth*, and her escorts to the South China Sea. Vessels from other allied countries have joined the French and British in the region.

For the US, such activity establishes the presumption that if anything goes wrong in the Indo-Pacific, the Europeans will act as allies. In turn, they should expect to be treated as such, with higher levels of information-sharing if not full consultation. Most importantly, in a war perceptions count double: if the Europeans are not in the Indo-Pacific physically, they will be out of the picture; in that case, American forces in Europe could be more readily withdrawn.

There are additional reasons for a European presence in the Indo-Pacific: 2.7m European citizens live and vote there, and some 10m square kilometres of France's exclusive economic zone lie in the region, which makes France's the largest maritime presence in the South Pacific (larger than Australia's). Given Chinese designs in the South Pacific, one would expect greater Australian and American interest in France's role than that displayed in the AUKUS affair.

Russia and Europe's 'three-body problem'

In *The Three-body Problem*, Chinese science-fiction writer Liu Cixin describes the fate of a planet that is subject to the gravitational pull of three different stars: it experiences sudden and unpredictable forces that frequently have egregious effects on the inhabitants of the planet.[25] Such a tripolar situation is also a fitting analogy for what can happen when international relations are dominated by a handful of great powers, such as the United States, China and Russia, with Europe caught in their intersecting ambitions.[26] The parallel may underestimate the lack of European agency and overrate the capabilities of post-Soviet Russia, but it works quite well as an analytical lens.

China has switched strategic allegiances three times since the creation of the People's Republic, from the initial Sino-Soviet alliance (1949–57) to its recusal after 1958 to the rapprochement with the US during the 1970s. Washington helped secure Beijing's recognition as the representative of China in the United Nations and was a party to the compromise which eventually led to the 'one country, two systems' formula. This created conditions for regional stability, and what followed: China's economic take-off and the triumph of globalisation. Washington's and Moscow's positions have also shifted but with their own logics, as the US retained superpower status while Russia's lustre has faded since the collapse of the Soviet Union.

Europe has been an essentially passive spectator of these permutations. They did not greatly matter for European security as long as China was a kind of dwarf star. Times have changed. As China extends its predatory grasp into Europe, the US pushes its allies to participate in a global coalition against China, and Russia presses its revisionist agenda, Europe acutely feels the impact of the three-way interaction. Furthermore, China and Russia have been deepening their rapprochement, and the US may be looking for ways to counter this alignment.

One approach, voiced by Macron in 2019 and 2020, is to attempt a European–Russian rapprochement with a view to weakening what he called the 'alliance' between Beijing and Moscow.[27] In the absence of a broader European consensus, he launched a French–Russian strategic dialogue. This included 2+2 ministerial meetings on defence and foreign affairs, and covers areas such as the Ukrainian nexus and arms control. Two years later, this hasn't yielded any tangible results on those issues, nor has it produced any hint of a distancing between Moscow and Beijing. This is not surprising, if only because the Russia–China partnership was not created for Europe-related reasons, and Macron's Russian interlocutors have not viewed what he could put on the table as relevant.

The US, which more clearly drives the Sino-Russian partnership and has potentially more to offer, may also be tempted to woo Russia. Such at least is the thinking of analysts as different as Graham Allison, Charles Kupchan and John Mearsheimer, among others.[28] There appears to be no indication that this sort of thinking is inspiring policymakers in Washington, Beijing or Moscow. However, such an approach, which would presumably affect European interests, is no more implausible than other strategic somersaults, from the Molotov–Ribbentrop accords to the Sino-Soviet split to the US–China rapprochement. Europeans would be suffering serious historical amnesia were they to dismiss the possibility of a US–Russia rapprochement along these lines, especially considering that post-Biden scenarios could include a second Trump term. It is yet another contingency against which Europeans may need to hedge.

The other approach is for NATO to view Russia and China as a single threat. Recent language from NATO Secretary-General Jens Stoltenberg suggests a possible drift in this direction: 'The whole idea of distinguishing so much between China, Russia, either the Asia-Pacific or Europe – it is one big security environment and we have to address it all together.'[29] It would be a strategic error to fold Russia and China into the same threat universe, akin to the self-damaging policies advocated by many in London and Paris after the Molotov–Ribbentrop accords, with Édouard Daladier and Neville Chamberlain pondering whether to bomb the Baku oil wells or deploy an expeditionary force to Finland to defend it against the Red Army, oblivious to the fact that wars are not won by uniting one's antagonists but by dividing them.

Such an approach is also a category error: China and Russia are not, at least not yet, true allies. China is not sending soldiers to Donbas to support Russia against Ukraine, nor is Russia sending troops to the Himalayas to support China against India. Treating the two powers as if they were allies might only encourage them to transform the partnership into a fully fledged Sino-Russian, anti-American or anti-Western alliance.

The way forward must surely be to work with or around the current, admittedly imperfect, status quo rather than attempting to change it.

*   *   *

Historically, the contest between a rising hegemon and a status quo great power is a dangerous and fraught process. Some of the prerequisites for a successful outcome of the sort stated earlier will call for familiar ingredients of good statecraft. Careful diplomacy with one's potential antagonists, policy informed by dispassionate and depoliticised intelligence, defence built on credible yet unprovocative military preparations, the ability to manage complexity internally and externally, respect for the interests of allies and partners: these should all be on the menu. Some will be even more important than they were during the Cold War given the salience of the three-body problem.

During the Cold War, there was also a sense of clear and present danger, most obviously in the form of what was rightly called the nuclear 'balance of terror' from the mid-1950s onward.[30] This did not suffice to make the nuclear powers reasonable actors, but it created a sense of limits, of brinks that could be approached but not crossed. Even the sharpest disagreements between allies – the Suez Crisis, the *Skybolt* missile affair, the Vietnam War and France's withdrawal from NATO's integrated command structure – were kept within manageable bounds. The Third World War did not break out between the superpowers. Fear was the key moderating ingredient. But the generation of the Second World War is fast disappearing, with Queen Elizabeth II as the last head of state with personal memories of that era's horrors. The actors in the climactic moments of the Cold War are also leaving the scene; the Cuban Missile Crisis and the multiple West Berlin showdowns are now present only in the recollections of those long retired. Resentment, suspicion and arrogance are abundantly present in the China–US nexus, but the pervasive, gripping fear of nuclear annihilation that helped keep the Cold War cold is notably absent.

Trust, especially among allies, is therefore paramount. The AUKUS affair may have the saving virtue of reminding us of the volatile and fragile nature of that quality, hard to build and easy to lose. The careful, patient work of nurturing and tending trust – the strategic version of gardening – is an essential component of the complex, dangerous and undoubtedly protracted period we entered a decade ago.

Notes

1 White House, 'Remarks by President Obama to the Australian Parliament', 17 November 2011, http://obamawhitehouse.archives.gov.

2 See, for example, Simon Shuster, 'As World Leaders Prepare to Remember D-Day, Diplomacy over Ukraine Takes Center Stage', *Time*, 4 June 2014, https://time.com/2823444/as-world-leaders-prepare-to-remember-d-day-diplomacy-over-ukraine-takes-centerstage/.

3 Formally, the US expanded its Pacific Command area of operations into the Indo-Pacific space with the establishment of the Indo-Pacific Command (USINDOPACOM) on 30 May 2018. France took a similar decision at the time.

4 See, for instance, Jasper Becker, *Made in China: Wuhan, Covid and the Quest for Biotech Supremacy* (London: C. Hurst & Co., 2021).

5 For example, China has suggested that the virus is a product of US biowarfare research, echoing Soviet

propaganda and active measures regarding the origin of AIDS. See Chen Qingqing and Cao Siqi, 'China Asks WHO to Investigate Fort Detrick, UNC Bio Labs Through Diplomatic Channel', *Global Times*, 25 August 2021, https://www.globaltimes.cn/page/202108/1232467.shtml.

6   See 'China's Q3 Economic Growth Slows to 4.9% amid Power Crunch, Supply Bottleneck', *Global Times*, 18 October 2021, https://www.globaltimes.cn/page/202110/1236577.shtml. That official figure is year-on-year (Q4 2020 to Q3 2021); China does not provide official quarter-on-quarter annualised rates, but business sources estimate Q3 annualised growth to range from –0.1% to +2%. See, for instance, Stella Wong and Takeshi Kihara, 'China GDP to Slow to 5% in Q3 amid Property Woes: Nikkei Survey', *Nikkei Asia*, 7 October 2021, https://asia.nikkei.com/Economy/China-GDP-to-slow-to-5-in-Q3-amid-property-woes-Nikkei-survey.

7   As of 23 October 2021, under the COVID-19 Vaccines Global Access (COVAX) worldwide initiative directed by Gavi, the Vaccine Alliance, the Coalition for Epidemic Preparedness Innovations and the World Health Organization, only 394 million doses had been distributed to 144 low- and middle-income countries. See UNICEF, 'COVID-19 Vaccine Market Dashboard', http://unicef.org/supply/covid-19-vaccine-market-dashboard.

8   The term comes from a speech by Robert Zoellick, then deputy US secretary of state, in September 2005. See Robert B. Zoellick, 'Whither China: From Membership to Responsibility?', US State Department Archives, 21 September 2005, https://2001-2009.state.gov/s/d/former/zoellick/rem/53682.htm.

9   See Edward Wong, 'Former Carter Adviser Calls for a "G-2" World', *New York Times*, 2 January 2009, https://www.nytimes.com/2009/01/12/world/asia/12iht-beijing.3.19283773.html.

10   That phrase is often, though inconclusively, attributed to Franklin D. Roosevelt in reference to Anastasio Somoza Garcia of Nicaragua, but it captures the flavour of Cold War geopolitics.

11   Graham Allison, *Destined for War: Can America and China Escape Thucydides's Trap?* (Boston, MA, and New York: Houghton Mifflin Harcourt, 2017).

12   Charles P. Kindleberger, *The World in Depression 1929–1939*, revised edition (Berkeley, CA: University of California Press, 1986).

13   For a compelling fictional treatment, see Kim Stanley Robinson, *The Ministry for the Future* (London: Orbit, 2020).

14   See Bruno Le Maire, 'The United States Has Only One Strategic Concern, China … We, We Consider that We Have to Be Independent', *L'Opinion*, 23 September 2021.

15   See Anatol Lieven, 'Climate Change and the State: A Case for Environmental Realism', *Survival*, vol. 62, no. 2, April–May 2020, pp. 7–26.

16   See 'AUKUS: EU Considers Postponing Major Summit with US amid France Submarine Deal Row', *Euronews*, 21 September 2021, https://www.euronews.com/2021/09/21/eu-considers-postponing-major-cooperation-summit-with-us.

17 See, for example, 'Emmanuel Macron Warns Europe: NATO Is Becoming Brain-dead', *The Economist*, 7 November 2019, https://www.economist.com/europe/2019/11/07/emmanuel-macron-warns-europe-nato-is-becoming-brain-dead.

18 See François Heisbourg, 'NATO 4.0: The Atlantic Alliance and the Rise of China', *Survival*, vol. 62, no. 2, April–May 2020, pp. 83–102.

19 On NATO's role regarding China and the Alliance's Russian priority, see Jens Ringsmose and Sten Rynning, 'NATO's Next Strategic Concept: Prioritise or Perish', *Survival*, vol. 63, no. 5, October–November 2021, pp. 147–68.

20 In a joint statement following their September phone conversation, Biden and Macron noted that 'the United States also recognizes the importance of a stronger and more capable European defence that contributes positively to transatlantic and global security and its complementarity to NATO'. White House, 'Joint Statement on the Phone Call Between President Biden and President Macron', 22 September 2021, https://www.whitehouse.gov/briefing-room/statements-releases/2021/09/22/joint-statement-on-the-phone-call-between-president-biden-and-president-macron/.

21 See 'France Suspends Role in NATO Naval Mission over Tensions with Turkey', France 24, 1 July 2020, https://www.france24.com/en/20200701-france-suspends-role-in-nato-naval-mission-over-turkish-warship-incident.

22 US Department of Defense, 'Secretary of Defense Lloyd J. Austin III Participates in Fullerton Lecture Series in Singapore', 27 July 2021, https://www.defense.gov/News/Transcripts/Transcript/Article/2711025/secretary-of-defense-lloyd-j-austin-iii-participates-in-fullerton-lecture-serie/. See also Anatol Lieven, 'The US Doesn't Need Europe's Help in the "Indo Pacific"', Responsible Statecraft, 30 July 2021, https://responsiblestatecraft.org/2021/07/30/the-us-doesnt-need-europes-help-in-the-indo-pacific/.

23 See Ringsmose and Rynning, 'NATO's Next Strategic Concept'.

24 See Xavier Vavasseur, 'French SIGINT Ship Dupuy de Lôme Makes Rare Taiwan Strait Transit', Naval News, 13 October 2021, https://www.navalnews.com/naval-news/2021/10/french-sigint-ship-dupuy-de-lome-taiwan/.

25 Liu Cixin, *The Three-body Problem* (New York: Tor Books, 2014). Netflix has ordered a series based on the book.

26 I have used the analogy before in this context. See Heisbourg, 'NATO 4.0', pp. 91–2. See also Niall Ferguson, *Doom: The Politics of Catastrophe* (New York: Penguin, 2021), chapter 11.

27 For an unabridged English-language exposition at the February 2020 Munich Security Conference, see 'Emmanuel Macron at Munich Security Conference 2020 (English version)', YouTube, 15 February 2020, https://www.youtube.com/watch?v=9aQjUf_LwPI.

28 See Graham T. Allison and Dmitri K. Simes, 'A Sino-Russian Entente Again Threatens America', *Wall Street Journal*, 29 January 2019, https://www.wsj.com/articles/a-sino-russian-entente-again-threatens-america-11548806978;

Charles A. Kupchan, 'The Right Way to Split China and Russia: Washington Should Help Moscow Leave a Bad Marriage', *Foreign Affairs*, 4 August 2021, https://www.foreignaffairs.com/articles/united-states/2021-08-04/right-way-split-china-and-russia; and John J. Mearsheimer, 'Bound to Fail: The Rise and Fall of the Liberal International Order', *International Security*, vol. 43, no. 4, Spring 2019, p. 50.

29 'Transcript: "China Is Coming Closer to Us" – Jens Stoltenberg, Nato's Secretary-General', *Financial Times*, 18 October 2021, https://www.ft.com/content/cf8c6d06-ff81-42d5-a81e-c56f2b3533c2.

30 On this theme, Winston Churchill said in his March 1955 address to the House of Commons: 'It may well be that by a process of sublime irony we have reached a state in this world where safety is the sturdy child of terror and survival the twin brother of annihilation.' See UK Parliament, 'The Hydrogen Bomb: Churchill's Last Major Speech in Parliament', https://www.parliament.uk/about/living-heritage/transformingsociety/private-lives/yourcountry/collections/churchillexhibition/churchill-the-orator/hydrogen/. For the classic policy treatment, see Albert Wohlstetter, 'The Delicate Balance of Terror', *Foreign Affairs*, vol. 37, no. 2, January 1959, pp. 211–33.

Copyright © 2021 The International Institute for Strategic Studies

Getting Restraint Right: Liberal Internationalism and American Foreign Policy

Daniel Deudney and G. John Ikenberry

Editor's note

In the August–September issue of *Survival*, Daniel Deudney and G. John Ikenberry critiqued what they called the 'Quincy coalition' in an essay titled 'Misplaced Restraint: The Quincy Coalition Versus Liberal Internationalism'. In the October–November issue, Anatol Lieven, a senior research fellow at the Quincy Institute for Responsible Statecraft, responded in an essay titled 'Vindicating Realist Internationalism'. In this essay, Deudney and Ikenberry reply to Lieven.

In an earlier essay in *Survival*, 'Misplaced Restraint: The Quincy Coalition Versus Liberal Internationalism', we examine the three parts of the Quincy coalition – libertarianism, balance-of-power realism and left-progressivism – in historical, theoretical and policy terms.[1] We focus on their central argument that liberalism and liberal internationalism, particularly since the end of the Cold War, are the root causes of major American foreign-policy mistakes and disasters, especially the Iraq War. We argue that their critique is seriously deficient in their understanding of liberalism and liberal internationalism, and in their interpretation of important historical events. Furthermore, we argue that the Quincy foreign-policy agenda is quite inadequate for meeting contemporary and emerging challenges. Our analysis also seeks to illuminate the weaknesses of these three schools of thought by considering

Daniel Deudney is a Professor of Political Science at Johns Hopkins University. **G. John Ikenberry** is the Albert G. Milbank Professor of Politics and International Affairs at Princeton University.

Survival | vol. 63 no. 6 | December 2021–January 2022 | pp. 63–100   https://doi.org/10.1080/00396338.2021.2006452

their basic ideas in relationship to those of liberalism and its republican precursors. Looking ahead, we say that 'responsible statecraft' in the twenty-first century will require new types of restraints and commitments that are outside the conceptual frameworks and intellectual imagination of the libertarian, balance-of-power realist and anti-imperial left traditions. It will require more – not less – liberal internationalism, and a reimagination of the rules and institutions required for global problem-solving.[2]

In response to our essay, Anatol Lieven offers a wide-ranging and passionately polemical critique of what he takes to be 'liberal internationalism' and its influence on American foreign policy and the world.[3] In his critique, Lieven deploys the key arguments that have been developed by leading restraint realists, libertarians and progressive critics of liberal internationalism in recent decades. Lieven almost entirely ignores our extensive critique of libertarianism and arguments about the role of hegemonic realism as the wellspring of disasters in American foreign policy. His critique of liberal internationalism is based on what he calls 'ethical realism', a familiar hybrid.[4] And he candidly acknowledges that many of his views are not shared by other members of the Quincy coalition. Lieven's case is a portmanteau of arguments that have been made by some members of the Quincy coalition as well as by many liberals and liberal internationalists. The Quincy contingent and Lieven emphasise the virtues of 'restraint' as a neglected but needed part of foreign-policymaking. A great many disasters in American foreign policy are attributed to the absence of such an approach. But Lieven does not engage our central proposition: that liberal internationalism offers a superior – that is, more complete and up-to-date – set of restraints to guide American foreign policy.

No one can doubt that liberal internationalism has often fallen short, at least in its implementation, and it has sometimes been used for the wrong purposes. Over the last two centuries, liberalism and its various internationalist projects have been entangled in other forces and movements, including imperialism, racism and great-power politics. Nevertheless, on balance, over the long term, liberal internationalism, as a global vision and foreign-policy guide, has had a profoundly progressive – even revolutionary – impact on the shaping of the post-war world order, helping to further the ideological and political forces for the grand transition from a world of empire to a world of nation-states, building an infrastructure of rules and institutions to foster and protect liberal democracy, and generating international coalitions and projects for tackling the gravest threats to world order and humanity. A central claim of our essay is that, unlike the schools of thought that make up the Quincy coalition, liberal internationalism places at the centre of its vision the cooperative organisation of international order – led by the United States and other liberal democracies, allies and partners – to defend shared liberal values and institutions and handle global problems of interdependence.

To advance the debate, this essay seeks to outline the ways in which liberalism and its republican precursors have produced an elaborate and rounded understanding of restraints in political order. This body of restraint theory and practice is superior to realism because it is more complete and incorporates the historical accomplishments of liberal-democratic polities and their international projects. On account of their commitment to restraint, liberal internationalists share with the three schools of the Quincy coalition an aversion to American military intervention and support for the ideal of responsible statecraft. Furthermore, many of what seem to be the most telling arguments of the critique offered by the different schools of the Quincy coalition against liberalism and liberal internationalism are actually liberal in character. Just as communism with Chinese characteristics looks a lot like capitalism, so too restraint realism looks a lot like liberalism.

Liberal internationalists share an aversion to American intervention

This paper explores restraint both theoretically and in key historical cases. We do not purport to provide either a comprehensive statement on liberalism and its internationalism, or a full assessment of the merits and impacts of American and liberal foreign policy in the modern era. Nor do we offer a full vision of a renewed and reformed liberal internationalism for America and its liberal allies in the twenty-first century. But we do hope to clear up some prevalent theoretical and historical misconceptions about liberalism and its record.

Republicanism, liberalism, realism and restraint

A central claim of contemporary realist thought about US foreign policy has been that liberal internationalism has led US foreign policy astray and contributed to many costly mistakes, most notably the Iraq War. More generally, the realists associated with the Quincy coalition claim to be champions of restraint, and they hold that liberals have an inferior understanding of politics because they lack an adequate appreciation of the role of restraints, especially in international affairs.

The labels 'liberalism' and 'realism' are imperfect guides for thinking about the Western tradition of restraint because both these terms are early-nineteenth-century inventions. Before that point, the fullest security theory came from writers who thought of themselves as 'republicans' focused on understanding 'republics'. The central problem of republican theory and practice was how to create, maintain and improve polities in a way that preserved the security, interests and freedoms of the people as a whole.[5] Thus, the foundational 'security liberalism' of republicanism is essentially a long exploration of how to fashion arrangements of political restraint in the service of individual and collective security for the people generally of a polity. This entailed an elaborate political science of power and restraint, making 'restraint' a central concept in ancient and early-modern republican thought.

Republican polities were rare and often precarious, and republican power-restraint theory emerged out of reflections on the political struggles, problems and institutional development of a small handful of ancient and early-modern regimes (most notably ancient Athens and Rome, next the early-modern European city-states of Venice, Florence and Holland, and then, at larger scale, England) provided by a vast array of practitioners and thinkers. Here was an explosion of ideas that remain central to political science and the institutions of free government – concepts such as democracy, vetoes, balance of power, mixed regimes, limited-government constitutionalism, freedom of religion, separation of church and state, assemblies and parliaments, popular sovereignty, representation, militias and popular arms control, free trade, commerce, rights of all sorts (cosmopolitan, natural and human) and unions, to mention some of the most prominent. This sprawling proto-liberalism constitutes the fullest theory and practice of power restraint.[6]

Across the nineteenth and twentieth centuries, these concepts and institutions of restraint spread in numerous ways, propelled by a global quest for freedom. This emancipatory project – along with its internationalisms – has been arguably the most distinctive and novel feature of the late-modern world. Within the global story of the development and expansion of popular government, the United States has played an outsized role. The founding of the American republic is the crowning achievement of early-modern republican theory and practice. The American founders viewed themselves as making a decisive innovation with the construction of a new, enlarged and uniquely survivable republican union capable of solving perennial and debilitating problems of inter-republican war and resisting recurrent predation of large kingdoms and empires.[7] The liberal internationalism that had been such a distinctive and innovative, but never full, driver of American foreign policy is essentially the manifestation of these republican and proto-liberal practices and institutions on the larger, sometimes very dangerous, global playing field, and in tumultuously modernising circumstances.

The reasons for thinking this liberal tradition and its internationalism are superior to realism for understanding restraint, security and political order are quite straightforward, and can be boiled down to three simple points. Firstly, it provides a fuller profile of threats and a fuller menu of restraints. Secondly, it presents a fuller account of interdependence and better mechanisms for accommodating changes in levels of interdependence. Thirdly, unlike realism, the liberal tradition offers a theory and practice for large-scale political orders and systems that are neither anarchical nor hierarchical.

The basic idea of the restraint theory of republicanism and its liberal descendants is that the extremes of anarchy and hierarchy should be avoided. Absent such restraints, domination occurs. In this way of thinking, the first right is to life, and the first responsibility of republican government is to secure individuals and the general population against predatory, arbitrary and unchecked violence. Republicans and modern liberals, in sharp contrast to core realists, hold that the people in general are the ultimate sovereign. Republicans and liberal democrats developed the restraints that the people needed to protect themselves. This thinking about restraint spawned ideas about balances and divisions as checks on power. These architectures of restraint are fundamentally different in their design and purpose from those that mark hierarchies.[8] In republics, restraints serve the people, while in hierarchical polities, restraints serve an elite.

Ideas about restraint and political order initially aimed to replace tyranny with distributed and accountable power. Then, in Enlightenment Europe, they became the basis of the first general 'system-level' international theory, of the 'natural republic' of Europe.[9] In this view, the balance of power served as a constraint against imperial consolidation. Then, in the nineteenth century, this idea – stripped of its terminological linkages to popular revolutionary movements for more accountability and popular rule within states – was incorporated into the first self-described realpolitik understandings of the patterns of politics that gave order to the European 'system'.

A second reason liberalism trumps realism in theorising restraint stems from its insights about problems posed by interdependence.[10] At the centre of canonical Western conceptions of anarchy, violence and security is the recognition that the magnitude of the capacity of actors to do lethal damage to one another matters fundamentally for the type and scope of governments needed to provide security, and for the prospects for creating them. Thus, anarchy – understood as the absence of authoritative government – is likely to be fundamentally insecure, and avoiding it is the paramount challenge for security politics. Vivid classical portrayals of this situation include Thucydides' account of the Corcyrean civil war and Thomas Hobbes's 'state of nature'. It is to avoid such perils that governments must be established and maintained. Thus, interdependence sits at the heart of the case for the creation of governments to order, restrain and secure.[11]

Since the late nineteenth century, the foundation of liberal thinking has been the recognition of rapidly rising levels of violence and other forms of interdependence brought about by the Industrial Revolution. First in Europe and then globally, it led to increasingly extreme levels of violence interdependence. War in industrial-era Europe was fundamentally different than war in early-modern Europe because, quite independently of the balance of power, the destruction caused by war became so much greater in absolute terms.[12] In the middle of the twentieth century, nuclear weapons produced another revolutionary leap in the scope of violence interdependence, making inter-state anarchy a threat of civilisational magnitude.[13]

Given these realities, liberals have argued that institutional change is necessary to avoid disasters and realise basic interests. As American political theorist John Dewey saw it, the problems generated by cascading waves of interdependence, interaction and vulnerability generated by industrial modernity call for successively more extensive forms of government and community.[14] Reaching farther back, the cascades of interdependence and vulnerability in Europe moved late-nineteenth-century liberals to argue for Europe-wide institutions that would authoritatively apply binding international law through permanent organisations to ensure security – an imperative at the heart of the European Union.

Realists often downplay interdependence

Indeed, the recognition of intensifying interdependence is the foundation of the arms-control, disarmament and global-institution-building theories and projects of liberal internationalists. In contrast, realists often downplay interdependence and focus mainly on relative power.

Thirdly, liberal internationalists hold that large-scale political orders that are neither anarchic state systems nor empires of dominance can be, have been and should be created. For liberals, non-hierarchical unions formed by consent are the basis of just polities, and a central focus of liberal-republican theory and practice has been on building free unions at successively larger scales.[15] Far from being just aspirational, this project has produced robust approximations of such orders. When Samuel P. Huntington observed that the inter-state political order of the democracies was a combination of 'confederations, federations and regimes', he was registering the fact that this vast and populous space is governed in ways that are largely outside the realist universe of anarchies and hierarchies.[16] In this order, power politics has not ended; it has been domesticated. Balancing is channelled and muffled, rather than raw and violent. While the earlier language of unions has faded, liberals have conceptualised a wide variety of international unions in terms of 'regimes' and 'global governance'.

With these theories and historical experiences in mind, liberals believe that fundamental reforms in the world order remain both necessary and possible. In contrast, a hallmark of realist theory since the nineteenth century has been deep scepticism about the prospects for international cooperation to solve common problems. Kenneth Waltz and John Mearsheimer, widely recognised as two leading realists of the later twentieth century, have also stressed the ephemeral character of international institutions and the extreme difficulty of forging cooperation among states.[17]

Contemporary realism, however, can be seen as having incorporated key republican and liberal ideas, in particular the balance of power. Many realists have also voiced general support for nuclear arms control and cooperative international problem-solving. Lieven underscores that key members of the Quincy Institute for Responsible Statecraft have championed the Iran nuclear deal and support the resumption of nuclear arms-control negotiations with Russia. And he underlines the importance of combatting climate change and the need for international cooperation to do so. But these admirable positions have their intellectual origins in the liberal tradition. As a result, the world view that Lieven champions against the perceived limitations of liberal internationalism is in fact republican and liberal in character. Overall, 'restraint realism' looks more like liberalism than old-school realism.

But this restraint-centred vision of order premised on the distribution of power is not the only thriving version of realism. Realism sits alongside its near antithesis: the earlier notion that order emerges from concentrations of power, classically voiced in Thucydides' 'Melian Dialogue' as the 'strong do what they have the power to do and the weak accept what they have to accept'.[18] In this view, international order comprises islands of hierarchy in a sea of anarchy. Major realist thinkers have continued to advance this view. Hegemonic realism – not liberal internationalism – permeated the thinking of the key architects of the Iraq War, and informs many contemporary advocates of global American military primacy.

Liberalism, tragedy and the maladies of power

A recurrent feature of the realist world view is the insistence that the human condition – especially the realm of international politics – is inescapably tragic in character, marked by inexorably painful, substantially zero-sum choices and trade-offs.[19] Numerous flaws in humans – some intrinsic to humanity and some rooted in political dynamics – recurrently and inescapably produce outcomes that are costly and disastrous. In this tragic world view, the good is perpetually difficult to achieve, and the best-laid plans frequently come to naught. With this sensibility, realists repeatedly criticise liberalism as naive. The liberal ideal of progress is a special realist target because it seems to be utopian and to create unrealisable expectations. Furthermore, realists, starting with Thucydides, argue that democratic states are in many ways ill suited to life in international anarchy, and are prone to dangerous lapses and irresponsible statecraft. More damningly, they say, liberal progressivism engenders crusades of betterment, leading to international meddling, foreign interventions and even war. The American global liberal project is thus prone to producing what Stephen Walt has called a 'hell of good intentions'.[20]

Liberals do believe that there can be – and has been – progress. And liberals think that some polities, and some international orders, are demonstrably better than others at producing peace, freedom and prosperity.[21] At the same time, liberals are keenly aware of the many limitations of human decision-making, and the many pitfalls to which statecraft is susceptible. Indeed, a major part of the liberal programme and its precursors is an institutional agenda to make statecraft more competent and restrained. For example, liberals have advanced constitutional control of war-making by representative and accountable bodies as preferable to authoritarian control by individuals whose competence and character could be and often is deficient.[22] Animating republican constitutional theory is Lord Acton's observation that 'power corrupts and absolute power corrupts absolutely'. [23]

Liberals also believe that transparency and public bureaucracies staffed by professionals enhances the quality of statecraft. Furthermore, liberal democracies have advanced and refined civilian control of militaries. Even so, the statecraft of liberal regimes remains vulnerable to forms of psychological and organisational dysfunction related to misperceptions, cultural blindness and groupthink, as well as corruptions of judgement that stem from fear and uncertainty. But arrogance, hubris and hypocrisy are endemically human, and there is little evidence that American decision-making has been exceptionally cursed with these recurrent maladies. Liberals hold that the glare of publicity, the demands of competitive elections and elaborate checks and balances on governmental authority can at least temper these maladies, but concentrated power cannot.

The Second World War was a telling case study in the comparative competence of liberal and non-liberal states. Historians and theorists have minutely debated the great powers' every move in this conflict. There is no doubt the leaders of all the warring states made significant and costly mistakes. But the strategic performance of the liberal democracies – the United States and the United Kingdom – was markedly better than that of the fascist and communist states, whose performance was deficient in ways that shaped the outcome of the war.[24]

Adolf Hitler's behaviour was erratic and he made many disastrous bold strokes, especially on the Eastern Front. He delayed Germany's full industrial mobilisation, while his unprovoked declaration of war against the United States seriously diminished prospects for a Nazi victory. Josef Stalin made comparable blunders, such as the purging of the officer corps and failing to act despite ample warning of imminent German attack, that were extraordinarily costly to the Soviet Union. Both leaders – for good reasons – were obsessed with domestic enemies, and their violently totalitarian and ideologically rigid political systems were ill suited to gathering and competently analysing information. Italy and Japan also made first-order errors that stemmed from their dysfunctional internal systems.[25]

At the other end of the spectrum, while the United Kingdom's record under Winston Churchill was mixed, Franklin Delano Roosevelt (FDR) masterfully orchestrated rapid mobilisation, coalition diplomacy and military strategy in both the European and Pacific theatres.[26] Realist critiques of liberal regimes generally fail to appreciate the relative success of the great strategies of liberal states.[27]

Recognition of tragic trade-offs has been a central part of liberal American thinking about the great mobilisations of American state power during the Cold War as well as the Second World War. Realists, libertarians and progressives in the Quincy coalition and elsewhere point to the ways in which these mobilisations have damaged limited government, individual rights and democratic accountability in the United States. But liberals in both the Republican and Democratic parties first raised these concerns. They have been a central feature of American republican and liberal thought since the country's founding.[28]

Forced to survive in an often predatory and anarchical system, republics have had to generate, sustain and employ military power. Coercive responses to external exigencies have been seen as necessary but also fraught with potentially tragic consequences. Republicans and liberals have viewed large militaries, and the governments to support and wield them, as a major threat to popular government. The founders argued on behalf of constitutional union as a remedy to potential wars among the American states, which would in turn fatally compromise the republican constitutional orders within the states. During the military mobilisations of the mid-twentieth century, some feared that the leviathan of the new American security state – ominously dubbed the 'military-industrial complex' by Dwight D. Eisenhower himself – while necessary for the survival of the country, might also produce an American garrison state.[29]

Thus, for American liberal republicanism, there has been a tragedy of American great-power globalism. On the one hand, democracy at home and abroad has been successfully secured against powerful anti-liberal adversaries. On the other hand, the national-security state that arose from long wars exhibits many of the dangers that previous generations feared. All of this is to underscore that when libertarians, progressives and even realists make arguments about the maladies of American great power, they are essentially reiterating a core point of republican liberalism. At the same time, they underplay the fact that the many of the illiberal features of American foreign policy have been lesser evils necessary for the larger good. In sum, critics of the liberal-international project have failed to grasp liberals' own sense of tragedy and its salience in American foreign-policy thinking.

Realists and others also fail to fully register the ways in which the vulnerabilities of republics have motivated liberals to promote increasingly binding forms of international law and organisation. While the liberal-internationalist programme is ultimately revolutionary with respect to the state system and the illiberal regimes that populate it, it seeks to serve a conservative domestic agenda of republican constitutional preservation. If America cannot ultimately change the world, the world will surely change America. Thus, the liberal programme is explicitly geared to slowly but surely develop alternative ordering arrangements that diminish the severe demands of raw anarchic systems.

While keenly attentive to the dynamics of anarchy, liberals ultimately reject realist convictions that world politics cannot fundamentally be changed. They also have different views of interdependence. Realists' almost exclusive emphasis is on the distribution of power, but liberals stress that increased interdependence in areas such as defence, economics, health and ecology are simply part of the modern world, and the anarchic system must give way to a new one marked by inter-state associations on an increasingly global scale short of creating a world state. Liberals maintain that this evolution is necessary to avoid disasters, as well as to come closer to a world consistent with universal human rights. For liberals, the real tragedy of realism is the prospect that these necessities and possibilities will be neglected due to outmoded realist thinking about the inevitable recurrence of conflict.

Liberalism, empire and hegemony

The central grievance of all three groups of the Quincy coalition against liberal internationalism and American foreign policy is that it is imperial. Drawing on a large revisionist historical and analytic literature by progressives and radical thinkers, as well as some realists, Lieven sees the American-led international system as a form of empire, and American foreign policy as essentially imperial. In this view, the United States has sought global domination, and liberal internationalism serves to motivate and legitimate the American imperial project both at home and abroad, providing ethically elevated justifications for dubious aggrandisement.

This view is fundamentally inaccurate. Over most of recorded human history, empire has been the dominant political form.[30] Early-modern political thinkers such as Niccolò Machiavelli and John Locke viewed empire as a normal feature of international politics. The decisive theoretical break occurred in the work of Montesquieu and other Enlightenment thinkers, who offered the first sustained critique of empire and imperialism.[31] National self-determination, not imperial expansion, was the hallmark of eighteenth- and nineteenth-century liberal thinking.[32]

The United States, across its history, has played – on balance – an important role in thwarting imperialism and dismantling empires. American liberals have vigorously opposed US imperialism since the founding.[33] The American Revolution and its theoretical justifications were strongly anti-imperial. The American struggle for independence was the first successful anti-colonial war of national liberation against a European world empire.[34] In an overall ledger sheet of its imperialism and anti-imperialism across two centuries, the US has a decidedly mixed record. US expansion across the continent and in the Western Hemisphere in the eighteenth and nineteenth centuries was imperial. But support for it was strongest among southern slaveholders, a powerful anti-liberal force in the early republic. Liberals, for their part, voiced critiques against the Mexican War, Cuban annexation and the occupation of the Philippines. US territorial expansion in the Americas and beyond fell significantly short of what its great relative power made possible.[35] While the United States was arguably the most powerful state in the global system in the late nineteenth and early twentieth centuries, the other great powers, such as Britain, France and Russia, were far more active empire-builders.

In the twentieth century, American foreign policy and the liberal-international project helped steer the global system away from empire, and towards widespread national self-determination. The United States played an important – and at times decisive – role in thwarting late-imperial aspirants and dismantling existing empires. American intervention in the First World War helped prevent the imperial domination of Europe by Imperial Germany. During the Second World War, the United States played a key role in blocking the imperialism and destroying the empires of Imperial Japan, Fascist Italy and Nazi Germany. Following that war, the

United States prodded its European allies to accept the dismantlement of their globe-spanning colonial empires.[36] During the Cold War, the United States led the effort to thwart the imperial ambitions of the Soviet Union and the world communist movement. This American opposition to the empires of other great powers stemmed from a combination of liberal ideological commitment and balance-of-power logic.

Liberal internationalism also provided the vision for a post-imperial world order. Recognising that the world held many distinct nations, liberals championed the principle of national self-determination, arguing that each nation deserved independence and recognition as sovereign within a globalised Westphalian system. This principle and its corollaries of non-intervention and the prohibition of aggressive war were enshrined in the United Nations Charter. While the US has at times violated the principles of the charter, the UN would never have come into existence without the strong support of liberal internationalists in the Roosevelt and Truman administrations.[37]

> *Liberal internationalists led the advancement of human rights*

Similarly, liberal internationalists have led the advancement of universal human rights and building institutions to support them. The modern conception of human rights emerged in Enlightenment liberal thought.[38] The 'Universal Declaration of Human Rights' of 1948 embodied the liberal-internationalist vision, and American liberals, starting with Eleanor Roosevelt, played decisive roles in its creation.[39] Oppressed peoples all over the world have looked to these liberal principles for inspiration and support. During the second half of the twentieth century and beyond, they have legitimated and empowered social movements, dissidents and human-rights activists. Again, American foreign policy has sometimes violated these norms and principles; but without American liberal leadership they would be much weaker.

In its basic outline, the Quincy coalition's narrative of an American quest for global domination is essentially inaccurate. After the Second World War, at the peak of its relative power, the United States rapidly demobilised. It was only the threat of renewed imperial expansion – this time from the Soviet

Union – that led the United States to rebuild its military and pursue a global policy of containing Soviet and communist power. Similarly, after the end of the Cold War and the collapse of the Soviet Union, the United States again militarily demobilised. Lieven, like many critics from the left, views the extended American alliance system, built to contain Soviet and communist power, as a type of empire. But as Geir Lundestad concisely put it, this was an 'empire by invitation'; that is, it was a defensive alliance system designed to effect not domination but an anti-imperial balance of power.[40] Both American realists and liberals supported it during the Cold War and after.

Within this balance-of-power alliance the United States may be dominant, but its writ stops far short of empire. It is a hierarchical order with liberal characteristics – a mixed and complex system built around institutions, bargains, partnerships, alliances and norms of diffuse reciprocity.[41] What is distinctive about this type of order is that it is bargained, with the lead state providing services and frameworks for cooperation. In return, it invites participation and compliance by other states, starting with the subsystem of liberal democracies. In formal terms, there are three features of liberal hegemony that separate it from empire. Firstly, the leading state sponsors and operates in a system of negotiated rules and institutions. Power disparities still afford advantages to the hegemonic state, but the arbitrary and indiscriminate exercise of power is reined in to the degree required to keep the order going. Secondly, the leading state provides an array of public goods – or club goods – in exchange for the cooperation of other states. Historically, these have included security and support for an open trade regime.[42] Thirdly, the hegemonic order provides channels and networks for reciprocal communication and influence. These informal 'voice opportunities' arise from informal access to the policymaking process of the hegemonic state and the intergovernmental institutions that make up the system.[43] Alliances and multilateral institutions provide mechanisms for communication and 'pulling and hauling' between states within the order.[44] While formal decision-making is not shared, the system works more like a pluralist domestic regime than an empire.[45] The United States' hegemony does afford it asymmetrical power. While this leaves partners with less influence, it also facilitates collective decision-making.[46]

Those exhorting America to 'come home', motivated by a critique of America as empire, are arguing for a world order which will advance and not retard empire in the international system. The Quincy prescription of radically reducing the US global footprint is an invitation to other powers to extend their imperial reach. Other great powers, notably China and Russia, have been quite explicit in their ambition to extend their domination of neighbouring peoples and to create regional and world orders that reflect and support their anti-democratic, anti-liberal and kleptocratic qualities. The liberal order among democracies, led by the United States, remains the best middle path between anarchy and empire. For the United States to abandon it would mark a historic decline in the prospects for individual liberty, democratic accountability and social justice.

Liberalism, universalism and intervention

Realists such as E.H. Carr, George Kennan, Hans Morgenthau and Henry Kissinger have indicted liberal internationalism for effectively destabilising the international system by means of universalist crusades.[47] In the view of Lieven and others, the United States, animated by universalist liberal ideology, sees all non-liberal states as in some fundamental sense illegitimate. This provides the pretext for continual intervention into the internal affairs of other countries, involvement in civil wars and attempts to change regimes. Realists argue that liberal democracy and the desire for freedom are not universal but are parochial expressions of American nationalism and Western culture and civilisation. Some realists, including Lieven, even object to the promotion of democracy with information and aid campaigns, such as the National Endowment for Democracy, as programmes of international subversion disruptive of Westphalian norms of sovereignty.[48] Instead, they want the United States to abandon its universalistic ambitions, shed its sense of exceptionalism and become a normal country, capable of entering into peaceful and cooperative relations with other countries governed by different regime types and ideologies.

Realists are only partially correct in their characterisation of liberal universalism. Liberals do believe that there is a widespread human aspiration for fundamental rights and freedoms, which liberal democracies are best able to realise. Liberals believe that these aspirations have been held by peoples in all times and places, and that they are valid across civilisations, cultures and nations. Over time, with the expansion of liberal democracy and the development of liberal thought, the list of fundamental rights and freedoms has expanded to include freedom from the arbitrary use of state power and violence towards individuals; freedom of expression, association and the press; freedom to own property; and freedom from sickness, want and fear.

Yet liberals also acknowledge that these rights often conflict, and that much of the political life of liberal democracy is an ongoing struggle about how to balance and prioritise them. A distinctive feature of modern liberalism has been its commitment to freedom of inquiry and reliance on science to guide pragmatic public decision-making.[49] And twentieth-century liberals have emphasised the importance of reconfiguring public authorities and restraints to grapple with the rising scope of political and economic interdependence and complexity.

This liberal vision of the just and desirable society has had – and still has – powerful adversaries for whom hierarchy, domination, extreme nationalism or 'race' provide the appropriate basis for political order.[50] In the liberal narrative of world politics in the twentieth century and beyond, liberal democracy is in grand competition, sometimes lethal, with authoritarian and fascist adversaries on the right, and socialist and communist ones on the left. To the extent that Americans, and especially American liberals, have viewed the United States as playing a special and indispensable role in world affairs, it is largely because the geopolitical fate of the liberal effort has been so dependent on American power and purpose. As Tony Smith has observed, 'it is difficult to escape the conclusion that since World War I, the fortunes of democracy worldwide have largely depended on American power'.[51] If American liberalism has at times taken on a martial internationalist quality, it is because of the special burden that the great contest for the world has imposed.

Realists are thus correct in their claim that the animating idea of modern liberal democracy since its inception in the eighteenth century has been that non-liberal democracies are in fundamental ways illegitimate. But what this means for the foreign policy of the United States, or any other liberal democracy, for supporting freedom elsewhere has posed chronic dilemmas for American statecraft. Similar dilemmas have challenged the statecraft of other liberal and democratic states, such as Great Britain in the era of Benjamin Disraeli and Viscount Palmerston.[52] During the administration of George Washington, the question of whether to support the French Revolution sharply divided Americans. And such difficult questions continue to vex American foreign policy and domestic politics. Views span a spectrum. At one end is the position articulated by John Quincy Adams (and enshrined in the credo of the Quincy Institute): the United States should remain aloof from the promotion of liberty abroad. At the other end is the view, held by Thomas Paine, that the United States has the moral obligation to employ the full weight of its power to liberate oppressed people everywhere.[53] Most American liberals and democrats have occupied a middle position: the United States should act only against the most extreme violations of popular rights and freedoms, and it should involve itself militarily only when there is a strong likelihood that doing so will accomplish its goals, or when foreign revolutions have the potential to shift the global balance of power.

Contrary to the realist picture of American foreign policy as perpetually and eagerly interventionist, the pattern of American intervention has been quite mixed. In some cases, the United States has refrained from intervening even in the face of strong domestic popular agitation for forceful action.[54] In some cases of extreme oppression, including the massacre of Jews by the Third Reich in the early 1940s, the Cambodian genocide in 1975 and the Rwandan massacres in 1994, the United States stood by and did nothing. But in other cases, such as Cuba in 1898, Bosnia in 1992, Somalia in 1992 and Libya in 2011, the United States did militarily intervene. And it is often difficult for decision-makers to discern whether American power can achieve emancipatory objectives.

In the deliberations of American policymakers considering intervention, reluctance and ambivalence – not crusading enthusiasm and resoluteness – have tended to predominate. In the case of the former Yugoslavia, for example, American and Western statecraft was highly conflicted and extremely slow.[55] Only after the massacre at Srebrenica and, later, with the imminent prospect of ethnic cleansings in Kosovo did the United States forcefully step in. In Afghanistan, the United States intervened militarily only after the Taliban regime refused to hand over Osama bin Laden and shut down the training camps implicated in transnational terrorism. Regarding Libya, it was Muammar Gadhafi's brazen attempt to assassinate the leaders of the United Arab Emirates and his violent repression of a popular uprising that triggered NATO's air campaign.

The realist indictment also overlooks that fact that American liberals and their European counterparts have often opposed and criticised American interventions. The domestic American opposition to the Vietnam War was overwhelmingly the work of liberals such as Eugene McCarthy, George McGovern and Ted Kennedy.[56] Since the end of the Second World War, liberal internationalists have been opponents as often as advocates of intervention.

Liberal accomplishments

Critics like Lieven are quick to attribute the failures and misadventures of American foreign policy to liberalism. Any serious and fair analysis must look at the successes as well as the failures, and put them in comparative and historical perspective. Liberalism has not been the only ideology shaping American foreign policy. As Lieven himself points out in his fine book on American nationalism, liberalism has domestically struggled against powerful illiberal forces, including the South's white racial and ethnic nationalism, which has at times frustrated American liberalism and liberal foreign policy.[57] Overall, the positives significantly outweigh the failures, and the successes have grown as America's influence on the world stage has expanded.

In the nineteenth century, American liberals and democrats were the global vanguard of the expansion of individual freedom and political democracy. The US was born a radical experiment in the promise of freedom in a world marked by oppression, oligarchy and empire. Through long struggles, the franchise was broadened, first to include white males without property, and then, in the early twentieth century, women. Perhaps the greatest accomplishment of liberalism in the nineteenth century was the abolition of slavery, a movement spearheaded by British and American liberal and radical Protestant abolitionists and consummated in the Union victory in the Civil War.[58] Because of their precocious commitment to liberal democracy, Americans viewed themselves as special, as did people all over the world living under oppression.[59] Another major liberal accomplishment was an economic system based on widely held private property that produced prosperity on a large scale. Monarchs and aristocrats viewed the American liberal democracy as a paramount danger that challenged their legitimacy and moral authority.[60]

Since the middle of the twentieth century, as American power and influence has expanded, so have its liberal accomplishments. Over seven decades under American auspices, the post-war liberal international order has lifted more boats in terms of economic growth and rising incomes than any other order in world history. It provided a framework for struggling industrial societies in Europe and elsewhere to transform themselves into modern social democracies. Japan and West Germany were integrated into a security community and were able to fashion distinctive national identities as peaceful great powers. Western Europe subdued old hatreds and launched a grand project of union. With American prodding, European colonial rule in Africa and Asia largely came to an end. The G7 system of cooperation among Japan, Europe and North America fostered growth and managed a sequence of trade and financial crises.[61] Beginning in the 1980s, countries across East Asia, Latin America and Eastern Europe opened up their political and economic systems and joined the broader order. As the United States experienced its greatest success as a world power with the peaceful end to the Cold War, countries around the globe wanted more, not less, US leadership. These monumental developments are rarely mentioned in indictments of American liberal internationalism.[62]

Modern liberal states are built around various values that are sometimes in tension with one another – liberty and equality, individualism and community, openness and social stability, hierarchy and sovereign equality. The Western system provided a framework within which liberal states could manage these trade-offs. The post-war system of 'embedded liberalism' provided mechanisms and capacities for these states to define the terms of economic openness. Governments were given tools to reconcile and balance the benefits of open trade with demands for economic stability and social protection. The alliance system facilitated sharing the costs of security protection. Alliances – along with the wider system of multilateral institutions – produced greater solidarity and community among Western and rising non-Western liberal democracies. The bargains and institutions behind the liberal-international order gave these states the ability to balance hierarchy and sovereign equality. The United States used its pre-eminent position to underwrite and lead the order, but its binding institutional ties with other liberal states produced a restraint on its power.

The fostering of cooperation among the world's democracies did not eliminate old-style power politics, which the United States and other liberal states continued to practise inside and outside the Western system. But the deep accomplishment of the post-war liberal order was the construction of a cooperative environment in which liberal democracies could provide tools and capacities to enable governments to navigate economic and security interdependence, balance their often conflicting values and principles, and secure rights and protections for their societies.[63] This US-led order reflected liberal statecraft, rooted in republican and liberal theory. It was and remains a pragmatic and reform-oriented endeavour to strengthen the ability of liberal democracies to survive and flourish. In a world of rising interdependence and illiberal great-power challengers, liberal democracies will surely want to renew rather than abandon their distinctive, liberal-internationalist approach to order building.[64]

Liberalism and the Iraq War

The debacle of the Iraq War sits prominently at the centre of the Quincy coalition's indictment of liberal internationalism. Without that disaster, Quincy might not have been formed. The coalition's advice for American foreign policy is geared towards preventing another Iraq-like mistake. The fact that the war is so widely viewed as a monumental blunder gives this message enormous resonance and appeal. Key to the indictment is the claim that the Iraq War straightforwardly exposed liberalism and its baneful agendas.

Any realistic assessment of the origins of the Iraq War, however, must focus not on the content of liberal and realist theory but rather on the perceptions and attitudes of key officials in the US government. The political dispositions of the key players in the George W. Bush administration who initiated the war, and the circumstances and climate of opinion prevailing during this period, make it clear that liberalism was not steering statecraft. The Iraq War (as well as the Afghan War that preceded it) were not fundamentally undertaken to plant liberal democracy in those societies. The war was driven by essentially defensive motivations compounded by fear, desperation and urgency. All accounts of this period emphasise the centrality of the 9/11 terrorist attacks, the subsequent anthrax letters and the fear that the United States would be subject to jihadist attacks with weapons of mass destruction (WMD), which made any possibility that a Muslim leader might supply WMD to al-Qaeda seem dire.[65] The key leaders of the Bush administration made disastrously inaccurate assessments of Saddam Hussein's nuclear capability. The administration, like many Americans, viewed 9/11 as the most catastrophic attack on American soil since Pearl Harbor. And the anticipation that these attacks were precursors to nuclear or biological surprise attacks gave actions to forestall such strikes overwhelming urgency. Many realists and liberals alike saw the war, however misguidedly in retrospect, as a matter of self-defence.

The Quincy coalition's broader indictment of the American involvement in the Middle East portrays it as part of an essentially liberal globalist vision. This is historically inaccurate. The essential logic of the regional American role is that of hegemonic realism, not liberal internationalism. America's hegemonic project in the region dates back to the Second World War and the early Cold War, and was premised on the need for access to oil resources and fear that they would fall under the control of the Soviet Union or some hostile regional power.[66] The promotion of liberal democracy was never a primary goal. Indeed, the United States had a long record of supporting extremely illiberal, anti-democratic and theocratic regimes and movements, in particular Saudi Arabia during the Cold War. Key US officials in the drive to war in Iraq – in particular, Donald Rumsfeld and Dick Cheney – were hardly liberal internationalists. They had a straightforwardly realist understanding of the stakes involved for America's hegemonic project in the region.[67] They viewed Saddam as a military threat to that project and had visions of eliminating this military threat long before 9/11.[68]

Many of the realists in the Quincy coalition vigorously opposed the Iraq War on the basis of what they view as quintessentially realist ideas about restraint and balance of power. But they tend to overlook the fact that the architects of the Iraq War were also operating under a realist view of international politics in which hegemony plays a central and positive ordering role.[69] Liberalism enters the story insofar as the Bush administration, in making the case for the war to American domestic audiences, cast it as an opportunity to expand freedom. Just as American military power in the Second World War and the Cold War had been viewed as an instrument for both the protection and the advancement of the liberal-democratic freedom agenda, an American overthrow of the Iraqi dictatorship would expand the international frontier of freedom. The use of this justification says more about the Bush administration's view of American public opinion than it does about the administration's primary motives and purposes in going to war.

Nation-building was not a motivation for the Iraq War

As Lieven documents, though, many prominent American liberals also supported the war. Some were simply motivated by fears of WMD attack. Others supported the war due to Saddam's persistent violations of UN Security Council resolutions, and his use of chemical weapons against rebellious Kurdish groups. Still other liberals hoped that American arms could play a useful role in reducing tyranny and opening possibilities for liberalisation and democratisation. This aligned some liberals with neoconservatives. And many American liberal public figures no doubt also feared the electoral consequence of opposing a popular war, remembering the numerous liberal Democrats who had suffered at the polls for mounting principled opposition to the Gulf War a decade earlier. In the end, neoconservative and liberal supporters of the war adopted the same grievous misperceptions of Iraq and the region as the Bush administration. The vaunted goal of nation-building was not a motivation for the war, but rather an answer to the question of what to do after overthrowing the Iraqi regime.

Furthermore, many liberal internationalists in the United States and elsewhere did vigorously oppose the war – in particular, the Bush administration's unilateralism, the doctrine of preventive war and the large-scale use of force – on liberal grounds.[70] Some liberal politicians, at potential electoral risk, voted against the authorisation of the war. Most of America's allies in Europe – liberal-democratic states embracing liberal-internationalist ideas – were strongly against it.[71] Clearly liberal internationalism did not lead America to its Iraqi misadventure.

China, world order and liberal internationalism

How to deal with China is becoming the central question of American foreign policy. In recent years, relations between Beijing and Washington have deteriorated as their regional and global rivalry has grown. China is a formidable rival, with the world's largest population and by some measures its largest economy. It has a highly competent central state and a dynamic, partly capitalist economy. It has thrived in the global capitalist system and is now by far the world's largest trading state. It has a long-standing self-image as the Middle Kingdom and historical hegemon of East Asia. And China is governed by the dictatorship of the Communist Party, which, like other Marxist regimes, views itself as the champion and exemplar of a path in modernity superior to liberal-democratic capitalism.[72] In its official telling, China has been attempting to overcome and reverse the 'century of humiliation' during which Western powers dominated East Asia and even encroached onto China itself. In this view, China is the rightful hegemon of the East Asian region and the state best positioned to replace the United States in the heretofore Western-centred international system. Seized with this vision and on the move, China has become a major shaper of world order.[73]

Since the nineteenth century, when the United States and China first started interacting, US policy towards China has shifted back and forth between friendship and enmity. Prior to the communist revolution, America was generally a friend. The United States opposed European territorial predation of China, fought in the Second World War to thwart Japanese imperialism and colonialism in China, and supported China's bid for a permanent seat on the UN Security Council. But after the revolution, Sino-American relations quickly turned hostile over Taiwan, Korea and communist-inspired revolutions in the colonial world. Then, with the Nixon–Kissinger diplomatic breakthrough, the US and China became de facto allies against the Soviet Union. Following the economic reforms of Deng Xiaoping after 1978, American and Western investment poured into China. China rapidly industrialised, its export trade grew explosively and in 2000 China joined the World Trade Organization, with American support.[74] But since Xi Jinping became its paramount leader, China has made major expansionist moves in the South China Sea and politically repressive ones in Hong Kong. Domestically, the regime has turned back the clock on liberalisation and oppressed its Muslim minority. In response, over the course of the Obama, Trump and Biden administrations, the United States began a geopolitical pivot to Asia, imposed heavy tariffs on Chinese imports and sought to limit Chinese economic penetration, especially in high-technology areas. A grand strategic debate has emerged in the United States on the magnitude of the Chinese threat and the appropriate American foreign-policy response.

One position, which Lieven articulates, is that the United States should avoid a global rivalry with China. He blames liberal internationalism for fuelling an ideological cold war. According to him, communism in China is just another 'developmental state' model that can be accommodated within a pluralistic Westphalian system. Libertarians and neo-isolationists who want to avoid a major American mobilisation to restrain Chinese expansion have advanced a version of this view. Their general advice is for the United States to 'come home', shed its global military and political presence and abandon its promotion of liberal democracy abroad. In this view, the United States has no standing or responsibility to champion human rights for the Uighurs, Hong Kong residents or anyone else.

The problem with such a strategy is that it seriously underestimates Chinese expansionist aspirations to challenge liberal democracies. Over the last decade, as the third wave of democratisation has ebbed in the non-Western world, China's efficient autocracy, bolstered by modern information and surveillance technologies, offers other authoritarian and autocratic regimes an attractive model. Like the fascist states in the 1930s and 1940s, and the Soviet Union during the Cold War, China today seeks to build a regional and global order in which liberal democracies and the United States are diminished. In this situation, the neo-isolationist and libertarian strategy of turning inward to 'tend our own garden' and influencing the world mainly through the appeal of American domestic accomplishments is woefully insufficient.

A liberal-internationalist grand strategy, however, combines active counterbalancing across military, economic and ideological fronts with continuing efforts to find areas of common agreement with China to solve the problems of interdependence, especially climate change. This programme thus finds common ground with the realist strategy of maintaining a military balance of power in East Asia and strengthening alliances with countries potentially in the shadow of Chinese domination. This strategy is complicated by the reality that these threatened countries are also dependent on China for trade and investment, and on the United States for security. While anti-Chinese alliance partners need not be liberal democracies, alliances involving more liberal democracies – such as the Quadrilateral Security Dialogue, which includes Australia, India, Japan and the US – tend to be stronger and more coherent. As the recent bolstering of Australia's alliance with the United States suggests, Chinese attempts to convert economic interdependence into political subordination may backfire.[75]

In this setting, the liberal promotion of human rights and anti-corruption measures becomes vital for limiting the spread and influence of autocratic states attracted to the Beijing model.[76] Beyond military and ideological approaches, liberal-internationalist strategy would advance new trade regimes that incorporate human-rights provisions. The Trans-Pacific Partnership, negotiated by Barack Obama and rejected by Donald Trump, is a model. It restricts state-owned enterprises from subsidised dumping, protects intellectual property, outlaws human trafficking and requires the legalisation of independent trade unions and collective bargaining.

Success in competition between liberalism and authoritarianism is going to depend, as US President Joe Biden has stressed, on whether the United States and other democracies can show that democracy works. This will require strenuous domestic efforts. Just as FDR's New Deal programme in the 1930s provided the foundation for success against fascism and then communism, Biden's neo-Rooseveltian domestic agenda – embracing more equitable tax policies as well as increased funding for research and development, infrastructure, education and decarbonisation – is now vital for both domestic renewal and successful grand strategy.[77] As in the great struggles of the twentieth century, the libertarian agenda of dismantling the modern liberal state is a recipe for the historic failure of liberal democratic capitalism.

There are good reasons that a liberal-internationalist strategy can succeed. While China has formidable assets, the tendency of states, regardless of regime type, to balance against proximate and growing threats to their independence is an enormously powerful force in world politics that works against China. The fact that the United States is geographically distant helps assure its allies that their independence will not be jeopardised by American encroachment. Individual freedom from arbitrary power, accountable government and free expression are also powerful and appealing forces favouring the liberal-democratic model of modernity. Furthermore, in governing technologically complex modern societies, dictatorships are unlikely to be as adaptive, resilient and innovative as pluralistic, open and accountable liberal democracies.

Trump and restraint

Finally, there is the question of the relationship between Trump's presidency and agendas of restraint in American foreign policy. In important ways, Trump and Trumpism are *sui generis*, and do not easily map onto recent US foreign-policy debate. His demonisation of domestic enemies, personal insults, embrace of conspiracy theories and pseudo-science, strident immigrant-bashing and endorsement of torture are rightly condemned as divisive and subversive of American norms. His dalliance with white supremacists sits well outside the centre-right and centre-left mainstream. Trumpism is perhaps most akin to what Walter Russell Mead describes as the Jacksonian tradition of US foreign policy.[78]

The restraint coalition clearly diverges from Trumpism, as Lieven insists. Certainly libertarians were horrified by Trump's infatuation with and praise for authoritarian foreign leaders. They strongly oppose his disregard for constitutional checks and balances, and his casual indifference to the rule of law. Many realists also supported the Iran nuclear deal, which Trump abrogated. Realists understand the importance of allies, which Trump denigrated and neglected. And most recognise the centrality of competent bureaucratic organisation, which Trump sought to weaken and dismantle, for the successful conduct of foreign policy.[79] Trump's impulsively personalised, historically ignorant and culturally chauvinistic style of presidential decision-making is utterly anathema to the agenda of responsible statecraft.[80] For the progressive-left members of the restraint coalition, Trumpism is simply a nightmare. Domestically, he moved the country away from social and economic justice, environmental responsibility and tolerant cultural pluralism. Internationally, under the banner of 'America First', he abandoned human rights, assaulted international institutions and embraced illiberal and anti-democratic authoritarians. Individually and together, the three parts of the restraint coalition could never be equated with Trumpism.

Yet despite these strong differences and antipathies, there are several ways in which Trump's major foreign and domestic initiatives advanced agendas supported by members of the coalition, particularly libertarians. Trump's massive tax cuts, channelled primarily to wealthy individuals and corporations, furthered the libertarian agenda of dismantling the fiscal foundations of the liberal-democratic state. Trump's climate denialism, attack on environmental regulations and withdrawal from the Paris climate accord realised libertarian aims. So did his distaste for binding international agreements and strong international organisations, epitomised by his withdrawal of the United States from the World Health Organization in the middle of a pandemic. These libertarian advances have diminished the capacity of the United States, both at home and abroad, to solve the major problems of the twenty-first century.

There are also important overlaps between Trump's America First foreign policy and the restraint-realist agenda, especially in the area of alliance management. Many realists hold that the cost and magnitude of American commitments to allies in Europe and East Asia have been excessive. As a remedy, some have advocated an 'offshore balancing' strategy as an alternative to long-standing American defensive pacts with weaker liberal democracies.[81] Trump voiced many of the same doubts, and sought, usually incompetently and ineffectively, to pull the United States back from these commitments and institutions, reducing America's global footprint and shrinking its role as a security guarantor and an arbiter of international disputes. But despite these apparent affinities, it is an open question whether Trump was committed to a general posture of American restraint or to American primacy. His bellicose rhetoric towards North Korea, maximum-pressure campaign against Iran, pursuit of dominance in outer space and swaggering proclamations of American supremacy have little place in a restraint agenda.[82]

*   *   *

One unfortunate legacy of the Trump presidency has been the emergence of a new set of far-right actors, world views and agendas. The new Trumpian voices in the foreign-policy debate are ultra-nationalist, stridently anti-liberal and explicitly racist.[83] This new far right is not only gaining traction in the United States but is also extensively globally networked with anti-liberal and anti-democratic groups in Europe, South America and Russia. It sits outside the centre-right to centre-left mainstream that has been dominant in American politics since the middle of the twentieth century.

The ultimate survival of democracy, in America and more broadly, will depend on the forging of a new political core to confront and overcome the anti-liberal and anti-democratic forces that Trumpism has tapped. A broad majority of Americans will need to set aside their internal quarrels over different freedoms and restraints, and establish another version of the 'vital center' that Arthur Schlesinger, Jr, identified and championed in the late 1940s to counter the fascist right and the communist left.[84] The members of the Quincy coalition, along with liberals and liberal internationalists, fall within this vital centre, and they should draw together into a new and broader coalition of restraint to protect liberal democracy.

Notes

1   Daniel Deudney and G. John Ikenberry, 'Misplaced Restraint: The Quincy Coalition Versus Liberal Internationalism', *Survival*, vol. 63, no. 4, August–September 2021, pp. 7–32.

2   We acknowledge helpful comments and suggestions from David Hendrickson, Peter Trubowitz, Wesley Warren and Thomas Wright.

3   Anatol Lieven, 'Vindicating Realist Internationalism', *Survival*, vol. 63, no. 5, October–November 2021, pp. 7–34.

4   See Anatol Lieven and John Holeman, *Ethical Realism: A Vision for America's Role in the World* (New York: Alfred A. Knopf, 2006).

5   See Daniel Deudney, *Bounding Power: Republican Security Theory from the Polis to the Global Village* (Princeton, NJ: Princeton University Press, 2007). See also Judith Scholar, 'The Liberalism of Fear', in Nancy Rosenbaum (ed.), *Liberalism and the Moral Life* (Cambridge, MA: Harvard University Press, 1989), pp. 21–38.

6   See Scott Gordon, *Controlling the State: Constitutionalism from Ancient Athens to Today* (Cambridge, MA: Harvard University Press, 1999). For varieties and debates, see Joyce Appleby, *Liberalism and Republicanism in the Historical Imagination* (Cambridge, MA: Harvard University Press, 1992); Stephen Holmes, *Passions and Constraint: On the Theory of Liberal Democracy* (Chicago, IL: University of Chicago Press, 1995); Philip Pettit, *Republicanism: A Theory of Freedom and Government* (Oxford: Oxford University Press, 1997); and J.G.A. Pocock, *The Machiavellian Moment* (Princeton, NJ: Princeton University Press, 1976).

7   See Daniel H. Deudney, 'The Philadelphian System: Sovereignty, Arms Control, and Balance of Power in the American States-Union, 1787–1861', *International Organization*, vol. 49, no. 2, Spring 1995, pp. 191–228; Gottfried Dietze, *The Federalist: A Classic on Federalism and Free Government* (Baltimore, MD: Johns Hopkins University Press, 1960); and David C. Hendrickson, *Peace Pact: The Lost World of the American Founding* (Lawrence, KS: University Press of Kansas, 2003).

8   See Vincent Ostrom, *The Political Theory of a Compound Republic: Designing the American Experiment*, 2nd edition (Lincoln, NE: University Press of Nebraska, 1987), pp. 1–30.

9   See Deudney, *Bounding Power*, ch. 5; Deborah Boucoyannis, 'The International Wanderings of a Liberal Idea', *Perspectives on Politics*, vol. 5, no. 4, December 2007, pp. 703–23; and Edward Gulick, *Europe's Classical Balance of Power* (New York: W. W. Norton & Co., 1967).

10   For classic statements on interdependence and interaction, see Barry Buzan, Charles Jones and Richard Little, *The Logic of Anarchy: Neorealism to Structural Realism* (New York: Columbia University Press, 1993); Robert Keohane and Joseph Nye, *Power and Interdependence* (Boston, MA: Little, Brown, 1977); Edward Morse, *Modernization and the Transformation of International Relations* (New York: Free Press, 1976); and Ramsey Muir, *The*

Interdependent World and Its Problems (London: Macmillan, 1932).

11 See Ioannis D. Evrigenis, *Images of Anarchy: The Rhetoric and Science in Hobbes's State of Nature* (Cambridge: Cambridge University Press, 2014); and Stuart Sim and Daniel Walker, *The Discourse of Sovereignty, Hobbes to Fielding: The State of Nature and the Nature of the State* (Aldershot: Ashgate, 2003).

12 See E.H. Carr, *Conditions of Peace* (New York: Macmillan, 1942); E.H. Carr, *Nationalism and After* (London: Macmillan, 1945); and H.G. Wells et al., *The Idea of a League of Nations* (Boston, MA: Atlantic Monthly Press, 1919).

13 For early nuclear one-world thinking, now completely abandoned by realists, see John Herz, *International Politics in the Atomic Age* (New York: Columbia University Press, 1960); and Rens van Munster and Casper Sylvest, *Nuclear Realism: Global Political Thought During the Thermonuclear Revolution* (London: Routledge, 2017).

14 John Dewey, *The Public and Its Problems* (New York: Henry Holt, 1927).

15 For the long theoretical history, see Murray Forsyth, *Unions of States: The Theory and Practice of Confederation* (Leicester: Leicester University Press, 1981).

16 See Samuel P. Huntington, 'The West: Unique, Not Universal', *Foreign Affairs*, vol. 75, no. 6, November/December 1996, p. 43.

17 See John J. Mearsheimer, 'The False Promise of International Institutions', *International Security*, vol. 19, no. 3, Winter 1994–95, pp. 5–49; and Kenneth N. Waltz, *Theory of International Politics* (Reading, MA: Addison-Wesley, 1979).

18 Thucydides, *History of the Peloponnesian War* (New York: Penguin Books, 1972), p. 402. See also Thomas J. Johnson, 'The Idea of Power Politics: The Sophistic Foundations of Realism', *Security Studies*, vol. 5, no. 2, Winter 1995, pp. 194–247.

19 Richard Ned Lebow, *The Tragic Vision of Politics: Ethics, Interests and Orders* (Cambridge: Cambridge University Press, 2003); and Reinhold Niebuhr, *The Irony of American History* (New York: Scribner, 1952).

20 Stephen M. Walt, *The Hell of Good Intentions: America's Foreign Policy Elite and the Decline of US Primacy* (New York: Farrar, Straus and Giroux, 2018). See also Andrew J. Bacevich, *American Empire: The Realities and Consequences of American Diplomacy* (Cambridge, MA: Harvard University Press, 2002); John J. Mearsheimer, *The Great Delusion: Liberal Dreams and International Realities* (New Haven, CT: Yale University Press, 2018); Patrick Porter, *The False Promise of Liberal Order: Nostalgia, Delusion and the Rise of Trump* (Cambridge: Polity Press, 2020); and Christopher Preble, *The Power Problem: How American Military Dominance Makes Us Less Safe, Less Prosperous, and Less Free* (Ithaca, NY: Cornell University Press, 2009).

21 See, for example, Michael W. Doyle, *Liberal Peace: Selected Essays* (New York: Routledge, 2012); and Michael W. Doyle, *Ways of War and Peace: Realism, Liberalism, and Socialism* (New York: W. W. Norton & Co., 1997). See also Michael Mandelbaum, *The Ideas that Conquered the World: Peace, Democracy, and Free Markets in*

the *Twenty-first Century* (New York: PublicAffairs, 2002); and Bruce Russett and John R. Oneal, *Triangulating Peace: Democracy, Interdependence, and International Organizations* (New York: W. W. Norton & Co., 2001).

22 See Bruce Russett, *Controlling the Sword: The Democratic Governance of National Security* (Cambridge, MA: Harvard University Press, 1990).

23 For Lord Acton's essays, see William H. McNeill (ed.), *Lord Acton: Essays in the Liberal Interpretation of History* (Chicago, IL: University of Chicago Press, 1967).

24 See Azar Gat, *Victorious and Vulnerable: Why Democracy Won in the 20th Century and How It Is Still Imperiled* (Lanham, MD: Rowman & Littlefield, 2010); and Richard Overy, *Why the Allies Won* (New York: Norton, 1995).

25 See Seishiro Sugihara, *Between Incompetence and Culpability: Assessing the Diplomacy of Japan's Foreign Ministry from Pearl Harbor to Potsdam* (Lanham, MD: University Press of America, 1997).

26 See Jeffrey A. Engel (ed.), *Four Freedoms: FDR and the Evolution of an American Idea* (Oxford: Oxford University Press, 2016); Nigel Hamilton, *The Mantle of Command: FDR at War, 1941–1942* (Boston, MA, and New York: Houghton Mifflin Harcourt, 2014); Harvey J. Kaye, *The Fight for the Four Freedoms: What Made FDR and the Greatest Generation Truly Great* (New York: Simon & Schuster, 2014); and Gerhard L. Weinberg, *Visions of Victory: The Hope of Eight World War II Leaders* (Cambridge: Cambridge University Press, 2005).

27 See Matthew Kroenig, *The Return of Great Power Rivalry: Democracy Versus Autocracy from the Ancient World to the U.S. and China* (New York: Oxford University Press, 2020).

28 See Edward Corwin, *Total War and the Constitution* (Ann Arbor, MI: University of Michigan Press, 1947); Michael J. Hogan, *A Cross of Iron: Harry S. Truman and the Origins of the National Security State, 1945–1954* (Cambridge: Cambridge University Press, 1998); and James Ledbetter, *Unwarranted Influence: Dwight D. Eisenhower and the Military-industrial Complex* (New Haven, CT: Yale University Press, 2011).

29 See David Cineplex, *Liberalism in the Shadow of Totalitarianism* (Cambridge, MA: Harvard University Press, 2006); Aaron Friedberg, *In the Shadow of the Garrison State: America's Anti-statism and Its Cold War Grand Strategy* (Princeton, NJ: Princeton University Press, 2000); and Michael S. Sherry, *In the Shadow of War: The United States Since the 1930s* (New Haven, CT: Yale University Press, 1995).

30 See Stuart J. Kaufman, Richard Little and William C. Wohlforth, *The Balance of Power in World History* (London: Palgrave, 2007)

31 See Sankar Muthu, *Enlightenment Against Empire* (Princeton, NJ: Princeton University Press, 2003); Jennifer Pitts, *A Turn to Empire: The Rise of Imperial Liberalism in Britain and France* (Princeton, NJ: Princeton University Press, 2005); and Bernard Semmel, *The Liberal Ideal and the Demons of Empire: Theories of Imperialism from Adam Smith to Lenin* (Baltimore, MA: Johns Hopkins University Press, 1993).

32 See John Stuart Mill, *Considerations on Representative Government* (London: Parker & Son, 1861).

33 For debates on American empire, see David C. Hendrickson, *Union, Nation, or Empire: The American Debate over International Relations, 1789–1941* (Lawrence, KS: University Press of Kansas, 2009); and Andrew Priest, *Designs of Empire: America's Rise to Power in the Age of European Imperialism* (New York: Columbia University Press, 2021).

34 See David Armitage, *The Declaration of Independence: A Global History* (Cambridge, MA: Harvard University Press, 2007).

35 On domestic sources of restraint, see Jeffrey W. Meiser, *Power and Restraint: The Rise of the United States, 1898–1941* (Washington DC: Georgetown University Press, 2015); and Peter Trubowitz, *Defining the National Interest: Conflict and Change in American Foreign Policy* (Chicago, IL: University of Chicago Press, 1998).

36 See William Roger Louis, *Imperialism at Bay: The United States and the Decolonization of the British Empire, 1941–1945* (Oxford: Oxford University Press, 1978).

37 See Townsend Hoopes and Douglas Brinkley, *FDR and the Creation of the U.N.* (New Haven, CT: Yale University Press, 1997); and Paul Kennedy, *The Parliament of Man: The Past, Present, and Future of the United Nations* (New York: Random House, 2006).

38 See Lynn Hunt, *Inventing Human Rights* (New York: W. W. Norton & Co., 2008); and Christian Reus-Smit, *Individual Rights and the Making of the International System* (Cambridge: Cambridge University Press, 2013).

39 See Mary Ann Glendon, *A World Made New: Eleanor Roosevelt and the Universal Declaration of Human Rights* (New York: Random House, 2001).

40 Geir Lundestad, '"Empire by Invitation" in the American Century', *Diplomatic History*, vol. 23, no. 2, Spring 1999, pp. 189–217. See also Geir Lunstad, *The Rise and Decline of the American 'Empire'* (Oxford: Oxford University Press, 1990).

41 See G. John Ikenberry, *After Victory: Institutions, Strategic Restraint, and the Rebuilding of Order after Major Wars* (Princeton, NJ: Princeton University Press, 2001).

42 For hegemony in the world economy and trade system, see Charles P. Kindleberger, *The World in Depression, 1929–1939* (London: Allen Lane, 1973).

43 These three features of liberal hegemony are outlined in G. John Ikenberry, *Liberal Leviathan: The Origins, Crisis, and Transformation of the American World Order* (Princeton, NJ: Princeton University Press, 2011), pp. 71–3.

44 See Thomas Risse-Kappen, *Cooperation Among Democracies: The European Influence on U.S. Foreign Policy* (Princeton, NJ: Princeton University Press, 1997).

45 See Daniel Nexon and Thomas Wright, 'What's at Stake in the Empire Debate?', *American Political Science Review*, vol. 101, no. 2, May 2007, pp. 253–71.

46 For studies of the functioning of liberal hegemonic orders, see Alexander Cooley and Daniel Nexon, *Exit from Hegemony: The Unraveling of the American Global Order* (Oxford:

Oxford University Press, 2020); Daniel Deudney and G. John Ikenberry, 'The Nature and Sources of Liberal International Order', *Review of International Studies*, vol. 25, no. 2, April 1999, pp. 179–96; Ikenberry, *Liberal Leviathan*; and G. John Ikenberry (ed.), *Power, Order, and Change in World Politics* (Cambridge: Cambridge University Press, 2014). On the differences between hegemonic order and empire, see Charles S. Maier, *Among Empires: American Ascendency and Its Predecessors* (Cambridge, MA: Harvard University Press, 2006). On contemporary debates about hegemonic order, see G. John Ikenberry and Daniel H. Nexon, 'Hegemonic Studies, 3.0: The Dynamics of Hegemonic Orders', *Security Studies*, vol. 28, no. 3, Summer 2019, pp. 395–421.

47 See E.H. Carr, *The Twenty Years' Crisis, 1919–1939: An Introduction to the Study of International Relations* (New York: Macmillan, 1939); George F. Kennan, *American Diplomacy, 1900–1950* (Chicago, IL: University of Chicago Press, 2012); Hans J. Morgenthau, *Politics Among Nations: The Struggle for Power and Peace* (New York: Alfred A. Knopf, 1973); and Henry Kissinger, *Diplomacy* (New York: Simon & Schuster, 1994).

48 See Lieven, 'Vindicating Liberal Internationalism', pp. 20–1.

49 See Daniel Boorstin, *The Republic of Technology* (Boston, MA: Houghton Mifflin, 1978).

50 See Stephen Holmes, *The Anatomy of Antiliberalism* (Cambridge, MA: Harvard University Press, 1993); and Matthew Rose, *A World*

After Liberalism: Philosophers of the Radical Right (New Haven, CT: Yale University Press, 2021).

51 Tony Smith, *America's Mission: The United States and the Worldwide Struggle for Democracy in the Twentieth Century* (Oxford: Oxford University Press, 1994), pp. 9–10.

52 See Gary Bass, *Freedom's Battle: The Origins of Humanitarian Intervention* (New York: Vintage, 2009).

53 For a sweeping history of America's reluctant engagement with the global system, see Charles Kupchan, *Isolationism: A History of American Efforts to Shield Itself from the World* (New York: Oxford University Press, 2020).

54 See Steven Hahn, *A Nation Without Borders: The United States and Its World in an Age of Civil Wars, 1830–1910* (New York: Viking, 2016).

55 See Richard Ullman (ed.), *The World and Yugoslavia's Wars* (New York: Council on Foreign Relations, 1996).

56 For an exploration of the connections between American liberalism and the peace movement and opposition to the Vietnam War, reflected in the political life of George McGovern, see Thomas Knock, *The Rise of a Prairie Statesman: The Life and Times of George McGovern* (Princeton, NJ: Princeton University Press, 2016).

57 See Anatol Lieven, *America Right or Wrong: An Anatomy of American Nationalism* (Oxford: Oxford University Press, 2004).

58 See Eric Foner, *The Story of American Freedom* (New York: W. W. Norton & Co., 1998); and David Brion Davis, *Slavery and Human Progress* (New York: Oxford University Press, 1984).

59 See James T. Kloppenberg, *Toward Democracy: The Struggle for Self-rule in European and American Thought* (Oxford: Oxford University Press, 2016).

60 See James Caesar, *Reconstructing America: The Symbol of America in Modern Political Thought* (New Haven, CT: Yale University Press, 1997); and Don H. Doyle, *The Cause of All Nations: An International History of the American Civil War* (New York: Basic Books, 2015).

61 See Hugo Dobson, *The Group of 7/8* (Milton Park: Routledge, 2007); and Robert Putnam and Nicholas Bayne, *Hanging Together: Cooperation and Conflict in the Seven-power Summits* (Cambridge, MA: Harvard University Press, 1988).

62 See Timothy Garton Ash, *Free World: America, Europe, and the Surprising Future of the West* (New York: Random House, 2004); Elizabeth Borgwardt, *A New Deal for the World: America's Vision for Human Rights* (Cambridge, MA; Harvard University Press, 2005); Ikenberry, *Liberal Leviathan*; and Stewart Patrick, *The Best Laid Plans: The Origins of American Multilateralism and the Dawn of the Cold War* (Lanham, MD: Rowman & Littlefield, 2009).

63 See G. John Ikenberry, *A World Safe for Democracy: Liberal Internationalism and the Crises of World Order* (New Haven, CT: Yale University Press, 2020).

64 See Daniel J. Fiorino, *Can Democracy Handle Climate Change?* (Cambridge: Polity, 2020); and Rebecca Willis, *Too Hot to Handle? The Democratic Challenge of Climate Change* (Bristol, UK: Bristol University Press, 2020).

65 Kori Schake, who worked on the National Security Council during the Bush administration, captured this post-9/11 orientation: 'I went to work at the Bush White House not long after September 11th, and my strongest impression was how frightened people were, how fearful they were that they didn't understand the dimensions of the terrorist threat. And I think we made a lot of bad policy choices out of fear and out of ignorance about the nature and magnitude of the threat … We were fearful, we were trying to look tough.' 'Is the US Safer in the Aftermath of 9/11?', interview with Christiane Amanpour, 8 September 2021, CNN, https://www.cnn.com/videos/tv/2021/09/09/amanpour-us-afghanistan-iraq-war-kori-schake.cnn?utm_source=feedburner&utm_medium=feed&utm_campaign=Feed%3A+rss%2Fcnn_freevideo+%28RSS%3A+CNN+-+Video%29.

66 For the realist agenda, see Robert W. Tucker, 'Oil: The Issue of American Intervention', *Commentary*, January 1975, https://www.commentary.org/articles/tucker-robert-w/oil-the-issue-of-american-intervention/.

67 See Daniel Deudney and G. John Ikenberry, 'Realism, Liberalism and the Iraq War', *Survival*, vol. 59, no. 4, August–September 2017, pp. 7–26; and Elizabeth Drew, *Fear and Loathing in George W. Bush's Washington* (New York: New York Review of Books, 2004).

68 See Robert Draper, *To Start a War: How the Bush Administration Took America into Iraq* (New York: Penguin, 2020); and Jeffrey Record, *Wanting War: Why the Bush Administration Invaded Iraq* (Washington DC: Potomac Books, 2010).

69 On the centrality of hegemonic struggle, see John J. Mearsheimer, *The Tragedy of Great Power Politics* (New York: W. W. Norton & Co., 2001).

70 See G. John Ikenberry, 'America's Imperial Temptation', *Foreign Affairs*, vol. 81, no. 5, September/October 2002, pp. 44–60; and John Newhouse, *Imperial America: The Bush Assault on the World Order* (New York: Knopf, 2003).

71 See Peter J. Katzenstein and Robert O. Keohane (eds), *Anti-Americanisms in World Politics* (Ithaca, NY: Cornell University Press, 2007); and Elizabeth Pond, *Friendly Fire: The Near-death of the Atlantic Alliance* (Washington DC: Brookings Institution Press, 2003).

72 See Lingling Wei, 'Xi Jinping Aims to Rein in Chinese Capitalism, Hew to Mao's Socialist Vision', *Wall Street Journal*, 20 September 2021, https://www.wsj.com/articles/xi-jinping-aims-to-rein-in-chinese-capitalism-hew-to-maos-socialist-vision-11632150725.

73 See Rush Doshi, *The Long Game: China's Grand Strategy to Displace American Order* (New York: Oxford University Press, 2021).

74 For surveys of America's long engagement with Asia, see Michael J. Green, *By More than Providence: Grand Strategy and American Power in the Asia Pacific Since 1783* (New York: Columbia University Press, 2019); and James Thomson, *Sentimental Imperialists: The American Experience in East Asia* (New York: Harper & Row, 1981).

75 See Damien Cave and Chris Buckley, 'Why Australia Bet the House on Lasting American Power in Asia', *New York Times*, 16 September 2021, https://www.nytimes.com/2021/09/16/world/australia/australia-china-submarines.html.

76 For China's illiberal international order-building, see Tom Ginsburg, 'Authoritarian International Law?', *American Journal of International Law*, vol. 114, no. 2, February 2020, pp. 221–60.

77 See Daniel Deudney and G. John Ikenberry, 'The Intellectual Foundations of the Biden Revolution', *Foreign Policy*, 2 July 2021, https://foreignpolicy.com/2021/07/02/biden-revolution-roosevelt-tradition-us-foreign-policy-school-international-relations-interdependence/; and Robert Kuttner, 'The China Challenge', *American Prospect*, 5 October 2021, https://prospect.org/world/china-challenge/.

78 See Walter Russell Mead, 'The Jacksonian Revolt: American Populism and the Liberal Order', *Foreign Affairs*, vol. 96, no. 2, March/April 2017, pp. 2–7. See also Taesuh Cha, 'The Return of Jacksonianism: The International Implications of the Trump Phenomenon', *Washington Quarterly*, vol. 39, no. 4, Winter 2017, pp. 83–97.

79 See Hal Brands, Peter Feaver and William Inboden, 'In Defense of the Blob: America's Foreign Policy Establishment Is the Solution, Not the Problem', *Foreign Affairs*, 29 April 2020, https://www.foreignaffairs.com/articles/united-states/2020-04-29/defense-blob.

80 See Stephen M. Walt, 'The Tragedy of Trump's Foreign Policy', *Foreign Policy*, 5 March 2019, https://foreignpolicy.com/2019/03/05/the-tragedy-of-trumps-foreign-policy/.

81 See Christopher Layne, 'From Preponderance to Offshore Balancing:

America's Future Grand Strategy, *International Security*, vol. 22, no. 1, Summer 1997, pp. 86–124; and John J. Mearsheimer and Stephen M. Walt, 'The Case for Offshore Balancing: A Superior U.S. Grand Strategy', *Foreign Affairs*, vol. 95, no. 4, July/August 2016, pp. 70–83.

82 See Barry R. Posen, 'The Rise of Illiberal Hegemony', *Foreign Affairs*, vol. 97, no. 2, March/April 2018, pp. 20–7. See also Daniel Deudney, *Dark Skies: Space, Expansion, Planetary Geopolitics, and the Ends of Humanity* (Oxford: Oxford University Press, 2020).

83 See Jean-Francois Drolet and Michael C. Williams, 'America First: Paleoconservatism and the Ideological Struggle for the American Right', *Journal of Political Ideologies*, vol. 25, no. 1, January 2020, pp. 28–50.

84 Arthur M. Schlesinger, Jr, *The Vital Center: The Politics of Freedom* (Boston, MA: Houghton Mifflin, 1949). See also Joshua L. Cherniss, *Liberalism in Dark Times: The Liberal Ethos in the Twentieth Century* (Princeton, NJ: Princeton University Press, 2021).

Copyright © 2021 The International Institute for Strategic Studies

Negotiating with North Korea … Again

Robert L. Gallucci

We have been here before, contemplating the start of talks with North Korea, a number of times. We have done this under five different presidents, dealing with three different North Korean leaders. We should have learned something about what to do and what not to do.

Expectations and terms of reference

It is probably wise, in most negotiations, for the participants to agree on the objective of the talks. This is particularly the case now with respect to prospective negotiations between the United States and North Korea. The emerging consensus on the American side is that the real objective should no longer be the denuclearisation of North Korea. That ship, the argument runs, has sailed. Instead, Washington should be practical and reasonable, acknowledge that the North has dozens of nuclear weapons – and perhaps even thermonuclear weapons – and get on with arms control and deterrence. In other words, Washington should abandon the non-negotiable objective of total nuclear disarmament and embrace the worthy and obtainable objective of ensuring nuclear stability at the lowest possible level of arms.[1]

Although the fully developed version of this approach does not sound at all frivolous, it does carry large downside risks. Chief among them is

Robert L. Gallucci is a Distinguished Professor of the Practice of Diplomacy at the Edmund A. Walsh School of Foreign Service at Georgetown University. He served as Assistant Secretary of State for Political-Military Affairs and as Deputy Executive Chairman of the UN Special Commission following the Gulf War, and was the chief US negotiator during the North Korean nuclear crisis of 1994.

Survival | vol. 63 no. 6 | December 2021–January 2022 | pp. 101–106 https://doi.org/10.1080/00396338.2021.2006446

that it permanently supports an argument in Seoul and Tokyo that the acquisition of nuclear weapons by South Korea and Japan, respectively, is the only durable away for these countries to achieve their own security objectives because America's extended-deterrent assurance, enshrined in treaties with both countries, will be suspect so long as the US is vulnerable to attack by North Korean nuclear weapons – as indeed it now appears to be. If anyone doubts the salience of this point, they should recall the long road to establishing persuasive assurances for America's NATO allies in the face of Soviet, and then Russian, nuclear-weapons deployments. Sharpening the point further was the recent spate of angst at the start of the Trump administration over its derogatory characterisation of the United States' Asian allies, and its apparent doubts about the value of maintaining their non-nuclear status.

If this is not persuasive, consider the absence of any real certainty that we actually know what the North Koreans – now or in the past – regard as essential to their security. If conventional wisdom were our guide, we might be comfortable believing that the North learned from America's adventures in Iraq and Libya that the only way to be safe from regime change is to have a nuclear deterrent. And, having worked so hard over decades to build its small but growing arsenal, together with sophisticated delivery capability, it will not give it away at the negotiating table.[2]

Again, this makes superficial sense, but it may still be wrong. If so, forgoing denuclearisation would be a serious pre-emptive surrender of an essential objective. Thirty years ago, the North Koreans said that they wanted America to end its hostile policy towards them and replace it with normal political and economic relations. For this, they said that they would forswear nuclear-weapons acquisition. Pyongyang has made that argument consistently over decades, adjusting the offer to abandoning the nuclear weapons it has acquired in the absence of normalisation. So, it may be that North Korea would give up its nuclear weapons if it became confident that it had achieved political, economic and diplomatic integration into the international community and true normalisation of its relations with the US.

Obviously, all that could not happen quickly, much less over lunch in Singapore or Hanoi.[3] It would take years. It would be politically plausible only through an incremental process, involving reciprocal steps, designed specifically to promote confidence on both sides. Among the obstacles to overcome would be Pyongyang's approach to domestic dissent, which is to brutally violate citizens' human rights. When this point was made to a North Korean during an intense 'Track 1.5' meeting a few years ago, he said: 'There you go again, insisting on regime change.' Maybe, but maybe not. If a political process could be sustained with slow but steady progress through the steps of denuclearisation and normalisation, the scope of what is politically plausible might be expanded beyond the current expectation of leaders in Washington and Pyongyang.

The negotiating process

This brings us to the elements of performance for both sides. Much has been said on this subject, but the details will probably have to wait until negotiations begin. We can speculate on the steps to denuclearisation, which would likely involve, for example, dismantlement of fissile-material production facilities, cessation of nuclear-weapons development activity and destruction of related facilities, and destruction of ballistic missiles beyond a certain range and related production capacity. The steps to normalisation would eventually include an end to sanctions of all kinds, replacement of the armistice between North and South Korea with a treaty of peace, demilitarisation of the now heavily militarised areas around the Demilitarized Zone and, more broadly, a raft of confidence- and security-building measures specifically affecting force deployments and exercises.

Some caution is warranted here. In approaching denuclearisation, some analysts argue that the essential first step should be a full and complete declaration by North Korea of its nuclear programmes. This seems to make sense and comport with our initial experience with the denuclearisation of Iraq after the Gulf War. United Nations Security Council Resolution 687 provided for just such a full and final declaration by Baghdad at the start of the UN Special Commission inspection process.[4] Saddam Hussein agreed to it, having just lost a war.

But Iraq's full and final declarations were repeatedly revised as successive inspections revealed their deliberate incompleteness. North Korea has not lately been defeated in battle. It has not lost a war. The declaration some analysts dream of would indeed be useful in designing an inspection effort aimed at verification of denuclearisation. But political reality would have that declaration come at the end of the process, a slow engagement over years that builds confidence on both sides. US insistence on an opening declaration has sounded more like a request for a target list for a preventive strike than the first step in the reciprocal implementation of a negotiated agreement.[5]

In thinking about any agreement that links denuclearisation with normalisation, it is natural to view the first as what we get and the second as what we give. It would be better, though, for the US to view normalisation as something we get too. It should be a joint objective of the US and North Korea, and we should say so publicly for domestic consumption in both countries. We should want negotiations to remove the need for sanctions – that is, the need to punish Pyongyang for pursuing dangerous policies internationally and horrendous policies at home. A successful negotiation would do that.

The process of negotiation should also make it possible to sustain domestic support in Congress and from the American public over a period of years and, ideally, across administrations. In the first instance, that means we should seek an early, substantive success to demonstrate the value of diplomacy as a means of protecting American security. Although it seemed a popular talking point in press commentaries to disparage an offer by the North to shut down and dismantle nuclear facilities at Yongbyon, such a step would have eliminated the only plutonium-producing facility in North Korea and one of its uranium-enrichment facilities, as well as other facilities that are part of a large nuclear complex. The North Koreans put this on the table at Hanoi in 2019, but because it wasn't everything, it was characterised as being nothing. That was a mistake we should not repeat.

The Clinton administration's model for managing foreign-policy crises was to name a relatively senior bureaucratic player to lead diplomacy with other governments abroad and manage policy development in the inter-agency process at home, serving as the principal advocate for policy with Congress, the press and the American public. This was the model for negotiations on Bosnia and the Middle East as well as North Korea. While not completely unproblematic, the model does afford the US government a ready way of integrating policy and maintaining popular support for what will likely be a lengthy and contentious journey.

*   *   *

The United States cannot expect to succeed at negotiating with North Korea if it does not manage to insulate the negotiations, as much as possible, from the divisive political atmosphere in Washington. Being tough on North Korea takes no political courage, and claiming that would-be negotiators are soft-headed diplomats willing to compromise national security to make a deal is commonplace. Unfortunately, when policymakers try to compensate for an exposed right flank, they can do material damage to the effort to improve relations with a negotiating partner. The temptation to pander will have to be resisted.

This is all to argue that getting off on the right foot is crucial to success. The Biden administration needs to take its time in figuring out what success means when negotiating with the North Koreans over the nuclear issue, and to prepare at home and abroad for an arduous process.

Acknowledgements

This article was written as part of an International Institute for Strategic Studies project on North Korea's nuclear and ballistic-missile capabilities, with generous support from the John D. and Catherine T. MacArthur Foundation.

Notes

[1] See 'Colloquium: Deterring a Nuclear North Korea', *Survival*, vol. 62, no. 1, February–March 2020, pp. 29–59.

[2] See, for instance, Sue Mi Terry, 'North Korea's Nuclear Family: How the Kims Got the Bomb and Why They Won't Give It Up', *Foreign Affairs*, vol. 100, no. 5, September/ October 2021, pp. 115–27.

[3] See Mark Fitzpatrick, 'Kim Jong-un's Singapore Sting', *Survival*, vol. 60, no. 4, August–September 2018, pp. 29–36.

[4] UN Security Council Resolution 687, S/Res/687, 8 April 1991, https:// www.un.org/Depts/unmovic/ documents/687.pdf.

[5] See, for example, Edward Ifft, 'Lessons for Negotiating with North Korea', *Survival*, vol. 62, no. 1, February– March 2020, pp. 96–7.

Copyright © 2021 The International Institute for Strategic Studies

The Perspective from Pyongyang: Limits of Compromise

Andrei Lankov

One of the most frequently repeated descriptions of North Korea's behaviour is 'paranoid'. Those who use this adjective assume that North Korean leaders live in a dangerous fantasy world, but that they can be bribed, persuaded or blackmailed into joining the real world, where they will be able to reap great benefits through supposedly 'rational' behaviour. The idea is that if they surrender their nuclear weapons, their economy will grow rapidly and they will enjoy the benefits that the Chinese elite have enjoyed since the 1980s.

Such an approach is dangerously misleading. The people in charge of North Korea are not naive ideologues, and they are by no means paranoid. If anything, they are simply Machiavellian, which their regime's improbable long-term survival tends to confirm. North Korean decision-makers, based on a sound analysis of their peculiar situation, see themselves as living under a grave and deadly threat. Indeed, a critical but unmet precondition of fruitful negotiations to reduce the North Korean nuclear threat is to understand how the North Korean elite's threat perceptions relate to the compromises they might be willing to make.

Andrei Lankov is a Professor of History at Kookmin University and is Director of the Korean Risk Group. This work was supported by the Laboratory Program for Korean Studies through the Ministry of Education of the Republic of Korea and the Korean Studies Promotion Service of the Academy of Korean Studies (AKS-2019-LAB-1250001).

Survival | vol. 63 no. 6 | December 2021–January 2022 | pp. 107–118 https://doi.org/10.1080/00396338.2021.2006447

Decades of living dangerously

The overwhelming concern of the North Korean political class is survival. For most states, this means maintaining the 'territorial integrity and the autonomy of their domestic political order'.[1] North Korea, however, is one of very few states in the modern world that faces the real threat of being fully absorbed into a powerful neighbour, with its current rulers being marginalised at best and imprisoned or even killed at worst. The perception of this threat colours everything that the North Korean elite do. The threat to their survival is a by-product of Korea's 1945–48 division into two separate states whose respective economic and political trajectories and resulting achievements have been vastly different.

In the early 1940s northern Korea was arguably the most developed industrial region in East Asia other than Japan, while southern Korea remained an agricultural backwater. In 1940, the territory of the future North Korea produced an estimated 88% of the country's chemicals, 85% of its metals and 70% of its cement, as well as almost all of Korea's electricity.[2] But North Korea's Leninist economy stagnated and then disintegrated, while South Korea's experienced a long period of swift growth with few historical precedents. In 2017, North Korea's nominal per capita GDP was $1,214, roughly the level of Bangladesh, according to its own, probably somewhat inflated, semi-official estimates.[3] The South boasted nominal per capita GDP of $31,617, roughly the level of Italy, according to the World Bank.[4] Thus, the South's per capita GDP is a startling 26 times larger than that of the North – one of the largest gaps between any two countries that share a land border. Living standards differ accordingly. This is the single most important factor determining the policy and strategy of the North Korean ruling elite.

Since at least the 1990s, many a foreign and, especially, South Korean observer has insisted that North Korea should learn from China and launch its own version of an 'openness and reform' policy. Pyongyang's stubborn refusal to heed this advice has been frequently explained as a product of ideological bias. Yet North Korean leaders' reluctance to tread the Chinese path demonstrates that they understand the facts of their situation remarkably well.

Suppose North Korean leaders did decide to follow the Chinese example, opening their country to foreign investment, and therefore to greater interaction with the outside world. Such a development would undoubtedly attract capital and technology, so the North Korean economy would start growing fast, as happened in China and Vietnam. However, it would also immediately import information about the prosperity of the outside world and, above all, that of South Korea. This could produce highly destabilising resentment and agitation among North Korea's general population.

In China, the spread of similar information has not created acute political problems because there is no more prosperous 'second China' of similar size, Taiwan being too small to compel serious comparison. Throughout the 'reform and openness' period, the Chinese people learned about prosperity in what were clearly foreign countries. They could not construe the economic success of Japan, the United States or Germany as proof of the Chinese Communist Party's inefficiency and ineptitude. But in North Korea, people who had learned about South Korea's impressive standard of living would likely hold North Korea's political class responsible for their country's plunge from being the most advanced country in the region to a pathetic basket case.

Furthermore, the North Korean public would likely believe that unification with the affluent South on Seoul's conditions – essentially, German-style unification by absorption – would readily solve the North's manifold economic and social problems. This hope might be naive, but it is bound to be politically very powerful and, from the point of view of the North Korean elite, profoundly threatening. Hence they feel compelled to silence the sirens of 'reform and openness' to prevent revolutionary collapse on the order of East Germany's, which would be followed by the destruction of North Korea's statehood. It is worth remembering that the per capita GDP ratio between the two German states at the time of German unification was merely 1:2 or 1:3 – a far cry from the yawning 1:26 gap between the two Koreas today.[5]

In Eastern Europe and the former Soviet Union, of course, the fall of communist regimes did not lead to radical changes in the composition of political elites. By and large, the putative *nomenklatura* shook off stale

Marxist–Leninist rhetoric and declared themselves nationalists or democrats (depending on the country and situation), while retaining political power or exchanging power for property.[6]

The present-day North Korean elite would not fare as well in a unified Korean state. They would not have the experience and knowledge necessary to maintain positions of authority in a developed, twenty-first-century country and, with their state gone, they would be unable to rely on political institutions to prop them up. Many of the key positions, especially in industrial management, would likely be taken over by South Korean business leaders, who would have the full backing of any unified government.

The current elite could not even hope for quiet retirement, which many East German party officials and Stasi operatives enjoyed. Unlike East Germany, which underwent its de-Stalinisation in the mid-1950s, North Korea has for decades remained a brutal, hyper-Stalinist regime that has committed human-rights abuses on a truly massive scale. South Korean researchers estimate that in the early 2010s the number of political prisoners in North Korea was between 80,000 and 120,000.[7] These estimates are supported by the US State Department.[8] Assuming they are correct, the ratio of political prisoners to the total population in North Korea now is similar to that of the Soviet Union in Josef Stalin's final years.

Members of North Korean leader Kim Jong-un's cohort are understandably afraid that after collapse and unification, they would be held accountable for their misdeeds, drawing on their knowledge of how North Korea treated those who cooperated with American or South Korean forces during the Korean War. Many of them believe that if they were not shot immediately or sent to die in prison, they would spend their entire lives at hard labour in remote locales, and that their descendants would remain pariahs.

Small wonder that since the late 1950s the North Korean authorities have implemented a 'closed door' information policy on a scale unmatched in any other communist-bloc country. Since the 1960s, all non-technical foreign publications have been kept in a special section of libraries, accessible only to those with proper security clearances. Freely tuneable radios have been banned since around the same time, and the mere possession of such a radio is a crime.[9] North Korea remains one of few countries without internet access: the nationwide network is not connected to the World Wide Web, and internet access is allowed only to a handful of trusted officials.[10] Private overseas trips are rare, and inside North Korea interaction between locals and expatriates or tourists is discouraged. In recent years, Kim has introduced even harsher measures, aimed at increasing the country's self-isolation. These include stricter border controls, crackdowns on foreign videos and music, and tougher punishment for reproducing or consuming uncensored information.[11]

In this light, it is quite rational for North Koreans in positions of power to believe that they and their families would be unable to survive politically, and perhaps even physically, if they let their state disintegrate. This belief greatly influences their actions.

The limits of the possible

Since North Korean decision-makers face a grave threat to the survival of their system and themselves, there are matters on which they will not compromise. The North Korean state is likely to continue to adhere to three major policies, all of them vexing to outside parties.

Firstly, while calibrated Chinese-style market-oriented reforms are possible – they were tried in 2000–05 and again in 2012–18, with some success[12] – the country will remain sealed off from the outside world to keep the populace ignorant about the prosperity of other countries.

Secondly, the North Korean regime will continue to be harsh in dealing with real or potential dissent, employing police terror, omnipresent surveillance and large-scale imprisonment. It cannot afford to improve the human-rights situation even to the dubious level of Xi Jinping's China.

Thirdly, the regime's survival requires it to go (and then remain) nuclear. The North Korean nuclear-weapons programme has had several functions. Sometimes it has been a tool for diplomatic blackmail, at other times a notional lever of forced unification under the Kim family's authority. However, its most important role has been that of deterrence. Nuclear weapons were developed mainly to ensure that North Korea is not attacked or invaded, and to preclude attempted regime change.[13]

Again, it is difficult to attribute its attitude to mere paranoia. From the North Korean point of view, Libya serves as a stark lesson, vindicating the elite's concerns about a denuclearisation outcome. In the early 2000s, Libyan leader Muammar Gadhafi agreed to surrender his nuclear-weapons programme under essentially the same conditions that have been suggested to the North Koreans, in exchange for improving economic relations with the outside world. Initially it worked, but in 2011 a mass revolution erupted. NATO countries, citing the 'responsibility to protect' humanitarian principle, intervened and precipitated Gadhafi's military defeat, whereupon he was brutally lynched. The North Korean government has evidently concluded that the NATO countries would not have intervened had Gadhafi possessed nuclear weapons. After his ugly demise, North Korea's foreign-ministry spokesman stated:

> The present crisis teaches the international community a serious lesson. It was fully exposed before the world that 'Libya's nuclear dismantlement' much touted by the US in the past turned out to be a mode of aggression whereby the latter coaxed the former with such sweet words as 'guarantee of security' and 'improvement of relations' to disarm itself and then swallowed it up by force. It proved once again the truth of history that peace can be preserved only when one builds up one's own strength if high-handed and arbitrary practices go on in the world.[14]

Neither the carrots nor the sticks presented by the US and its allies have been enough to substantially alter North Korea's insistence on retaining a nuclear-weapons capability. Their approaches have oscillated between hard and soft, with some emphasising sanctions and others economic benefits. If success is seen as the complete, verifiable, irreversible denuclearisation of North Korea, as some have defined it, strategic success is unlikely.

Sanctions usually work indirectly, by creating hardship in the general population and depriving elites of their perks, impelling them to press for or acquiesce to reforms. Such a dynamic is unlikely to take hold in North Korea, where all political outlets for popular protest are closed off and the political elite is united in its fear of exposure to the outside world.[15] Lee

Jones, in his recent study of the tenuous efficacy of sanctions, notes that 'sanctions could not generate powerful political oppositions where none previously existed; nor, despite sometimes inflicting massive economic damage, could they shatter ruling coalitions where they were not already in decay'.[16] In the North, the entire elite has good reason to believe that nuclear deterrence protects its vital group interests in isolation. Most have never heard of Benjamin Franklin, but they would surely act in accordance with the famous dictum ascribed to him, that 'we must, indeed, all hang together, or, most assuredly, we shall all hang separately'.

The hopes some pin on economic incentives as a source of strategic leverage are as unrealistic as the sanctions-related expectations harboured by others. No doubt the North Korean leadership cares about economic growth, but only as long as such growth does not jeopardise regime stability. During the 2018 US–North Korea summit in Singapore, US president Donald Trump showed Kim Jong-un a video produced by the US National Security Council staff depicting North Korea in an imaginary future of abundant prosperity, with high-rise buildings erected after Pyongyang's denuclearisation.[17] But Trump was pushing the wrong button. Massive foreign investment would also mean an increase in interactions with the outside world, which would quickly erode the ruling elite's power and hasten the people's vengeance. While its members want to be rich, and might not mind if their subjects live well, they would be loath to court an economic boom if they would see it only through the bars of prison cells.

Security guarantees that might be extended as part of a denuclearisation deal are unlikely to be much more availing. The North Koreans see them as nothing more than pieces of paper and understand that no US or other foreign government would protect them against domestic disturbances.[18]

There are clear and likely non-negotiable limits to possible concessions. North Korea will inexorably remain closed, repressive and nuclear-armed. But while the complete, verifiable, irreversible denuclearisation of North Korea is a pipe dream, some concessions on the size of its nuclear arsenal or the degree of its repressiveness are conceivable and should be encouraged.

Space for compromise

North Korea's nuclear project has many goals, but not all of them are equally important. Its major role is to serve as an absolute deterrent against military coercion and attempted regime change. For these purposes, North Korea needs only a limited number of nuclear warheads and delivery systems. Even the existing nuclear arsenal might be excessive from this point of view. So at least some of it should be expendable – if and when the price is right.

It is conceivable that North Korean leaders could negotiate a deal and agree to freeze or even dismantle their nuclear research-and-development (R&D) and production facilities. However, under such an arrangement, North Korea would still implicitly maintain control over enough nuclear warheads and delivery systems to make any military attack or intervention in a domestic crisis prohibitively risky. True denuclearisation would not be on the cards, and the deal would be tantamount to conditional acceptance of North Korea as a nuclear state. Thus, irreversible disarmament may be practically infeasible. But, with the appropriate inducements, Pyongyang might accept the physical destruction of the existing R&D and manufacturing facilities and equipment, making any breakout from the arrangement as costly and difficult as possible. North Korean leaders would expect generous compensation for making even such a partial sacrifice, including assorted aid packages and manifold political concessions, as well as the lifting of the UN sectoral sanctions.

What can the US and its partners offer to the North that might be attractive enough? Concessions on the US presence in the region should be avoided, as, say, a significant withdrawal of US forces from South Korea would damage the US–South Korea alliance. Economic incentives are more promising, especially given the toll that COVID-19 and failed harvests have taken on North Korea. The country's leaders are interested in measures that can boost economic performance without jeopardising the population's isolation and quiescence.

One possibility would be the reopening of the special economic zones (SEZs). When Kim came to power in the early 2010s, apparently with optimistic expectations and modest enthusiasm for reform, he launched a number of these zones. By 2015, there were 25 official SEZs in the country.

The enterprise was stifled by a nuclear crisis, and by the unrealistic expectations and ineptitude of North Korean officials.[19] But they might now be open to restarting the SEZ programme. From the North Korean standpoint, SEZ-based foreign investment would carry minimal political risk, since it would place foreigners in controllable environments in which they would be able to interact only with selected North Koreans and be subject to constant monitoring at low cost. The high-rises in the 2018 Singapore summit video would be far more attractive if they were located behind the barbed wire of a well-guarded SEZ.

The North Koreans pin great hopes on the development of the tourist industry. Kim was impressed by Switzerland's tourist industry when he was at school there as a teenager and seeks to emulate it in his country. A North Korean tourist industry would not draw many Western visitors, but it could attract many Chinese visitors, as well as some South Koreans. The two Korean states ran a joint tourist project in the Kumgang Mountains in 1998–2008. North Korean authorities created what was then essentially a tourist ghetto in a picturesque region: South Korean tourists were bused in and enjoyed their time there, hiking and bathing in spas while being supervised by carefully selected North Korean personnel and plainclothes security police. Over a million South Koreans reportedly visited the resort, and it was sometimes used for North–South family reunions. Seoul ended the visits in 2008 after a South Korean visitor was shot and killed after straying beyond the boundaries of the resort.[20]

There may be additional possibilities. According to the Pyongyang Joint Declaration of September 2018 following the North–South summit meeting, 'the two sides agreed, as conditions mature, to first normalize the Gaeseong industrial complex and the Mt. Geumgang [aka Kumgang] Tourism Project, and to discuss the issue of forming a west coast joint special economic zone and an east coast joint special tourism zone'.[21] Other possible steps were mentioned, such as breaking ground on north–south roads and railway lines on the east and west coasts. Family reunions have increased.[22] The fact remains, however, that only proposals that North Korean leaders do not perceive as potentially threatening to their political system would be plausible, and musings about condos on the beach won't help.

*   *   *

The opportunities for North Korea's denuclearisation, if they ever existed, were lost many years ago, and the real choice has long been between letting the North Korean nuclear programme grow unchecked or introducing arms control that will halt or slow its growth. That will be neither cheap nor easy. Time seems to be on North Korea's side: the later a deal is made, the more costly and less satisfactory it is going to be to South Korea, the United States and their allies and partners. Furthermore, having seen what it considers the West's perfidious manipulations of Libya and Iraq, Pyongyang still finds it difficult to trust democratic countries to keep their word due to unpredictable changes in their governments. This factor may further constrain the ability of the United States and others to strike a single grand bargain in the short term, and militate in favour of small steps pursuant to relatively narrow agreements, executable in finite time frames, that might build the mutual trust required to meaningfully reduce the risks of conflict and nuclear use on the Korean Peninsula in the longer term.

Acknowledgements

This article was written as part of an International Institute for Strategic Studies project on North Korea's nuclear and ballistic-missile capabilities, with generous support from the John D. and Catherine T. MacArthur Foundation.

Notes

[1] John J. Mearsheimer, *The Tragedy of Great Power Politics* (New York: W. W. Norton & Co., 2001), p. 31.

[2] George McCune, *Korea Today* (Cambridge, MA: Harvard University Press, 1950), p. 57.

[3] 'North Korea's Economy Grows 3.7% in 2017', Kyodo News, 12 October 2018, https://english.kyodonews. net/news/2018/10/46a852b7c627- n-koreas-economy-grows-37-in- 2017-professor.html.

[4] World Bank, 'GDP Per Capita (Current US$) – Korea, Republic', https://data.worldbank.org/indicator/ NY.GDP.PCAP.CD?locations=KR.

[5] Halle Institute for Economic Research, *The Economic Integration of East Germany* (Halle: Halle Institute, 2016), p. 40.

[6] See Lawrence King and Ivan Szelenyi, 'Post-communist Economic Systems', in Neil Smelser and Richard Swedberg

(eds), *Handbook of Economic Sociology*, 2nd edition (Princeton, NJ: Princeton University Press, 2005), pp. 205–29.

7   Sookyung Kim et al., *White Paper on Human Rights in North Korea* (Seoul: Korean Institute for National Unification, 2019), p. 452.

8   US Department of State, 'Democratic People's Republic of Korea: 2017 Human Rights Report', https:// www.state.gov/wp-content/ uploads/2019/01/North-Korea.pdf.

9   See *2018 Pukhan ihae* [Understanding of North Korea in 2018] (Seoul: T'ongilpu, 2017).

10   See Daniel Pinkston, 'North Korea's Objectives and Activities in Cyberspace', *Asia Policy National Bureau of Asian Research,* vol. 15, no. 2, April 2020, pp. 81–2.

11   See Laura Bicker, 'Why Kim Jong-un Is Waging War on Slang, Jeans and Foreign Films', BBC News, 7 June 2021, https://www.bbc.com/news/ world-asia-57225936.

12   See Andrei Lankov, 'Is Byungjin Policy Failing? Kim Jong Un's Unannounced Reform and Its Chances of Success', *Korean Journal of Defense Analysis,* vol. 29, no. 1, March 2017, pp. 25–45.

13   With remarkable frankness, the North Korean foreign ministry officially expressed this view days before the country's first nuclear test in 2006: 'A people without reliable war deterrent are bound to meet a tragic death and the sovereignty of their country is bound to be wantonly infringed upon … The DPRK's nuclear weapons will serve as reliable war deterrent for protecting the supreme interests of the state and the security of the Korean nation from the U.S. threat of aggres-sion and averting a new war and firmly safeguarding peace and stability on the Korean peninsula under any circumstances.' 'DPRK Foreign Ministry Clarifies Stand on New Measure to Bolster War Deterrent', KCNA, 3 October 2006, https://www. globalsecurity.org/wmd/library/news/ dprk/2006/dprk-061004-kcna01.htm.

14   'DPRK Denounces US Military Attack on Libya', TwoCircles.net, 23 March 2011, http://twocircles.net/2011mar23/ dprk_denounces_us_military_attack_ libya.html. See also Frederic Wehrey, 'NATO's Intervention', in Peter Cole and Brian McQuinn (eds), *The Libyan Revolution and Its Aftermath* (New York: Oxford University Press, 2015), p. 105.

15   See Abel Escribà-Folch and Joseph Wright, 'Dealing with Tyranny: International Sanctions and the Survival of Authoritarian Rulers', *International Studies Quarterly,* vol. 54, no. 2, June 2010, pp. 335, 338.

16   Lee Jones, *Societies Under Siege: Exploring How International Economic Sanctions (Do Not) Work* (Oxford: Oxford University Press, 2015), p. 175.

17   See John Bolton, *The Room Where It Happened: A White House Memoir* (New York: Simon & Schuster, 2020), pp. 107, 111.

18   See 'DPRK Denounces US Military Attack on Libya'.

19   See Théo Clément, 'Between Economic Reform and Support of an "Independent National Economy": Special Economic Zones in North Korea', *North Korean Review,* vol. 16, no. 1, Spring 2020, pp. 27–54.

20   See Jon Herskovitz and Kim Junghyun, 'South Korean Tourist Shot Dead by North Soldier', Reuters, 11 July

2008, https://www.reuters.com/ article/us-korea-north-shooting-idUS-SEO14908720080711.

21 'Pyongyang Joint Declaration of September 2018', *Korea Times*, 19 September 2018, https:// www.koreatimes.co.kr/www/

nation/2018/09/103_255848.html.

22 See Choe Sang-Hun, 'Korean Families, Separated for 6 Decades, Are Briefly Reunited', *New York Times*, 20 August 2018, https://www.nytimes. com/2018/08/20/world/asia/north-south-korea-family-reunions.html.

Copyright © 2021 The International Institute for Strategic Studies

Engaging North Korea: The Warming-up Phase

Målfrid Braut-Hegghammer

The United States and North Korea are edging towards re-engagement. Now the two governments must decide how this process would start and work. Key challenges include the trust deficit between them and what appears to be a basic disagreement about how to proceed.[1]

'Off-stage' or 'warming-up' activities that precede the negotiation of a formal agreement can help states mitigate some of these challenges. These could include discussions towards a shared understanding of what a phased approach to risk reduction, arms control and denuclearisation could look like, and engagement between the technical and military communities to clarify the form and purpose of future confidence-building and verification measures. Past experiences with such warming-up activities involving the Soviet Union, some successful and some not, yield useful lessons that can inform the next stage of engagement.

Pairing objectives and activities

The warming-up phase is an opportunity to clarify key objectives, assess how proposed activities will contribute to fulfilling those objectives, and define the terms of their implementation or 'rules of the road'. These activities would come before any formal agreement.[2] While several of the components of the warming-up phase (for instance, familiarisation visits to

Målfrid Braut-Hegghammer is Professor of Political Science at the University of Oslo, where she directs the Oslo Nuclear Project.

Survival | vol. 63 no. 6 | December 2021–January 2022 | pp. 119–125 https://doi.org/10.1080/00396338.2021.2006448

facilities) resemble those that are likely to be required by formal agreements (say, on-site inspections to verify declarations or address non-compliance concerns), they serve different purposes. During the warming-up phase, they are primarily goodwill gestures and means of developing a shared working-level understanding of what specific implementation activities will entail.

Tools that have been effective in previous bilateral and multilateral warming-up efforts include simulations (such as table-top exercises on various scenarios for visits or inspections); demonstrations and expert discussions for arriving at practical understandings of key terms to be used in formal agreements; trial inspections; and even de facto inspections formally described as familiarisation visits. The precise number and combination of activities is not inherently important and should be determined according to the specific needs of the participants. The fundamental aim is for participants to develop a specific understanding of how these activities will work as part of a future formal agreement or series of arrangements, and to identify and address any problems that emerge and cope with them preventively.

Since the Biden administration signalled that it wants to pursue a pragmatic and phased approach, the North Korean side has appeared to be more positive.[3] At the same time, North Korean representatives have indicated that they are not interested in a dialogue for dialogue's sake, or in a process without a clearly specified set of objectives.[4] But there is real value in starting a dialogue when the alternative is no engagement. The warming-up phase does not require any concessions. These activities offer the participants an opportunity to demonstrate a willingness to engage and to raise specific concerns in a private setting. This prepares their respective technical and military bureaucracies for future activities, including verification. Even if warming-up activities are not followed by a formal agreement, there is nothing to lose from engaging in them.

More broadly, ongoing dialogue can ease tensions and contribute to regional stability.[5] In the current environment there is a need for activities that allow parties to explore steps that can contribute to risk reduction and dialogue without prior concessions.

Involving North Korean diplomatic and military personnel and technical managers – that is, officials charged with implementing future activities – from the outset helps facilitate the implementation of an eventual formal agreement. For example, senior managers of key facilities may fear being put in the position of losing face in front of their superiors or subordinates. Their participation in early discussions would enable them to head off such eventualities or at least minimise their likelihood.[6] It would also allow senior and lower-level officials to resolve misunderstandings and misinterpretations – for example, about the scope of outside parties' rights of access during visits or trial inspections – prior to a formal agreement.[7] A working dialogue at the scientific level could also reassure North Korea by showing how practical collaboration with US (and perhaps other) counterparts would work in practice. New technologies allow for less intrusive verification than previous formats have done.[8] Exploring how such technologies would actually operate could reduce concerns about the level of transparency or intrusiveness required as well as establish whether North Korea's understanding of the concept of verification is comparable to that of others.[9]

Lessons learned

Unilateral transparency efforts can help states demonstrate goodwill in the warming-up process. A pertinent example is the Soviet Union's phasing in of greater transparency during the negotiations of what became the Convention on the Prohibition of the Development, Production, Stockpiling and Use of Chemical Weapons and on their Destruction (CWC).

On 6 August 1987, Eduard Shevardnadze, then the Soviet foreign minister, gave a speech in Geneva in which he stated that the Soviet Union wanted to incorporate mandatory challenge inspections 'without right of refusal' by the inspected state party to the CWC. He added that to 'build an atmosphere of trust and in the interests of an early conclusion of an international convention, the Soviet side invites the participants in the chemical weapons negotiation to the Soviet military facility at Shikhany to see standard items of our chemical weapons and observe the technology of destroying chemical weapons at a mobile facility'.[10] This facility was a large chemical-weapons complex where the Soviet Union had developed and tested chemical weapons. The Soviet government hosted diplomats and technical experts from 45 countries at Shikhany in October 1987. This event included the first-ever demonstration of Soviet chemical weapons, as promised by Shevardnadze. The Soviets showed their guests what they called 'standard' chemical weapons, including chemical-filled munitions such as artillery shells, aerial bombs and missile warheads. They were then criticised, however, for refraining from revealing to their guests more advanced munitions within each category.[11] Whereas the Soviets considered 'standard' to mean every type of their chemical-weapons-filled munitions, other states assumed that this would mean showing all of their chemical weapons within each category. This offered an important lesson to the Soviets, which was to be as specific as possible about the purpose of a goodwill measure to avoid misunderstandings.

North Korea has also invited foreign scientists and journalists to selected facilities over the years.[12] These efforts have been met with scepticism, as they were orchestrated events that were limited in terms of both access and scope. Clearly such events are not a substitute for proper verification or inspections.[13] Taken for what they are, however, such unilateral initiatives can demonstrate a willingness to provide access, albeit limited, offer some opportunities for mutual exposure and information-gathering, and afford the hosts valuable experience in receiving foreign visitors.

For the Soviet Union, the 1987 visit to Shikhany helped acclimate its own mid-level officials to foreign experts. Ultimately, this inspired in the Soviets greater confidence in hosting foreigners at Soviet facilities, in terms of their ability to answer foreigners' questions and meet the logistical challenges of receiving foreign delegations at remote locations. The visit contributed to a significant change in the Soviet negotiating positions, leading to data exchanges and trial inspections. These began as national trials and progressed to bilateral and multilateral exercises culminating in the 1989 Wyoming Memorandum of Understanding between the Soviet Union and the United States, which provided for extensive and detailed data exchanges and reciprocal visits, as well as routine and challenge inspections. These experiences also served to reassure elites in Soviet bureaucracies and the Soviet military that inspections were not as threatening or difficult as the early negotiation of the CWC and the academic literature had suggested to them. Mid- and upper-level Soviet officials involved in this process became more active and comfortable with permitting greater openness at their respective levels.

This example demonstrates the value of warming-up exercises in giving states a concrete understanding of activities associated with verification under formal agreements – which cannot be gained from mere abstract descriptions – at an early stage. They can also relax concerns about the degree of transparency needed for verification.

A robust and effective warming-up process can allow the participants to raise or address specific concerns through unilateral or reciprocal initiatives. During the late stages of the Cold War, West Germany harboured a serious and long-standing concern about the Soviet Union's possible forward deployment of chemical weapons in six to eight suspected locations in East Germany.[14] In 1989, the Soviet Union invited West Germany to inspect any Soviet facility in East Germany on 24 hours' notice. In August 1990, West German officials executed a short-notice challenge inspection at a facility that they had chosen and found nothing. Subsequently, West German concerns about alleged Soviet forward deployment of chemical weapons faded.

Goodwill gestures like the one that the Soviet Union extended to West Germany show a willingness to assuage concerns. They can also help move discussions about disputed activities or specific concerns away from the public sphere to discreet settings more conducive to frank and candid dialogue.[15]

*   *   *

The Biden administration could take the initiative in outlining tentative plans for a warming-up process with North Korea and other interested parties. Such a process would not require concessions. Instead, it would provide them with opportunities to demonstrate goodwill and explore specific options. Such an initiative could build on unilateral steps that the parties have previously identified as options they are willing to consider.[16]

These steps could be scaled up from unilateral to coordinated measures. This is a flexible approach that can help the participants address sequencing issues and accommodate their different concerns. Any reciprocal measures do not have to be precisely equal in practice. For one participant, a familiarisation visit might be useful in providing information about a particular facility, whereas for another participant its main purpose might be to shed more light on how future inspections would unfold.

In particular, the United States could propose a trial exercise, inviting North Korea to a curated facility to conduct a simulated inspection under the scenario of an allegation that proscribed items were stored at this site. The site selected for the exercise should be specifically made to appear like a facility where prohibited activities might occur, or prohibited items or materials might be located. The selection of a civilian site would avoid any concerns about sensitive information. The North Korean side would then execute its own inspection procedures to search for any evidence of violations. Following the completion of the exercise, experts from both sides would discuss its value and shortcomings. They might consider, for example, whether less intrusive procedures could have achieved the inspecting parties' objectives, or whether more aggressive inspections were required. Such an experience could serve as a basis for establishing future verification arrangements and additional confidence-building measures. The essential goal is for the parties to cultivate a shared and reasonably detailed understanding of what they – separately and collectively – want to achieve.

Acknowledgements

This article was written as part of an International Institute for Strategic Studies project on North Korea's nuclear and ballistic-missile capabilities, with generous support from the John D. and Catherine T. MacArthur Foundation.

Notes

[1] See Daryl G. Kimball and Kelsey Davenport, 'Paths Forward on Action-for-action Process for Denuclearization and a Peace Regime for the Korean Peninsula', *Arms Control Today*, vol. 11, no. 3, 29 January 2019, https://www.armscontrol.org/issue-briefs/2019-01/ paths-forward-action-action-process-denuclearization-peace-regime-korean.

[2] See Geoffrey Forden, 'Designing Denuclearization Regimes: Agreement, Declarations, Objectives, and Inspections', *Arms Control Today*, vol. 48, no. 9, November

2018, pp. 10–15, https://www. armscontrol.org/act/2018-11/features/ designing-denuclearization-regimes- agreement-declarations-objectives.

3   See Sang-Min Kim, 'Biden Open to Talks with North Korea', *Arms Control Today*, vol. 51, no. 5, June 2021, pp. 31–2, https://www. armscontrol.org/act/2021-06/news/ biden-open-talks-north-korea.

4   See 'North Korea "Not Responding" to US Contact Efforts', BBC, 14 March 2021, from https://www.bbc.com/ news/world-asia-563914.

5   See 'A Principled US Diplomatic Strategy Toward North Korea', 38 North, 22 February 2021, https://www.38north. org/2021/02/a-principled-us-diplomatic- strategy-toward-north-korea/; and Vipin Narang and Ankit Panda, 'North Korea: Risks of Escalation', *Survival*, vol. 62, no. 1, February–March 2020, pp. 47–54.

6   See David C. Kelly, 'The Trilateral Agreement: Lessons for Biological Weapons Verification', in *Verification Yearbook 2002* (London: Verification Research, Training and Information Centre, 2002), p. 103, https:// www.vertic.org/media/Archived_ Publications/Yearbooks/2002/ VY02_Kelly.pdf.

7   See *ibid.*, p. 95.

8   See Rose Gottemoeller, 'Rethinking Nuclear Arms Control', *Washington Quarterly*, vol. 43, no. 3, Fall 2020, pp. 139–59.

9   See Andrew J. Coe and Jane Vaynman, 'Why Arms Control Is So Rare', *American Political Science Review*, vol. 114, no. 2, May 2020, pp. 342–55.

10 Eduard Shevardnadze, 'Speech at Geneva', *Soviet News*, 12 August 1987, p. 294.

11 See David Hoffman, *The Dead Hand: The Untold Story of the Cold War Arms Race and Its Dangerous Legacy* (New York: Doubleday, 2009), p. 306.

12 See, for instance, Siegfried Hecker, 'Report of Visit to the Democratic People's Republic of North Korea (DPRK)', Center for International Security and Cooperation, Stanford University, 14 March 2008, https:// fsi-live.s3.us-west-1.amazonaws.com/ s3fs-public/HeckerDPRKreport.pdf.

13 See Barbara Starr and Zachary Cohen, 'Kim's Tunnel Explosions a Good Will Gesture? Not So Fast', CNN, 1 June 2018, https://edition. cnn.com/2018/06/01/politics/ north-korea-nuclear-test-tunnel- gesture-propaganda/index.html.

14 See 'Verifying a Chemical Weapons Convention', *Chemical Weapons Convention Bulletin*, no. 9, September 1990, p. 14, http://www.sussex.ac.uk/ Units/spru/hsp/documents/Old%20 Bulletins/199009%20CBWCB09.pdf.

15 See Allison Carnegie and Austin Carson, 'The Spotlight's Harsh Glare: Rethinking Publicity and International Order', *International Organization*, vol. 72, no. 3, Summer 2018, pp. 627–57; and Reid B.C. Pauly, 'Deniability in the Nuclear Nonproliferation Regime: The Upside of the Dual- use Dilemma', *International Studies Quarterly*, May 2021.

16 See Kimball and Davenport, 'Paths Forward on Action-for-action Process for Denuclearization and a Peace Regime for the Korean Peninsula'.

Copyright © 2021 The International Institute for Strategic Studies

Noteworthy

Last chance?

'This twelfth edition of the United Nations Environment Programme (UNEP) Emissions Gap Report comes during a year of constant reminders that climate change is not in the distant future. Extreme weather events around the world – including flooding, droughts, wildfires, hurricanes and heatwaves – have continuously hit the news headlines. Thousands of people have been killed or displaced and economic losses are measured in the trillions … There is a fifty–fifty chance that global warming will exceed 1.5°C in the next two decades, and unless there are immediate, rapid and large-scale reductions in GHG [greenhouse-gas] emissions, limiting warming to 1.5°C or even 2°C by the end of the century will be beyond reach.

[…]

The twenty-sixth United Nations Climate Change Conference of the Parties (COP26) is charged with the growing urgency of accelerating global ambition and action on both mitigation and adaptation. This year, the spotlight is on the new and updated nationally determined contributions (NDCs) that countries were requested to submit in advance of COP26 … The new and updated NDCs are insufficient to achieve the temperature goal of the Paris Agreement.

[…]

New or updated NDCs and announced pledges for 2030 have only limited impact on global emissions and the emissions gap in 2030, reducing projected 2030 emissions by only 7.5 per cent, compared with previous unconditional NDCs, whereas 30 per cent is needed to limit warming to 2°C and 55 per cent is needed for 1.5°C. If continued throughout this century, they would result in warming of 2.7°C. The achievement of the net-zero pledges that an increasing number of countries are committing to would improve the situation, limiting warming to about 2.2°C by the end of the century. However, the 2030 commitments do not yet set G20 members (accounting for close to 80 per cent of GHG emissions) on a clear path towards net zero.'

> Extract from the United Nations Environment Programme's October 2021 report 'Emissions Gap Report 2021: The Heat Is On – A World of Climate Promises Not Yet Delivered'.[1]

Geopolitical risk

'When authoritarian regimes demonstrate expansionist tendencies, democratic countries should come together to stand against them. Taiwan is on the front lines.'

> Taiwanese President Tsai Ing-wen comments on what she sees as the threat from the People's Republic of China in an interview with CNN on 28 October 2021.[2]

'Taiwan is a critical partner to the United States and a democratic success story. Taiwan should have meaningful participation in the @UN system, especially as we face an unprecedented number of global challenges.'

> US Secretary of State Antony Blinken expresses his support via Twitter of Taiwan's inclusion in the United Nations.[3]

'We have a commitment to do that.'

US President Joe Biden answers a reporter's question about whether the United States would defend Taiwan if attacked by the People's Republic of China.[4]

'China urges the US to strictly abide by the one-China principle and the provisions of the China–US Three Joint Communiqués, be cautious in its words and deeds on the Taiwan issue, and refrain from sending any wrong signals to the separatist forces of Taiwan independence, so as not to seriously damage China–US relations, peace and stability across the Taiwan Strait.'

Wang Wenbin, spokesman for China's foreign ministry.[5]

Detention tensions

'Today marks four years since the ongoing detention of Osman Kavala began. The continuing delays in his trial, including by merging different cases and creating new ones after a previous acquittal, cast a shadow over respect for democracy, the rule of law and transparency in the Turkish judiciary system.

Together, the embassies of Canada, France, Finland, Denmark, Germany, the Netherlands, New Zealand, Norway, Sweden and the United States of America believe a just and speedy resolution to his case must be in line with Turkey's international obligations and domestic laws. Noting the rulings of the European Court of Human Rights on the matter, we call for Turkey to secure his urgent release.'

Ten embassies in Turkey call for the release of Osman Kavala, a Turkish businessman and philanthropist whose arrest on charges of seeking to overthrow the government is believed to have been politically motivated, in a statement released on 18 October 2021.[6]

'I gave the order to our foreign minister and said what must be done: these 10 ambassadors must be declared *persona non grata* at once.'

Turkish President Recep Tayyip Erdogan threatens to expel the diplomats responsible for the statement.[7]

'In response to questions regarding the Statement of October 18, the United States notes that it maintains compliance with Article 41 of the Vienna Convention on Diplomatic Relations.'

The US Embassy in Turkey, along with the other embassies that supported the statement, reaffirms its commitment 'not to interfere in the internal affairs' of the states in which its diplomats are based in a tweet released on 25 October.[8]

'Our aim was not to create a crisis, but to protect Turkey's honour, pride and dignity. With the statement made today by the ambassadors, their mistakes have been reversed. I believe that, in future, they will be more cautious about Turkey's sovereign rights.'

Erdogan backs down from his threat to expel the diplomats in a televised statement on 25 October.[9]

Sources

1 United Nations Environment Programme, 'Emissions Gap Report 2021: The Heat Is On – A World of Climate Promises Not Yet Delivered', p. iv, https://wedocs.unep.org/bitstream/handle/20.500.11822/36991/EGR21_ESEN.pdf.

2 Will Ripley, Eric Cheung and Ben Westcott, 'Taiwan's President Says the Threat from China Is Increasing "Every Day" and Confirms Presence of US Military Trainers on the Island', CNN, 28 October 2021, https://edition.cnn.com/2021/10/27/asia/tsai-ingwen-taiwan-china-interview-intl-hnk/index.html.

3 Antony Blinken (@SecBlinken), tweet, 26 October 2021, https://twitter.com/SecBlinken/status/1452997840825892881.

4 Kevin Liptak, 'Biden Vows to Protect Taiwan in Event of Chinese Attack', CNN, 22 October 2021, https://edition.cnn.com/2021/10/21/politics/taiwan-china-biden-town-hall/index.html.

5 *Ibid.*

6 US Embassy and Consulates in Turkey, 'Statement on Four Years of Osman Kavala's Detention', 18 October 2021, https://tr.usembassy.gov/statement-on-four-years-of-osman-kavalas-detention/.

7 Laura Pitel, 'Turkey's Erdogan Declares 10 Western Ambassadors "Persona Non Grata"', *Financial Times*, 24 October 2021, https://www.ft.com/content/5d0cec70-3c7e-46e7-a3cf-4330e72328ca.

8 US Embassy Turkey (@USEmbassyTurkey), tweet, 25 October 2021, https://twitter.com/USEmbassyTurkey/status/1452616273796419588; and Laura Pitel, 'Erdogan Backs Down in Row with 10 Western Ambassadors', *Financial Times*, 25 October 2021, https://www.ft.com/content/344dc375-abb2-4bc8-9165-82b41522d7a7.

9 Pitel, 'Erdogan Backs Down in Row with 10 Western Ambassadors'.

Copyright © 2021 The International Institute for Strategic Studies

China Looks at the Korean Peninsula: The 'Two Transitions'

Robert S. Ross

China's understanding of strategic trends on the Korean Peninsula has fundamentally changed over the past five years. A consensus has emerged among Chinese scholars and foreign-policy analysts in government think tanks that there are two power transitions under way on the peninsula. The first is the US–China power transition, reflecting China's emerging military parity with the United States and influence over the South Korean economy. This power transition is challenging South Korea's ability to rely solely on the US for security and prosperity. The second power transition reflects South Korea's development of an increasingly capable military that can mount an independent defence against North Korea. Together, Chinese argue, these two trends are encouraging South Korea to develop a policy of equidistance between the United States and China, and an independent policy toward North Korea that supports both South Korean and Chinese policy preferences.

China's understanding of these power transitions is reflected in its policy toward South Korea, North Korea and denuclearisation. China no longer contributes to North Korea's diplomatic isolation or to economic sanctions against it. With greater South Korean autonomy and common Chinese–South Korean interests vis-à-vis North Korea, China can pursue leadership on peninsular issues, including denuclearisation, undermining US coercive diplomacy.

Robert S. Ross is a professor of political science at Boston College and an associate of the John King Fairbank Center for Chinese Studies, Harvard University.

Survival | vol. 63 no. 6 | December 2021–January 2022 | pp. 129–158 https://doi.org/10.1080/00396338.2021.2006455

Chinese scholars and foreign-policy analysts argue that these trends in peninsular affairs reflect more than the results of Donald Trump's presidency or the election of Moon Jae-in as South Korean president in May 2017. Rather, they believe that changes in both the US–China balance of power – a 'structural change' in regional affairs – and South Korea's security policy have been under way since the Obama administration.[1]

A changing balance of power on the Korean Peninsula

China's rise as an economic and maritime power and the US–China power transition have influenced security affairs throughout Northeast Asia. As China has expanded its maritime capabilities, its presence in South Korean coastal waters has increased. Chinese scholars and think-tank analysts have paid close attention to the power transition and its contribution to China's interest in security cooperation with South Korea.

The US–China power transition

Shifts in the economic and military balance of power between the US and China have altered strategic trends on the Korean Peninsula. In economic affairs, China has been South Korea's most important partner since the turn of the century. In 2001, it became the leading recipient of South Korea's foreign direct investment. Between 2001 and 2003, South Korean investment in China increased by nearly 50%, and roughly 50% of all South Korean foreign direct investment was destined for China.[2] In 2002, China became South Korea's largest export market; exports to China increased by nearly 50% from 2001 to 2003. In contrast, between 2002 and 2003, South Korean exports to the United States stagnated. In 2003, more than 31% of South Korean exports went to China.[3] In 2019, 25% of South Korean exports went to China, while 14% went to the United States.[4]

In military affairs, China has long possessed ground-force capabilities strong enough to influence politics on the Korean Peninsula and to contend with US forces.[5] The changing US–China naval balance in the Yellow Sea is a more recent development, however, and means that China now dominates South Korea's maritime periphery. Moreover, China's modernisation of its air force, its deployment of ground-based anti-ship cruise missiles on the Shandong Peninsula and its bases in the Yellow Sea all add to China's growing superiority in South Korea's coastal waters.[6]

Since 2015, as South Korea considered deployment of the US Terminal High Altitude Area Defense (THAAD) system, China's People's Liberation Army Navy has increased the frequency and sophistication of live-fire naval operations in the Yellow Sea near South Korea.[7] Between January 2016 and February 2019, Chinese warships entered South Korea's exclusive economic zone (EEZ) 465 times. As tensions increased between China and South Korea in 2016 over US deployment of THAAD in Korea, Chinese incursions doubled.[8] In contrast, the US Navy, sensitive to Chinese capabilities, has reduced its operations in the Yellow Sea.[9]

In 2016, there was escalation in the China–South Korea maritime dispute over Socotra Reef in the Yellow Sea. In June, Chinese and South Korean fishing boats clashed, and South Korea detained two Chinese boats. In October, when approximately 40 Chinese fishing boats entered South Korean-claimed waters in the vicinity of Socotra Reef, a South Korean coastguard ship sank after colliding with a Chinese fishing boat.[10] Since then, Chinese observers have noted an increase in the attention paid by South Korea to Socotra Reef as a security issue in Chinese–South Korean relations.[11] The 'THAAD incident' made clear that becoming involved in US–China competition can bring harm to South Korea.[12]

Chinese confidence in China–South Korea relations

The implications of the US–China power transition for South Korean security policy have been carefully examined by Chinese observers. Some have argued that the Asia-Pacific's 'geopolitical structure has changed' and that the balance of power in East Asia now favours China rather than the US, with implications for South Korean decision-making. The rise of China as a maritime power is said to have 'smashed' the US military advantage on China's coastal periphery such that the decline in US power is now 'difficult to ignore'. China's role in peninsular stability has become 'indispensable', and China's 'each and every move in regional security affairs influences all aspects' of South Korean foreign policy.[13]

Many Chinese are thus confident in Beijing's ability to challenge American influence in South Korea. They argue that the increase in Seoul's strategic reliance on China already means that it would be difficult for South Korea to 'pull away from China'.[14] Cooperation with China is seen as especially important for South Korean management of the North Korean threat, including in the areas of crisis management, nuclear diplomacy and peaceful reunification. This trend is viewed as irreversible: as the US–China power gap continues to narrow, the pressure on South Korea to manage Chinese power will increase.[15]

Chinese analysts argue that China's economy has long been critical for South Korean economic growth, but the 2014 China–South Korea Free Trade Agreement has strengthened the countries' comprehensive economic cooperation. South Korean development is now seen as 'inseparable' from China–South Korea trade, there being 'no way to substitute' for China–South Korea cooperation.[16] Chinese observers have noted that in 2017, nearly 12% of South Korea's GDP came from exports to China.[17] The loss incurred by South Korea from Chinese economic retaliation against Seoul's deployment of THAAD underscored South Korean dependence on the Chinese economy. The reduction in Chinese tourism alone had a major impact on South Korea's GDP.[18]

Chinese analysts thus argue that China's rise has affected the costs to South Korea of US–South Korea alliance cooperation against Chinese interests. They contend that China can now impose significant costs on South Korea, while the United States' ability to offset Chinese policy is declining. This is compelling South Korea to reconsider its security posture.[19] Chinese writers understand that the US–South Korea alliance is critical for South Korean security, especially regarding North Korea, and that Seoul must avoid provoking Washington. But South Korea also must avoid provoking China – it must be 'prudent'. South Korean security is already reliant on Chinese policy, imposing an 'alliance dilemma' on Seoul in managing China's rise.[20]

South Korea now finds itself caught between the United States and China, obliging it to pursue the 'balanced development of great-power relations'.[21] It is thus moving toward equidistance; some Chinese observers have described South Korea as walking a 'kind of tightrope' between China and the United States.[22] South Korea requires the alliance with the United States to deal with the North Korean threat, but if it follows the US too closely, China will 'not be happy', and 'misunderstandings' could result.[23]

China's confidence in these findings reflects its analysis of its retaliation against the decision of Park Geun-hye's government to deploy THAAD despite Chinese opposition. In that instance, South Korea placed security cooperation with the United States over its interest in security and economic cooperation with China, thereby disrupting its strategic balance between the US and China. This resulted in the deterioration of South Korea's 'strategic environment' and imposed 'security costs' on the country. To restore China–South Korea stability, Chinese maintain that the Moon government declared the 'three nos': no additional THAAD deployments in South Korea; no integration of South Korea's THAAD system into the US missile-defence system; and no South Korean participation in US–Japan alliance cooperation. Chinese–South Korean tension over THAAD also prompted Seoul to promote summitry and improved trade relations with Beijing.[24]

Some Chinese have commented on South Korea's 'prudence' in refraining from aligning with the United States on regional issues. South Korea has not taken a stand on the sovereignty disputes in the South China Sea, despite US pressure.[25] It has been neutral in the Sino-Japanese territorial dispute over the Diaoyu/Senkaku islands. And, against American objections, South Korea joined the Asian Infrastructure Investment Bank and has participated in China's Belt and Road Initiative (BRI).[26]

South Korea's autonomous security policy

Just as China is a rising power vis-à-vis the United States, South Korea is a rising power vis-à-vis North Korea. The growth and modernisation of South Korea's military has allowed it to develop superior conventional capabilities, and therefore to reduce its reliance on the United States to deter and defend against a North Korean attack. Meanwhile, North Korea's conventional military capabilities have been largely stagnant, causing the North–South balance to shift. Chinese analysts have argued that this North–South power transition has enabled South Korea to develop an autonomous security policy and to strengthen its cooperation with China.

The North–South power transition

From 2005 to 2017, South Korea's defence budget nearly doubled. The average annual increase in defence spending during the Lee Myung-bak and Park administrations (2009–16) was 5.1% in nominal terms, rising to 7.5% during the Moon administration, which has plans to maintain this growth rate through 2023. In 2019, South Korean defence spending ranked tenth in the world, only slightly behind Japanese spending.[27]

In 2015, South Korea tested a conventional missile that could reach political and military targets throughout North Korea, the first step toward an independent retaliatory capability. It is developing missiles and radar systems to target North Korea's artillery deployments north of the Demilitarized Zone and an anti-missile system to intercept North Korean artillery.[28] The South Korean aircraft industry is developing the '4.5 generation' KF-X fighter aircraft, a near-equivalent to the F-35. It is expected to make its first flight in 2022. The KF-X will be armed with supersonic anti-ship missiles developed in South Korea.[29] The South Korean defence industry is also developing ship-based helicopters armed with anti-ship and anti-submarine capabilities. After purchasing 16 German submarines, South Korea is now manufacturing next-generation diesel submarines, with the first ship expected to enter operation in 2022. It has tested a submarine-launched conventional ballistic missile as well. In February 2021, South Korea began construction of *Aegis* destroyers equipped with land-attack missiles, as well as missile-defence and anti-submarine capabilities. A light aircraft carrier is also in development that will carry up to 15 F-35Bs.[30] Seoul has purchased US *Global Hawk* uninhabited aerial vehicles, and is developing indigenous rocket and satellite capabilities for reconnaissance of North Korean military activities.[31]

The superiority of South Korea's conventional capabilities is enhanced by the stagnation of North Korean conventional capabilities. Approximately one-half of North Korea's conventional weapons were designed in the 1960s; the other half are even older. South Korea's missiles can penetrate North Korea's missile-defence system. North Korea has a quantitative advantage in tanks, but uses older models, including Russian tanks that did not perform well 30 years ago in the 1991 Gulf War and are demonstrably inferior to South Korean tanks.[32] Moreover, North Korean soldiers are undernourished, which reduces their combat effectiveness and undermines North Korea's quantitative advantage in troop numbers.[33]

South Korea possesses an effective deterrent against a conventional attack from North Korea. It is also developing conventional capabilities, including missile-defence technologies, to deter a North Korean nuclear strike.[34] The United States' treaty commitment to South Korea and its troop presence there contribute to the deterrence of a North Korean nuclear strike against South Korea, so that the US–South Korean alliance remains important to South Korean security. Nonetheless, South Korea is developing an independent defence capability that contributes to its strategic autonomy.

China's assessment of South Korean strategic autonomy

Just as Chinese scholars and think-tank analysts have been assessing the US–China power transition and South Korea's 'alliance dilemma', they have also been paying close attention to the South Korea–North Korea power transition and the implications for South Korean security policy. They argue that this power transition has encouraged South Korea to pursue independent diplomatic initiatives and an 'autonomous' security policy regarding North Korea. As long as the North Korean threat exists, South Korea will require the support of the US–South Korea alliance, but it will seek greater authority within the alliance and a more balanced position between the United States and China.[35]

Chinese observers concur with American scholars that South Korea now possesses 'middle power' economic and military capabilities.[36] In East Asia, South Korea's economy and 'comprehensive national power' are ranked in third place, behind only China and Japan. South Korea's 'hard power' and 'soft power' alike are seen as having afforded it a greater role in regional diplomacy and a desire to exercise independent influence on peninsular affairs.[37] 'To give meaning to its middle power diplomacy', Chinese believe that South Korea will maintain 'friendly relations' with both the United States and China, rather than 'tilt toward one side or the other'. Cooperation with China is thus an 'important objective of South Korea's middle-power diplomacy'.[38]

Chinese observers are especially impressed by South Korea's improved defence capability. The country's military-modernisation programme is seen as an 'obvious' effort to develop an 'independent national defence' and 'to realise a balanced position within the alliance' while reducing its reliance on the United States.[39] This trend was first developed by the Park administration and extended by the Moon administration with its five-year defence-acquisitions plan and its Defense Reform 2.0 programme. What Chinese observers have called South Korea's 'indigenous defence revolution' is seen as contributing to a broad-based capability to deal with 'all kinds of threats', including the North Korean threat, and to take the lead for South Korean security within the US–South Korean alliance, all in support of 'balanced' diplomacy.[40] The Park administration's development of a South Korean missile-defence system contributed to its resistance to deployment of THAAD and underscored its preference for strategic autonomy.[41]

Chinese observers understand that South Korea's security has benefitted from the stagnation of North Korean weaponry. This trend has led to a 'wide disparity' between North and South Korea in terms of national power and advanced military technologies, a gap that affords South Korea greater independence in planning and implementing its North Korea strategy.[42]

With improved military capabilities and its middle-power status, South Korea, according to Chinese observers, is refusing to be cast as a 'chess piece' in the power struggles of Northeast Asia. It does not wish to become a mere sacrificial object in any great-power 'trial of strength'.[43] As one Chinese scholar wrote, South Korea feels some pressure to choose sides, but is concerned that any 'transformation of the international structure' would damage South Korean security.[44] As a 'front-line state ... under the flag of US containment of China', it is at risk of suffering intolerable costs in any conflict.[45]

Chinese similarly argue that South Korea's 'four-power strategy' reflects its effort to maintain balanced relationships with regional powers and to reduce its reliance on the United States. It focuses on developing cooperation with China, Japan and Russia, as well as with the United States. South Korea's 'northern policy' likewise aims at expanded cooperation with China, Mongolia and Russia. It places special emphasis on regional economic cooperation through expanded transportation infrastructure, including North–South rail links to connect South Korea with Russia. South Korea's participation in China's BRI reflects, in part, its focus on infrastructure development for economic diversity. These efforts also support South Korea's objective of easing North–South tension and expanding North–South economic cooperation. The United States has opposed such initiatives, but this has only increased South Korea's interest in autonomy.[46]

US resistance to South Korean policy independence

Chinese scholars and think-tank experts have focused on American resistance to South Korean strategic autonomy, arguing that the United States views South Korea as a critical asset for dealing with the rise of China and for encircling it militarily. As US–China competition has intensified, Chinese have argued that the US 'cannot accept defeat' and 'cannot tolerate' South Korea's balanced diplomacy, and is therefore seeking to disrupt China–South Korea cooperation.[47] Ongoing North–South tensions are seen as serving US interests.[48] American resistance to the transfer to South Korea of wartime operational control (OPCON) of South Korean military forces similarly reflects the United States' determination to maintain its troop presence in South Korea.[49]

Chinese observers believe the US has used a 'wedge strategy' to block closer China–South Korea cooperation and to maintain its presence in South Korea. US deployment of THAAD in South Korea is seen as a key element of this strategy. According to this logic, THAAD deployment was not for the defence of South Korea; rather, it was intended as a wedge to divide China and South Korea.[50] THAAD is ineffective against North Korean missiles, but it was useful to compel South Korea to 'make a choice' between China and the United States. Because of American pressure, South Korea had no other option but to agree to deploy THAAD.[51]

China also believes the United States has constrained South Korean development of independent policies toward North Korea, policies that align with Chinese preferences. Whereas the United States prioritises its geopolitical interest in US–China competition over North Korean denuclearisation and relies on sanctions to compel unconditional North

Korean concessions, South Korea, as well as China and North Korea, supports a negotiated and incremental strategy for denuclearisation, with reciprocal concessions by North Korea and the United States. China and South Korea also oppose reliance on sanctions to compel North Korean compromises. Instead, they advocate expanded economic cooperation with North Korea to promote stability. And whereas the United States has resisted improved North–South relations for fear that such an outcome would reduce the need for an American military presence in South Korea, China and South Korea promote North–South reconciliation.[52]

Chinese writers argue that when North–South tensions were beginning to ease, Trump announced sanctions that were heavier and of a greater scale than any that had gone before, revealing the 'sharp differences' between the United States and South Korea.[53] When South Korea considered easing sanctions on North Korea, the United States opposed this, contributing to South Korea's decision to abandon the idea. Similarly, the United States compelled South Korea to abandon resumed cooperation with North Korea at the Kaesong Industrial Zone.[54] Chinese writers have especially focused on US efforts to constrain South Korean autonomy. They observed that when South Korean companies shipped coal to North Korea, Mike Pompeo, then US secretary of state, insisted that any advances in North–South relations must not get ahead of US policy. They also noted that Steven Mnuchin, then US secretary of the treasury, bypassed the Korean government to speak directly to South Korea's seven commercial banks, warning that they needed to comply with sanctions against North Korea.[55] The United States established the US–South Korea working group to exercise control over South Korean policy, insisting that all South Korean policies toward North Korea be coordinated within the group.[56]

As the power differential between the United States and China continues to close and the competition between them intensifies, Chinese expect that the 'strategic space' occupied by South Korea between the two powers will contract, and that US efforts to constrain South Korea will become 'clearer and clearer'. Washington will pressure Seoul to accept deployment of US intermediate-range ballistic missiles, to integrate the THAAD system with US missile-defence systems, to expand security cooperation with Japan and to link its own regional foreign policy (known as the 'New Southern Strategy') with the US Indo-Pacific strategy. But China is confident that US resistance will only increase South Korea's commitment to autonomy.[57] The Moon administration's determination to assume OPCON from the United States demonstrates Seoul's resolve to reduce its reliance on Washington and to assume leadership in peninsular affairs.[58]

Opportunities for China on the Korean Peninsula

Chinese analysts have argued that the US–China and South Korea–North Korea power transitions are enhancing Chinese leadership in peninsular diplomacy.[59] South Korea's movement toward equidistance between the United States and China alleviates Chinese concerns that US–China differences over North Korean denuclearisation will lead to greater US–South Korea alliance cooperation. Moreover, China believes its own military expansion has balanced US military capabilities, so that any US effort to expand cooperation with South Korea to balance China's modernisation will fail. As one analyst told the author, 'China is winning'.[60] At the same time, South Korea's greater security vis-à-vis North Korea is allowing it to prioritise the implications of a rising China and to accommodate Chinese interests.[61] It is also allowing South Korea to pursue its own interests in North–South relations, contributing to Chinese leadership and to China–South Korea cooperation.

Chinese expectations of peninsular leadership

Chinese writers understand that, as a rising power, China has a responsibility to contribute to global order and to support nuclear non-proliferation. But Chinese analysts argue that these tasks are not China's most important objective. Rather, given that the United States is seen as working to contain China and to maintain its own 'forward deployments' in South Korea while downplaying non-proliferation, China cannot alter, much less abandon, its geopolitical considerations to itself pursue non-proliferation.[62]

It is in China's interest to weaken US alliances and to reduce the negative effects they have on China. Chinese writers have concluded that, just as the United States has pursued a wedge strategy to divide China and South

Korea, China can now drive a wedge between South Korea and the United States.[63] Beijing is seen as having sufficient leverage over South Korea to develop a 'counter-wedge' strategy: because security and economic cooperation with China are 'indispensable' for South Korea, China possesses 'dual levers' with which to 'exert leverage' on South Korea and to induce it to increasingly tilt toward China.[64]

Because China, South Korea and North Korea agree that nuclear stability requires incremental and reciprocal measures; because China and South Korea both stress the importance of scaling back economic sanctions and enhancing economic and cultural cooperation with North Korea; and because North Korea seeks expanded international economic cooperation, China believes it has an 'unshirkable responsibility' to be involved in peninsular diplomacy. Its proposals for peninsular easing 'should not be absent' from regional negotiations, and it can contribute to regional stability and improved North–South relations by serving as a 'go-between' in peninsular affairs.[65]

China's capacity for leadership, combined with increasing South Korean autonomy, is seen as enabling China and South Korea to play a 'mediating role' between North Korea and the United States. Chinese observers are encouraged by South Korean support for four-party talks on peninsular issues (involving China, North Korea, South Korea and the United States), rather than the US-supported three-party talks, which exclude China. China and South Korea can be conduits for back-channel signals, helping to bridge US–North Korea differences over nuclear diplomacy. They could even put forward joint proposals for easing peninsular tensions.[66]

The end of Chinese sanctions

The dual power transition has led China to reduce its cooperation with US coercive diplomacy toward North Korea and its support for sanctions. Instead, it prefers to focus on engagement with North Korea to promote economic reform in that country.

North Korean economic reform has been a long-standing interest of China's. Former North Korean leader Kim Jong-il's first visit to China in 2000 included a tour of a computer factory, during which he reportedly expressed amazement at the technologies on display. In later visits, Kim toured China's special economic zones.[67] Beginning in 2012, his son Kim Jong-un has introduced limited agricultural and industrial reforms that have created greater opportunity for Chinese engagement with North Korea's economy and society.[68] More recently, China–North Korea border trade has contributed to the development of local markets and independent economic enterprises in North Korea.[69] In the context of ongoing state control over North Korean society, China's export of consumer goods to North Korea has contributed to a more porous society open to influences beyond state propaganda.[70]

Nonetheless, until recently there has been a contradiction between China's support for North Korean reform and its opposition to North Korea's nuclear programme. Chinese engagement of North Korea was seen as promoting long-term reform, but also as undermining North Korea's incentive to curtail its nuclear programme and putting China at odds with the United States and South Korea. This contradiction led China to limit its cooperation with North Korea, lest it enable the United States to increase its strategic presence in South Korea and drive a wedge between China and South Korea.[71] Thus, China offered North Korea only enough economic assistance to maintain political stability.[72] As North Korea continued to develop its nuclear capability, China supported United Nations-led economic sanctions against the country.[73]

In 2018, however, China initiated a policy reversal. Beijing no longer wished to exercise restraint, but to develop China–North Korea diplomatic, economic and cultural cooperation. Now that China and South Korea agree on engagement, China has improved relations with North Korea with less fear of US retaliation or of undermining China–South Korea cooperation.

Between May 2018 and June 2019, China held five summits with North Korean leader Kim Jong-un. Kim's 2018 visit to Beijing was his first since taking power in 2011. In September 2018, Li Zhanshu, chairman of the Standing Committee of the National People's Congress, delivered a letter to Kim from Chinese leader Xi Jinping. In his letter, Xi pledged to strengthen China–North Korea cooperation.[74] Then, in June 2019, Xi carried out the first visit to Pyongyang by a Chinese leader since Hu Jintao's visit in January 2011. Xinhua reported that Xi had declared China–North Korea relations to have entered a 'new historical era' and claimed that the two countries had developed a 'blueprint' for expanded cooperation. In September 2021, on the occasion of the 73rd anniversary of North Korea's Workers' Party, Xi wrote to Kim that he not only attached 'great importance' to Chinese–North Korean relations, but wanted to work with Kim 'to promote long-term friendly relations and lift it to new levels'.[75]

Xi's visit to Pyongyang was followed by a surge in Chinese diplomacy. The two sides exchanged multiple delegations to promote cooperation between their communist parties, their public-security organisations and their legal communities. In August 2019, China resumed military ties with North Korea with a visit to Pyongyang by General Zhang Youxia, China's number-two military officer. Zhang declared that the Chinese military 'is willing to work with the [North Korean] side to ... promote cooperation and mutual support, so as to contribute to ... the development of bilateral relations'.[76] Renewed China–North Korea cooperation also included improved cultural ties.

Xi's visit was followed by a surge in diplomacy

In 2018, China sent delegations to Pyongyang led by Minister of the General Administration of Sport Gou Zhongwen and Minister of Culture and Tourism Luo Shugang.[77] The flurry of China–North Korea summits in 2018 led to a 75% increase in Chinese tourism to North Korea in 2019, providing a financial windfall for the North Korean tourist industry, including its restaurants, hotels and retail businesses. Increased tourism encouraged Kim Jong-un to build a ski resort, and led Air China and Air Koryo to open routes between Pyongyang and multiple Chinese cities, including Beijing, Chengdu, Dalian, Jinan and Xian.[78]

The most consequential change in China's policy is reduced support for US coercive diplomacy. In 2017, following North Korea's fourth nuclear test, China voted for and implemented strengthened UN sanctions against North Korea.[79] Chinese imports from North Korea in December 2017 declined by 83% over the previous December; and in April 2018 Chinese imports were 89% less than the previous April.[80] But in 2019 China not only joined with Russia to block UN criticism of North Korean sanctions violations, but also called for lifting some sanctions.[81] China also helped North Korea evade

UN sanctions. A 2020 UN report concluded that China had assisted North Korea in evading sanctions on coal exports by transporting North Korean coal on Chinese ships. China also helped North Korea evade sanctions on fish exports by allowing Chinese ships to pay North Korea to fish in North Korean waters.[82] In the first five months of 2020, 89 North Korean petroleum ships had called on Chinese ports in violation of UN sanctions.[83]

China also increased its investment in infrastructure to expand border trade. In 2018, it agreed to spend nearly $90 million for road construction in North Korea to connect the North Korean and Chinese markets. In 2019, after a six-year delay, China recommenced work on the nearly completed Yalu River bridge connecting the border cities of Dandong and Sinuiju. In June 2018, Chinese firms rushed to the annual Pyongyang Spring International Trade Fair in the expectation of expanded investment opportunities.[84] In the first half of 2019, China–North Korea trade had increased by 14.3% over the first half of 2018; North Korean exports had increased by 15.5%. In September 2021, when China and North Korea eased border restrictions imposed following the breakout of the COVID-19 pandemic, trade doubled over August 2019 and reached the highest level since December 2019.[85] As China–North Korea summitry developed and trade expanded, real-estate prices in Dandong surged.[86]

China's growing power and South Korea's increasing policy independence have allowed China to expand its cooperation with North Korea and South Korea simultaneously. South Korea's 2020 defence White Paper expressed its intent to 'steadily' develop bilateral ties with China 'to secure peace and prosperity on the Korean Peninsula'.[87] Shortly after Joe Biden's inauguration as US president, Xi spoke with Moon and expressed support for his North Korea initiatives. South Korea then called on the Biden administration to support sanctions relief on North Korea in exchange for a freeze on its nuclear programme, and to carry out the transfer of OPCON to South Korea. Soon afterwards, Chinese Foreign Minister Wang Yi spoke with South Korean Foreign Minister Chung Eui-yong to express full support for South Korean policy.[88] In 2021, South Korea reopened diplomatic communication with North Korea and called on China to use its close relations with both North and South Korea to promote improved

North–South relations.[89] In October 2021, as the United States restricted Chinese access to advanced technologies and as China moved to develop an independent semiconductor industry, South Korea's SK Hynix agreed to work with Wuxi, China, to develop 19 semiconductor-related projects at the China–Korea Integrated Circuit Industrial Park complex in that city.[90]

*   *   *

Chinese observers have calculated that the dual power transition on the Korean Peninsula has created a new great-power strategic order. They are confident that China's rise and improved South Korean defence capabilities have strengthened China's role in peninsular diplomacy and allowed Beijing to challenge the American presence on the peninsula. China has significantly reduced its cooperation with US sanctions against North Korea, while taking advantage of South Korea's interest in foreign-policy autonomy to improve its relations with Seoul at American expense.

Because of the two power transitions on the Korean Peninsula, the United States can no longer rely on China's interest in stable US–China relations to encourage Chinese cooperation with US sanctions policy. Likewise, the United States can no longer count on South Korea to support its North Korea policy or to serve as a reliable asset in its competition with China. Whereas the post-Second World War strategic order on the Korean Peninsula reflected a division between a Chinese sphere of influence encompassing North Korea and a US sphere of influence encompassing South Korea, the latter is now tending toward equidistance between the two great powers.

Since the Korean War, US policy has aimed to isolate North Korea diplomatically and economically in a bid to coerce political change. Since 1992, the US has implemented increasingly restrictive unilateral and UN sanctions to compel North Korea to abandon its nuclear proliferation. But Pyongyang has continued to develop nuclear weapons and nuclear-capable missiles.[91] Even at the height of American power in the post-Cold War era, when China was cooperative with US policy and there was extensive US–South Korea political and defence cooperation against North Korea, the United States was not able to prevent North Korean nuclear proliferation.

Chinese views of the two power transitions are reflected in the changes in Chinese policy toward North Korea. As it develops, US sanctions policy will become increasingly ineffective. Chinese economic cooperation with North Korea continues to reduce the latter's isolation. South Korea can be expected to continue to advance its own economic and political cooperation with both North Korea and China, while North Korea will consolidate its nuclear capabilities. The United States lacks the leverage to coerce North Korea to abandon its nuclear weapons, and any incentives Pyongyang may have had to do so will continue to weaken.[92]

Given that coercion has failed and North Korea is now a nuclear state, the United States' objective should be threat moderation. Cooperation with China and South Korea in four-party negotiations should be directed at an agreement for reciprocal and incremental steps for reduced sanctions in exchange for a freeze on North Korea's nuclear and missile programmes.[93] There is no guarantee that engagement will be successful, but more than 65 years of US-led economic and political isolation have failed to moderate North Korean politics or its nuclear proliferation.

Engaging North Korea would have other advantages. As China and South Korea move ahead with bilateral engagement, the United States may find itself increasingly marginalised should it persist in its sanctions policy. Participation in four-party talks would give the United States a greater voice in peninsular diplomacy. By engaging with North Korea, the US might gain opportunities to participate in North Korea's economy and society, exposing the North Korean people to the benefits of capitalism and to American political values. Kim Jong-un will want to retain full political control over North Korean society, but he also wants sanctions relief and greater access to the international economy. Kim's interest in economic cooperation with other countries presents an opportunity for the US to make contact with North Korean society.

US engagement with North Korea would also give Pyongyang an alternative to total economic and political dependence on China. Given that China and North Korea share a border, US influence in North Korea will necessarily remain secondary to Chinese influence. Nonetheless, it is in the United States' interest that North Korea come out from under China's shadow.

The power transitions on the Korean Peninsula require the United States to negotiate with North Korea as a nuclear state. Once it begins to do so, Washington will be able to develop policies that can contribute to political and economic reform in North Korea with a view to reducing the risk of war. If it does not do so, the US may lose its voice in the region's security affairs.

Notes

1   See, for example, Zhao Yihei and Zheng Hua, 'Quanli Bianqian Shijiao xia de Mei Han Tongmeng Kunjing' [The US–ROK Alliance Dilemma in a Power-shift Perspective], *Guoji Luntan* [International Forum], no. 4, 2020, p. 58.

2   James Brooke, 'Koreans Look to China, Seeing a Market and a Monster', *New York Times*, 10 February 2004, https://www.nytimes.com/2004/02/10/business/koreans-look-to-china-seeing-a-market-and-a-monster.html.

3   'China Emerges as Biggest Export Market of South Korea', *People's Daily*, 14 November 2002, http://english.peopledaily.com.cn/200211/14/eng20021114_106796.shtml. See also Statista, 'Value of Goods Exported from South Korea to China from 2000 to 2020', https://www.statista.com/statistics/657617/south-korea-exported-goods-value-to-china-since-free-trade-agreement/; and Statista, 'Value of Goods Exported from South Korea to the United States from 2000 to 2020', https://www.statista.com/statistics/656522/south-korea-exported-goods-value-to-united-states-since-free-trade-agreement/.

4   This data is from Trading Economics, 'South Korea Exports', https://tradingeconomics.com/south-korea/exports.

5   See Susan M. Puska, 'Rough but Ready Force Projection: An Assessment of Recent PLA Training', in Andrew J. Scobel and Larry M. Wortzel (eds), *China's Growing Military Power: Perspectives on Security, Ballistic Missiles, and Conventional Capabilities* (Carlisle, PA: Strategic Studies Institute, US Army War College, 2002).

6   On the shifting balance in Chinese coastal waters, see Eric Heginbotham et al., *The US–China Military Scorecard: Forces, Geography, and the Evolving Balance of Power, 1996–2017* (Santa Monica, CA: RAND Corporation, 2015), chapter 13, http://www.rand.org/content/dam/rand/pubs/research_reports/RR300/RR392/RAND_RR392.pdf.

7   See 'China Holds "Unprecedented" Live-fire Drills in Yellow Sea', Yonhap, 4 July 2015, https://en.yna.co.kr/view/AEN20150704000900315; Sarah Zheng, 'Beijing Sends Warning with Second Naval Drill in Yellow Sea', *South China Morning Post*, 5 August 2017, https://www.scmp.com/news/china/article/2105483/beijing-sends-warning-second-naval-drill-yellow-sea;

'China Holds Simultaneous Military Drills in Four Seas, Again', Reuters, 28 September 2020, https://www.reuters.com/article/us-china-defence/china-holds-simultaneous-military-drills-in-four-seas-again-idUSKBN26J1KW; and Jina Kim, 'China and Regional Security Dynamics on the Korean Peninsula', in Chung Min Lee and Kathryn Botto (eds), *Korea Net Assessment 2020: Politicized Security and Unchanging Strategic Realities* (Washington DC: Carnegie Endowment for International Peace, 2020).

8   See Kim, 'China and Regional Security Dynamics on the Korean Peninsula'.

9   See David Lague and Benjamin Kang Lim, 'The China Challenge: Ruling the Waves', Reuters, 30 April 2019, https://www.reuters.com/investigates/special-report/china-army-navy/.

10   See 'S. Korea to Urge China for Strong Measures on Illegal Fishing', Arirang, 10 June 2016, http://www.arirang.com/News/News_View.asp?nSeq=192125; Lisa Collins, 'Between a Rock and a Grey Zone: China–ROK Illegal Fishing Disputes', Asia Maritime Transparency Initiative, Center for Strategic and International Studies, 6 July 2016, https://amti.csis.org/rock-grey-zone-china-rok-illegal-fishing-disputes/; and 'South Korea Vows Armed Crackdown Against Chinese Fishing Boats After Sinking of Coast Guard Ship', *South China Morning Post*, 11 October 2016, https://www.scmp.com/news/china/diplomacy-defence/article/2027042/seoul-summons-chinese-envoy-over-sinking-coast-guard. For an analysis of the Socotra dispute, see Senan Fox, *China, South Korea, and the Socotra Rock Dispute: A Submerged Rock and Its Destabilizing Potential* (Singapore: Palgrave, 2019).

11   On the 'sensitivity' of Socotra Reef for South Korean security, see Tang Ke and Zhao Zhiguo, 'Shi Lun Wen Zaiyin xia de Hanguo Guojia Anquan Zhanlüe' [Korea's National Security Strategy Under Moon Jae-in's Rule], *Guoji Yanjiu Cankao* [International Studies Reference], no. 5, 2019, p. 43; and Zhang Chi, 'Hanguo dui Diaoyudao Zhengduan de Renshi, Lichang yu Yingxiang' [South Korea's Perspective and Position on the Diaoyu Islands Dispute and Its Influence], *Taipingyang Xuebao* [Pacific Journal], no. 11, 2017, p. 22.

12   See Zhao and Zheng, 'Quanli Bianqian Shijiao xia de Mei Han Tongmeng Kunjing', pp. 56, 58; and Liu Shengxiang and Jiang Jiamin, 'Zhong Mei Guanxi Shiyu xia de Hanguo Juese Lunxi' [An Analysis of the Role of South Korea from the Perspective of Sino-US Relations], *Taipingyang Xuebao*, vol. 26, no. 3, March 2018, p. 35.

13   Zhang Huizhi, 'Zhong Mei Jingzheng Geju xia de Zhong Han, Mai Han Guanxi Zouxiang yu Hanguo Xuanze' [The Trend in China–South Korea and US–South Korea Relations in the Structure of China–US Competition and South Korean Choice], *Dongbei Ya Luntan* [Northeast Asia Forum], no. 2, 2019, pp. 27–8.

14   Liu and Jiang, 'Zhong Mei Guanxi Shiyu xia de Hanguo Juese Lunxi', pp. 30, 36.

15   See Wang Junsheng, 'Chuyu Zhuanzhe qi de Chaoxian Bandao: Guoji Hezuo yu Zhongguo Juesi' [The Korean Peninsula at the Turning Point:

International Cooperation and China's Role], *Dongbei Ya Xuekan* [Journal of Northeast Asian Studies], no. 2, March 2020, p. 47; Song Wenzhi, 'Tixi Yali, Weixie Renzhi yu Hanguo zai Zhong Mei zhijian de Zhanlüe Xuanze' [South Korea's Strategic Choice in US–China Relations Under Systemic Pressure and Threat Perception], *Dongbei Ya Luntan*, no. 4, 2019, pp. 88, 90; and Liu and Jiang, 'Zhong Mei Guanxi Shiyu xia de Hanguo Juese Lunxi', p. 36.

[16] Zhang, 'Zhong Mei Jingzheng Geju xia de Zhong Han, Mai Han Guanxi Zouxiang yu Hanguo Xuanze', p. 27.

[17] See Zhao and Zheng, 'Quanli Bianqian Shijiao xia de Mei Han Tongmeng Kunjing', p. 54.

[18] For analyses of the impact of Chinese sanctions, see Darren J. Lim, 'Chinese Economic Coercion During the THAAD Dispute', Asan Forum, 28 December 2019, http://www.theasanforum.org/chinese-economic-coercion-during-the-thaad-dispute/; and Yul Sohl, 'South Korea Under the United States–China Rivalry: Dynamics of the Economic–Security Nexus in Trade Policymaking', *Pacific Review*, vol. 32, no. 6, 2019, pp. 1,030–1.

[19] See Zhao and Zheng, 'Quanli Bianqian Shijiao xia de Mei Han Tongmeng Kunjing', p. 58.

[20] Liu and Jiang, 'Zhong Mei Guanxi Shiyu xia de Hanguo Juese Lunxi', pp. 30, 36; Ling Shengli, 'Chaoxian Bandao Zhanlüe Zizhuxing de Tisheng ji qi Yingxiang' [The Rise of Korean Peninsula Strategic Autonomy and Its Influence], *Dangdai Hanguo* [Contemporary South Korea], no. 4, 2018, p. 3; and Dai Weilai, 'Hanguo Zhongdeng Qiangguo Waijiao Zhanlüe ji qi dui Zhongguo de Yingxiang' [South Korea's Middle Power Diplomatic Strategy and Its Influence in China], *Dangdai Yatai* [Journal of Contemporary Asia-Pacific Studies], no. 2, 2016, p. 150.

[21] Zhang, 'Zhong Mei Jingzheng Geju xia de Zhong Han, Mai Han Guanxi Zouxiang yu Hanguo Xuanze', p. 25. Recent US scholarship on South Korea's policy dilemmas includes Ellen Kim and Victor Cha, 'Between a Rock and a Hard Place: South Korea's Strategic Dilemmas with China and the United States', *Asia Policy*, no. 21, January 2016; and Scott A. Snyder, *South Korea at the Crossroads: Autonomy in an Era of Rival Powers* (New York: Columbia University Press, 2018), particularly chapter 9.

[22] See Bi Yingdao, 'Wen Zaiyin Zhengfu de Zizhu Zhanlüe: Jinzhan yu Tiaozhan' [Moon Jae-in Government's Independent Strategy: Development and Challenges], *Guoji Wenti Yanjiu* [International Studies], no. 4, 2020, p. 129; and Ling, 'Chaoxian Bandao Zhanlüe Zizhuxing de Tisheng ji qi Yingxiang', p. 3.

[23] Liu and Jiang, 'Zhong Mei Guanxi Shiyu xia de Hanguo Juese Lunxi', pp. 31, 36; and Dai, 'Hanguo Zhongdeng Qiangguo Waijiao Zhanlüe ji qi dui Zhongguo de Yingxiang', p. 150.

[24] See Zhang, 'Zhong Mei Jingzheng Geju xia de Zhong Han, Mai Han Guanxi Zouxiang yu Hanguo Xuanze', p. 24; Zhang Chi, 'Gongtong Minzhudang de Duiwai Zhengce Zhuzhang yu Wen Zaiyan Shiqi Zhong Han Guanxi de Fazhan Fangxiang' [The Foreign Policy of

the Democratic Party of South Korea and the Developing Direction of Sino-Korean Relations in the Moon Jae-in Period], *Hanguo Yanjiu Luncong* [Journal of South Korean Studies], no. 1, 2018, pp. 65–6; and Bi, 'Wen Zaiyin Zhengfu de Zizhu Zhanlüe: Jinzhan yu Tiaozhan', p. 131. See also David Josef Volodzko, 'China Wins Its War Against South Korea's US THAAD Missile Shield – Without Firing a Shot', *South China Morning Post*, 18 November 2017, https://www.scmp.com/week-asia/geopolitics/article/2120452/china-wins-its-war-against-south-koreas-us-thaad-missile.

25   See Lü Chenyun, 'Shilun Hanguo Wen Zaiyin Zhengfu de Dongnan Ya Waijiao' [On the Southeast Asian Diplomacy of South Korea's Moon Jae-in Government], *Heping yu Fazhan* [Peace and Development], no. 4, 2020, pp. 99–101; and Bi Yingdao, 'Chaoxian Bandao Xin Xingshi xia Shenhua Zhong Han Anquang Hezuo de Sikao' [Thoughts on Deepening China–South Korea Security Cooperation in the New Situation on the Korean Peninsula], *Xiandai Guoji Guanxi* [Contemporary International Relations], no. 10, 2019, p. 37.

26   See Bi, 'Chaoxian Bandao Xin Xingshi xia Shenhua Zhong Han Anquang Hezuo de Sikao'; and Song, 'Tixi Yali, Weixie Renzhi yu Hanguo zai Zhong Mei zhijian de Zhanlüe Xuanze', p. 90.

27   See 'S. Korea's 2020 Defense Budget Rises 7.4% to over 50tr Won', *Korea Herald*, 11 December 2019, http://www.koreaherald.com/view.php?ud=20191211000099#; and Nan Tian et al., 'Trends in World Military Expenditure, 2019', Stockholm International Peace Research Institute, 20 April 2020, https://www.sipri.org/sites/default/files/2020-04/fs_2020_04_milex_0.pdf.

28   See 'South Korea Test-fires Missile that Can Strike All of the North', Reuters, 3 June 2015, https://www.reuters.com/article/us-southkorea-missile/south-korea-test-fires-missile-that-can-strike-all-of-the-north-idUSKBN0OJ0YM20150603; Jeff Jeong, 'South Korea to Deploy "Artillery Killer" to Destroy North Korean Bunkers', Defense News, 19 March 2018, https://www.defensenews.com/global/asia-pacific/2018/03/19/south-korea-to-deploy-artillery-killer-to-destroy-north-korean-bunkers/; Chad O'Carroll, 'South Korea to Develop Iron Dome-style Artillery Interceptor System for Defense', NK News, 10 August 2020, https://www.nknews.org/2020/08/south-korea-to-develop-iron-dome-style-artillery-interceptor-system-for-defense/; and Jeff Jeong, 'South Korea Moves to Kick Its Missile Defense Shield Up a Notch', Defense News, 14 August 2019, https://www.defensenews.com/global/asia-pacific/2019/08/14/south-korea-moves-to-kick-its-missile-defense-shield-up-a-notch/.

29   See 'S Korean KF-X Jet Prototype Roll-out in April', Defenseworld.Net, 31 January 2020, https://www.defenseworld.net/news/28866/S_Korean_KF_X_Jet_Prototype_Roll_out_in_April#.YEAeEGhKiUl; Gabriel Dominguez and Dae Young Kim, 'South Korea Confirms First KF-X Prototype To Be Rolled Out in April', *Janes*, 2 March 2021, https://www.janes.

com/defence-news/news-detail/ south-korea-confirms-first-kf-x- prototype-to-be-rolled-out-in-april; and Xavier Vavasseur, 'New Supersonic Anti-ship Missile for South Korea's KF-X Breaks Cover', Navalnews, 15 February 2021, https://www.navalnews. com/naval-news/2021/02/ new-supersonic-anti-ship-missile-for- south-koreas-kf-x-breaks-cover/.

30 See Oh Seok-min, 'S. Korea Successfully Tests SLBM from New Submarine', Yonhap, 7 September 2021, https://en.yna.co.kr/view/ AEN20210907001900325; Xavier Vavasseur, 'South Korea Selects MH-60R Helicopter for ROK Navy', Navalnews, 15 December 2020, https://www.navalnews. com/naval-news/2020/12/ south-korea-selects-mh-60r-helicopter- for-rok-navy/; 'South Korean Submarine Capabilities', NTI, 22 February 2021, https://www.nti. org/analysis/articles/south-korea- submarine-capabilities/; Xavier Vavasseur, 'South Korea's DSME Launches 2nd KSS III Submarine for ROK Navy', Navalnews, 10 November 2020, https://www. navalnews.com/naval-news/2020/11/ south-koreas-dsme-launches-2nd- kss-iii-submarine-for-rok-navy/; Xavier Vavasseur, 'South Korea's HHI Cut Steel of New KDX III Batch II Destroyer for ROK Navy', Navalnews, 3 March 2021, https://www. navalnews.com/naval-news/2021/03/ south-koreas-hhi-cut-steel-on-new- kdx-iii-batch-ii-destroyer-for-rok- navy/; and Robert Farley, 'The South Korean Navy Has Big Plans Ahead',

Diplomat, 23 August 2019, https:// thediplomat.com/2019/08/the-south- korean-navy-has-big-plans-ahead/. For a comprehensive and analytical perspective on South Korean naval modernisation, see Ian Bowers, The Modernisation of the Republic of Korea Navy (London: Palgrave, 2019).

31 See Dae Young Kim, 'US Delivers Fourth and Final RQ-4 Global Hawk UAV to RoKAF', Janes, 15 October 2020, https://www.janes. com/defence-news/news-detail/ us-delivers-fourth-and-final- rq-4-global-hawk-uav-to-rokaf; and Kelsey Davenport, 'South Korea to Pursue Military Satellites', Arms Control Today, 20 September 2020, https://www. armscontrol.org/act/2020-09/news/ south-korea-pursue-military-satellites.

32 Andrew H. Cordesman, 'The Conventional Military Balance in the Koreas and Northeast Asia', Center for International and Strategic Studies, 2 August 2016, pp. 23, 65, 71, https://csis- website-prod.s3.amazonaws.com/ s3fs-public/publication/160802_ Korea_Conventional_Balance.pdf.

33 See Dylan Tan, 'Kim Jong Un Wants to Change How North Korea's Soldiers Eat', Business Insider, 26 July 2018, https://www.businessinsider.com/ kim-jong-un-wants-to-change-how- north-koreas-soldiers-eat-2018-7; and Eunjung Cho, 'Study Finds Little Change in N. Korean Diet over 50 Years', Voice of America, 3 February 2015, https://www.voanews.com/a/ study-little-change-north-korean- diet/2627515.html.

34 See Ian Bowers and Henrik Stålhane

Hiim, 'Conventional Counterforce Dilemmas: South Korea's Deterrence Strategy and Stability on the Korean Peninsula', *International Security*, vol. 45, no. 3, Winter 2020–21.

35 See Dai, 'Hanguo Zhongdeng Qiangguo Waijiao Zhanlüe ji qi dui Zhongguo de Yingxiang', p. 146.

36 On South Korea as a middle power, see Snyder, *South Korea at the Crossroads*, chapter 8.

37 See Liu and Jiang, 'Zhong Mei Guanxi Shiyu xia de Hanguo Juese Lunxi', pp. 31, 33; Lü, 'Shilun Hanguo Wen Zaiyin Zhengfu de Dongnan Ya Waijiao', pp. 101, 106; Li Li, 'Yi Zhongdeng Guojia Waijiao Shentan Hanguo dui "Baohu de Ziren" de Lichang' [Using Middle-power Diplomacy to Explore South Korea's Position on 'Responsibility to Protect'], *Wuhan Keji Daxue Xuekan* [Journal of Wuhan University of Science and Technology], vol. 19, no. 2, April 2017; and Zhang Dongming and Zhang Peng, 'Hanguo zai Dongya diqu de Zhongdeng Qiangguo Waijiao Zhengce: Lilun yu Shijian' [South Korea's Middle-power Diplomacy: Theory and Practice], *Dongjiang Xuekan* [Dongjiang Journal], vol. 36, no. 4, October 2019.

38 Dai, 'Hanguo Zhongdeng Qiangguo Waijiao Zhanlüe ji qi dui Zhongguo de Yingxiang', pp. 146, 151.

39 Yang Lühuì and Zhao Weiníng, 'Han Mei Lianmeng Shiyu xià de Hanguo Zizhuxìng Yanjiu' [A Study of South Korea Autonomy from the Perspective of the US–South Korea Alliance], *Dangdai Hanguo*, no. 3, 2019, pp. 3, 13; and Liu Yucheng, 'Hanguo Wen Zaiyin Zhengfu Guojia Anquan Zhanlüe Jiadu' [Decoding the National-security Policy of the South Korean Moon Jae-in Government], *Junshi Wenzhai* [Military Digest], April 2019, p. 35.

40 Lü Chunyan, 'Lun Bandao Jushi Zhuanhuan xia Han Mei Xin Dongtai' [On the New Trend in South Korea–US Alliance in the Context of Peninsular Developments], *Dongbei Ya Xuekan*, no. 1, January 2010, pp. 40–1; Zhao and Zheng, 'Quanli Bianqian Shijiao xia de Mei Han Tongmeng Kunjing', pp. 50, 58; and Tang and Zhao, 'Shi Lun Wen Zaiyin xia de Hanguo Guojia Anquan Zhanlüe', pp. 38–9. See also Mike Yeo, 'Reform Efforts in South Korea Create Ecosystem for Defense Industry Growth', Defense News, 17 August 2020, https://www.defensenews.com/top-100/2020/08/17/reform-efforts-in-south-korea-create-ecosystem-for-defense-industry-growth/; 'Moon Jae-in's Five-year Road Map Unveiled', *Korea Herald*, 19 July 2017, http://www.koreaherald.com/view.php?ud=20170719000825; and 'S. Korean Defense Ministry Released 2020 White Paper', KBSWorld, 2 February 2021, http://world.kbs.co.kr/service/news_view.htm?lang=e&Seq_Code=159319.

41 See Bi, 'Wen Zaiyin Zhengfu de Zizhu Zhanlüe: Jinzhan yu Tiaozhan', p. 131; and Zhao and Zheng, 'Quanli Bianqian Shijiao xia de Mei Han Tongmeng Kunjing', p. 52. On South Korea's missile-defence programme, see Sebastien Roblin, 'Meet South Korea's Very Own Killer S-300 Air Defense System', *National Interest*, 24 February 2019, https://nationalinterest.org/blog/buzz/

meet-south-koreas-very-own-killer-s-300-air-defense-system-45477; and Jeong, 'South Korea Moves to Kick Its Missile Defense Shield Up a Notch'.

42 Chen Yue, 'Chao Han Junli Duibi: Nanfeng Yadao Beifeng haishi Beifang Yadao Nanfeng' [Comparison of North Korea–South Korea Military Power: The Southern Wind Overwhelms the Northern Wind or the Northern Wind Overwhelms the Southern Wind?], *Shijie Zhishi* [World Knowledge], October 2016, pp. 26–7; Zhang, 'Zhong Mei Jingzheng Geju xia de Zhong Han, Mai Han Guanxi Zouxiang yu Hanguo Xuanze', pp. 27–8; and Tang Ke and Li Qingbin, 'Jin Zhengen Jingji Gaige Fenxi' [Analysis of Kim Jong-un's Economic Reform], *Guoji Yanjiu Cankao*, no. 4, 2020, p. 43.

43 Liu and Zhang, 'Zhong Mei Guanxi Shiyu xia de Hanguo Juese Lunxi', p. 34; Zhao and Zheng, 'Quanli Bianqian Shijiao xia de Mei Han Tongmeng Kunjing', p. 53; and Zhang, 'Zhong Mei Jingzheng Geju xia de Zhong Han, Mai Han Guanxi Zouxiang yu Hanguo Xuanze', pp. 24, 31.

44 Zheng Jiyong, 'Hanguo Anquan Xian Zhengcai Fasheng Bianhua' [South Korea's Security Outlook Is Changing], *Huanqiu Shibao* [Global Times], 4 February 2021, https://3w.huanqiu.com/a/de583b/41mponaQk11.

45 Liu and Zhang, 'Zhong Mei Guanxi Shiyu xia de Hanguo Juese Lunxi', p. 34; Zhao and Zheng, 'Quanli Bianqian Shijiao xia de Mei Han Tongmeng Kunjing', p. 53; and Zhang, 'Zhong Mei Jingzheng Geju xia de Zhong Han, Mai Han Guanxi Zouxiang yu Hanguo Xuanze', pp. 24, 31.

46 See Lü, '2019–2020 Nian Han Mei Guanxi: Huigu yu Fazhan', p. 41; Zhao Yiran, 'Wen Zaiyin Zhengfu de "Xin Beifang Zhengce"' [Moon Jae-in Government's 'New Northern Policy'], *Guoji Yanjiu Cankao*, no. 7, 2020, pp. 46–7, 51; Bi, 'Wen Zaiyin Zhengfu de Zizhu Zhanlüe: Jinzhan yu Tiaozhan', p. 126; Ling, 'Chaoxian Bandao Zhanlüe Zizhuxing de Tisheng ji qi Yingxiang', p. 2; and Xue Li, 'Wen Zaiyin Zhengfu "Xin Beifang Zhengce" Pingxi' [Comment on Moon Jae-in Government's 'New Northern Policy'], *Shijie Zhishi*, no. 9, 2018, p. 73.

47 Lin Limin, 'Chaoxian He Wenti de Zhanlüe Benzhi: Fan Kuosan hai shi Diyuan Zhengzhi Boyi' [Strategic Essence of the North Korean Nuclear Problem: Non-proliferation or Geopolitical Game?], *Xiandai Guoji Guanxi*, no. 2, 2018, pp. 13–16; Liu and Jiang, 'Zhong Mei Guanxi Shiyu xia de Hanguo Juese Lunxi', p. 31; Wang, 'Chuyu Zhuanzhe qi de Chaoxian Bandao: Guoji Hezuo yu Zhongguo Juesi', p. 48; and Zhang Huizhi, 'Wen Zaiyin Zhengfu de Duiwai Zhengce: Jiyu yu Tiaozhan' [The Foreign Policy of the Moon Government: Opportunities and Challenges], *Dongbei Ya Luntan*, no. 2, 2018, p. 44.

48 See Zhao and Zheng, 'Quanli Bianqian Shijiao xia de Mei Han Tongmeng Kunjing', p. 52; Fang Xiaozhi, 'Meiguo zai Hanguo Bushu Gengduo Zhanlüe Wuqi you Yong Ma' [Is US Deployment of More Strategic Weapons in South Korea Useful?], *Shijie Zhishi*, no. 23, 2017, p. 29; and Liu Chong, 'Meiguo Yunniang zai Han Bushu "Sade" Xitong Banxi' [Analysis of US Deployment of the THAAD

System in South Korea], *Xiandai Guoji Guanxi*, no. 5, 2015.

49 See Zhang, 'Wen Zaiyin Zhengfu de Duiwai Zhengce: Jiyu yu Tiaozhan', p. 44.

50 See Ling Shengli, 'Shuangzhong Fenhua: Meiguo dui Chaoxian Bandao de Xiezi Zhanlüe' [Dual Divide: US Wedge Strategy Toward the Korean Peninsula], *Dongbei Ya Luntan*, no. 5, 2017, pp. 52, 54.

51 Zhang, 'Zhong Mei Jingzheng Geju xia de Zhong Han, Mai Han Guanxi Zouxiang yu Hanguo Xuanze', p. 26; Liu and Jiang, 'Zhong Mei Guanxi Shiyu xia de Hanguo Juese Lunxi', p. 31; and Zhao and Zheng, 'Quanli Bianqian Shijiao xia de Mei Han Tongmeng Kunjing', p. 52. For a US view on the ineffectiveness of THAAD for South Korean defence, see Theodore Postol and George N. Lewis, 'Illusion of Missile Defense: Why THAAD Will Not Protect South Korea', *Global Asia*, vol. 11, no. 3, September 2016.

52 See Meng Yueming and Wang Yinan, '2019–2020 Nian Zhong Han Guanxi: Huigu yu Fazhan' [2019–2020 China–South Korean Relations: Retrospect and Prospects], *Dangdai Hanguo*, no. 1, 2020, p. 10; Wang, 'Chuyu Zhuanzhe qi de Chaoxian Bandao: Guoji Hezuo yu Zhongguo Juesi', pp. 47; Bi, 'Chaoxian Bandao Xin Xingshi xia Shenhua Zhong Han Anquang Hezuo de Sikao', pp. 36–7; and Zhang, 'Zhong Mei Jingzheng Geju xia de Zhong Han, Mai Han Guanxi Zouxiang yu Hanguo Xuanze', p. 26.

53 Zhang Chi, 'Chaoxian Bandao Jushi Fazhan Qianzhan yu Zhongguo de Zuoyong' [Prospects for Developments on the Korean Peninsula and China's Role], *Guoji Wenti Yanjiu*, no. 2, 2020, p. 116.

54 See Zhang, 'Chaoxian Bandao Jushi Fazhan Qianzhan yu Zhongguo de Zuoyong', p. 116; and Lü, 'Shilun Hanguo Wen Zaiyin Zhengfu de Dongnan Ya Waijiao', p. 34.

55 Zhang, 'Wen Zaiyin Zhengfu de Duiwai Zhengce: Jiyu yu Tiaozhan', p. 48.

56 See Bi, 'Wen Zaiyin Zhengfu de Zizhu Zhanlüe: Jinzhan yu Tiaozhan', p. 133; and Khang Vu, 'US–South Korea: Working Group Blues', Interpreter, Lowy Institute, 31 July 2020, https://www.lowyinstitute.org/the-interpreter/us-south-korea-working-group-blues.

57 See Li Nan, 'Hanguo "Xin Nanfang Zhengce" Weihe xiang Meiguo "Yintai Zhanlüe" Kaolong' [Why Is South Korea's 'New Southern Strategy' Moving Closer to the US 'Indo-Pacific Strategy'?], *Shijie Zhishi*, no. 23, 2009, p. 27; Song, 'Tixi Yali, Weixie Renzhi yu Hanguo zai Zhong Mei zhijian de Zhanlüe Xuanze', p. 90; Bi, 'Wen Zaiyin Zhengfu de Zizhu Zhanlüe: Jinzhan yu Tiaozhan', p. 136; and Lü, 'Shilun Hanguo Wen Zaiyin Zhengfu de Dongnan Ya Waijiao', p. 112.

58 See Zhang, 'Zhong Mei Jingzheng Geju xia de Zhong Han, Mai Han Guanxi Zouxiang yu Hanguo Xuanze', p. 30; Lü, 'Lun Bandao Jushi Zhuanhuan xia Han Mei Xin Dongtai', p. 40; Bi, 'Wen Zaiyin Zhengfu de Zizhu Zhanlüe: Jinzhan yu Tiaozhan', pp. 125, 129; and Zhao and Zheng, 'Quanli Bianqian Shijiao xia de Mei Han Tongmeng Kunjing', p. 52. See also 'US Says

OPCON Transfer Will Be Impossible by 2022', *Dong-A Ilbo*, 22 October 2020, https://www.donga.com/en/article/all/20201022/2218349/1/U-S-says-OPCON-transfer-will-be-impossible-by-2022; and 'Defense Minister to Expedite 2nd Stage FOC for OPCON Transfer', *Dong-A Ilbo*, 25 December 2020, https://www.donga.com/en/article/all/20201225/2325742/1/Defense-minister-to-expedite-2nd-stage-FOC-for-OPCON-transfer. On the merits of the OPCON transfer, see Shin Beomchul, 'South Korea's Military Readiness Under Moon', in Lee and Botto (eds), *Korea Net Assessment 2020*.

59 See, for example, Wang, 'Chuyu Zhuanzhe qi de Chaoxian Bandao: Guoji Hezuo Juesi', p. 44.

60 Interviews with Chinese policy analysts, January 2021. The interview subjects reported Chinese confidence regarding the US–China balance of power.

61 See Song, 'Tixi Yali, Weixie Renzhi yu Hanguo zai Zhong Mei zhijian de Zhanlüe Xuanze'.

62 Lin, 'Chaoxian He Wenti de Zhanlüe Benzhi', p. 16.

63 See Zhang Yunling, 'Chaoxian Bandao Wenti yu Zhongguo de Zuoyong' [Korean Peninsula Issues and China's Role], *Shijie Zhishi*, no. 11, 2016, pp. 28–9; Lin, 'Chaoxian He Wenti de Zhanlüe Benzhi', p. 13; and Ling, 'Shuangzhong Fenhua: Meiguo dui Chaoxian Bandao de Xiezi', p. 48.

64 Ling, 'Shuangzhong Fenhua: Meiguo dui Chaoxian Bandao de Xiezi', p. 55.

65 Meng and Wang, '2019–2020 Nian Zhong Han Guanxi: Huigu yu Fazhan', p. 10; Zhang, 'Chanxian Bandao Jushi Fazhan Qianzhan yu Zhongguo de Zuoyong', p. 119; and Wang, 'Chuyu Zhuanzhe qi de Chaoxian Bandao: Guoji Hezuo Juesi', p. 44.

66 See Wang Junsheng, 'Chaoxian Bandao Heping Jizhi Goujian yu Zhong Han Hezuo de Yiyi' [Constructing Peace Mechanisms on the Korean Peninsula and the Significance of China–South Korean Cooperation], *Shijie Zhishi*, no. 19, 2018, p. 29.

67 See John Pomfret, 'North Korean Leader Amazed by Computers During Trip to China', *Washington Post*, 2 June 2000, https://www.washingtonpost.com/archive/politics/2000/06/02/north-korean-leader-amazed-by-computers-during-trip-to-china/c5417847-625e-49ca-9b95-eda39df328c6/; and Wonhyuk Lim, 'Kim Jong Il's Southern Tour: Beijing Consensus with a North Korean Twist?', Brookings Institution, 13 February 2006, https://www.brookings.edu/articles/kim-jong-ils-southern-tour-beijing-consensus-with-a-north-korean-twist/.

68 For a Chinese analysis, see Tang and Li, 'Jin Zhengen Jingji Gaige Fenxi'.

69 See James Reilly, *Orchestration: China's Economic Statecraft Across Asia and Europe* (New York: Oxford University Press, 2021), chapter 5; and James Reilly, 'China's Market Influence in North Korea', *Asian Survey*, vol. 54, no. 5, 2014.

70 On China's role in North Korean society, see Daniel Tudor and James Pearson, *North Korea Confidential: Private Markets, Fashion Trends, Prison Camps, Dissenters, and Defectors* (Rutland, VT: Tuttle, 2015).

71 On Chinese understanding that

Beijing's support for North Korea undermined China–South Korea cooperation, see Song, 'Tixi Yali, Weixie Renzhi yu Hanguo zai Zhong Mei zhijian de Zhanlüe Xuanze', p. 92.

72 For more on this dynamic, see Tat Yan Kong, 'China's Engagement-oriented Strategy Toward North Korea: Achievements and Limitations', *Pacific Review*, vol. 31, no. 1, 2018.

73 On China's behaviour toward North Korea during the Clinton, Bush and Obama administrations, see Stephan Haggard and Marcus Noland, *Hard Target: Sanctions, Inducements, and the Case of North Korea* (Stanford, CA: Stanford University Press, 2017), pp. 214–21; and Bonnie S. Glaser and Liang Wang, 'The North Korea Nuclear Crisis and US–China Cooperation', in Suisheng Zhao (ed.), *China and the United States* (New York: Palgrave Macmillan, 2008).

74 See 'China's Top Legislator Presents Xi's Letter to DPRK Leader', Xinhuanet, 10 September 2018, http://www.xinhuanet.com/english/2018-09/10/c_137456693.htm; and Rachel Zhang, 'China's Xi Jinping Vows to Take "Valuable Friendship" with North Korea to New Heights', *South China Morning Post*, 9 September 2021, https://www.scmp.com/news/china/diplomacy/article/3148136/chinas-xi-jinping-vows-take-valuable-friendship-north-korea?utm_source=email&utm_medium=share_widget&utm_campaign=3148136.

75 'Spotlight: Xi's DPRK Visit Writes New Chapter of Friendship, Promotes Peninsula Stability', Xinhuanet, 21 June 2019, http://www.xinhuanet.com/english/2019-06/21/c_138162907.htm. See also Scott Snyder and See-Won

Byun, 'China Reaffirms Tradition: DPRK Friendship and Recovery of South Korean Ties', *Comparative Connections*, vol. 20, no. 3, January 2019, http://cc.pacforum.org/2019/01/china-reaffirms-tradition-dprk-friendship-and-recovery-of-south-korean-ties/.

76 'N. Korea, China Demonstrate Military Ties in High-level Talks', Yonhap, 18 August 2019, https://en.yna.co.kr/view/AEN20190818000451325. See also Scott Snyder and See-Won Byun, 'A New Chapter?', *Comparative Connections*, vol. 21, no. 2, September 2019, http://cc.pacforum.org/2019/09/a-new-chapter/.

77 See Snyder and Byun, 'China Reaffirms Tradition'.

78 See Chad O'Carroll, 'How a Massive Influx of Chinese Visitors Is Changing North Korean Tourism', NK News, 1 November 2019, https://www.nknews.org/2019/11/how-a-massive-influx-of-chinese-visitors-is-changing-north-korean-tourism/; Oliver Hotham, 'North Korea's Air Koryo to Begin Twice-weekly Pyongyang–Macau Flights in August', NK News, 23 July 2019, https://www.nknews.org/2019/07/north-koreas-air-koryo-to-begin-twice-weekly-pyongyang-macau-flights-in-august/; 'Air China to Resume Beijing–Pyongyang Flights', Hankyoreh, 6 June 2018; Heesu Lee and Sam Kim, 'Kim Jong Un's Ski Resort Ambitions in North Korea Are Melting', Bloomberg, 12 February 2020, https://www.bloomberg.com/news/articles/2020-02-12/kim-jong-un-s-ski-resort-ambitions-in-north-korea-are-melting; and Mercedes Hutton, 'Chinese Tourists

in North Korea: "Almost a Necessary Evil"', *South China Morning Post*, 6 November 2019, https://www.scmp.com/magazines/post-magazine/travel/article/3036406/chinese-tourism-north-korea-booming-not-everyone.

79 See 'China to Enforce UN Sanctions Against North Korea', *Guardian*, 23 September 2017, https://www.theguardian.com/world/2017/sep/23/china-to-enforce-un-sanctions-against-north-korea.

80 Benjamin Katzeff Silberstein, 'Sanctions Enforcement and Fuel Prices in North Korea: What the Data Tells Us', 38 North, February 2019, p. 5, https://www.38north.org/wp-content/uploads/pdf/38-North-SR-1902-BKS-China-NK-Fuel.pdf.

81 See 'China and Russia Thwart US-led Bid to Call Out North Korea on UN Sanctions Violations', 19 June 2019, *South China Morning Post*, https://www.scmp.com/news/china/diplomacy/article/3015153/china-russia-thwart-un-accusation-north-korea-sanctions; and Michelle Nichols, 'China, Russia Propose Lifting Some U.N. Sanctions on North Korea, US Says Not the Time', Reuters, 17 December 2019, https://www.reuters.com/article/us-northkorea-usa-un/china-russia-propose-lifting-some-u-n-sanctions-on-north-korea-u-s-says-not-the-time-idUSKBN1YK20W.

82 See 'North Korea Defies Sanctions with China's Help, UN Panel Says', *Guardian*, 17 April 2020, https://www.theguardian.com/world/2020/apr/18/north-korea-defies-sanctions-with-chinas-help-un-panel-says; and Choe Sang-Hun, 'Defying US Ban, Chinese Ships Pay North Korea to Fish in Its Waters', *New York Times*, 14 August 2020, https://www.nytimes.com/2020/07/22/world/asia/north-korea-squid-sanctions-china.html.

83 Ariel Cohen, 'North Korea Illegally Trades Oil, Coal, with China's Help', *Forbes*, 21 March 2020, https://www.forbes.com/sites/arielcohen/2019/03/21/north-korea-illegally-trades-oil-coal-with-chinas-help/.

84 See 'China to Invest in Infrastructure in N. Korea, May Violate Sanctions', Kyodo, 20 July 2018, https://english.kyodonews.net/news/2018/07/e12d0ea5c940-china-to-invest-in-infrastructure-in-n-korea-may-violate-sanctions.html; Colin Zwirko, 'Homes Demolished in Path of Long-stalled Sino-DPRK "Bridge to Nowhere": Imagery', NK Pro, 26 September 2019, https://www.nknews.org/pro/homes-demolished-in-path-of-long-stalled-sino-dprk-bridge-to-nowhere-imagery/; and 'Chinese Firms Rush to N. Korea to Discuss Economic Cooperation', Yonhap, 22 June 2018, https://en.yna.co.kr/view/AEN20180622003100315.

85 Lee Jeong-ho, 'China–North Korea Trade Up 14.3 Per Cent in First Half to US$1.25 Billion', *South China Morning Post*, 24 July 2019, https://www.scmp.com/news/china/diplomacy/article/3019940/chinas-first-half-trade-north-korea-recovers-old-allies; and Christian Davies 'North Korea–China Trade Hits Highest Level Since Start of Pandemic', *Financial Times*, 20 October 2021, https://www.ft.com/content/a8f270ae-5cce-4ef3-a179-244b3d40311b?shareType=nongift.

86 See Yuan Yang, 'China's Dandong Property Prices Jump on Korea Talks', *Financial Times*, 2 May 2018, https://www.ft.com/content/ffcae376-4dda-11e8-8a8e-22951a2d8493.

87 See Park Chan-kyong, 'South Korea Affirms Cool Japan Relations, Warm China Ties in Defence White Paper', *South China Morning Post*, 3 February 2021, https://www.scmp.com/week-asia/politics/article/3120359/south-korea-affirms-cool-japan-relations-warm-china-ties-defence.

88 See 'Xi Expresses Support for Korean Denuclearization in Phone Talks with Moon: Cheong Wa DaeOn', Yonhap, 27 January 2021, https://en.yna.co.kr/view/AEN20210127006452315; Hyonhee Shin, 'North Korea, US Should Aim for Initial Nuclear Freeze: South Korea', Reuters, 28 January 2021, https://www.reuters.com/article/us-southkorea-politics-northkorea/north-korea-u-s-should-aim-for-initial-nuclear-freeze-south-korean-pm-idUSKBN29X13Y; Oh Seok-min, 'Defense Ministry Vows Push for Regular Inter-Korean Military Talks, Swifter OPCON Transfer', Yonhap, 21 January 2021, https://en.yna.co.kr/view/AEN20210121006600325; and 'China's Wang Urges Peace Push in Call with New South Korea Foreign Minister', Reuters, 16 February 2021, https://www.reuters.com/article/us-china-southkorea/chinas-wang-urges-peace-push-in-call-with-new-south-korea-foreign-minister-idUSKBN2AG1QK.

89 See Choe Sang-Hun, 'North and South Korea Reopen Communication Hotlines After a Tense 14 Months', *New York Times*, 27 June 2021, https://www.nytimes.com/2021/07/27/world/asia/north-korea-south-reopen-hotlines.html?smid=em-share; 'S.Korea Minister Expects China to Play Role in N.Korea Peacemaking', Reuters, 3 April 2020, https://www.reuters.com/article/us-china-southkorea/s-korea-minister-expects-china-to-play-role-in-n-korea-peacemaking-idUSKBN2BQ064; and Chae Yun-hwan, 'Nuke Envoys of S. Korea, China Discuss End-of-war Declaration for NK Dialogue', Yonhap, 1 November 2021, https://en.yna.co.kr/view/AEN20211101007000325.

90 Tracy Qu, 'New China–Korea Semiconductor Industrial Complex Starts Construction amid Beijing's Push for Tech Self-reliance', *South China Morning Post*, 8 October 2021, https://www.scmp.com/tech/tech-war/article/3151684/new-china-korea-semiconductor-industrial-complex-starts-construction?utm_source=email&utm_medium=share_widget&utm_campaign=3151684.

91 See Michelle Nichols, 'North Korea Developed Nuclear, Missile Programs in 2020: U.N. Report', Reuters, 8 February 2021, https://www.reuters.com/article/us-northkorea-sanctions-un/north-korea-developed-nuclear-missile-programs-in-2020-u-n-report-idUSKBN2A82G2; and Joby Warrick and Simon Denyer, 'As Kim Wooed Trump with "Love Letters", He Kept Building His Nuclear Capability, Intelligence Shows', *Washington Post*, 30 September 2020, https://www.washingtonpost.com/national-security/trump-kim-north-korea-nuclear/2020/09/30/2b7305c8-

032b-11eb-b7ed-141dd88560ea_
story.html.

92   For a contrary view that endorses
     sanctions, see Victor Cha and Katrin
     Fraser Katz, 'The Right Way to Coerce
     North Korea: Ending the Threat
     Without Going to War', *Foreign
     Affairs*, vol. 97, no. 3, May/June 2018,
     https://www.foreignaffairs.com/
     articles/north-korea/2018-04-01/
     right-way-coerce-north-korea.

93   See David Kang's contributions in
     Victor D. Cha and David C. Kang

(eds), *Nuclear North Korea: A Debate
on Engagement Strategies* (New York:
Columbia University Press, 2018),
chapters 2, 4; Markus Garlauskas, 'It's
Time to Get Real on North Korea',
United States Institute of Peace, 9
February 2021, https://www.usip.
org/publications/2021/02/its-time-get-
real-north-korea; and Hongyu Zhang
and Kevin Wang, 'A Nuclear-armed
North Korea Without ICBMs: The Best
Achievable Objective', *Nonproliferation
Review*, vol. 26, nos 1–2, 2019.

Copyright © 2021 The International Institute for Strategic Studies

Strengthening the US Partnership with the Syrian Democratic Forces

Federico Manfredi Firmian

Almost a year into US President Joe Biden's term of office, his administration still lacks a clear Syria policy. In and of itself, that is not a novelty. Neither Barack Obama nor Donald Trump ever managed to develop a consistent Syria policy. But the persistent lack of one carries several problematic implications. Sweeping US sanctions have helped push millions of Syrians to the brink of starvation, while doing little to curb the power of Syrian President Bashar al-Assad's brutal regime.[1] In Idlib, millions remain under the sway of Hayat Tahrir al-Sham and other salafi-jihadist organisations, including al-Qaeda affiliate Hurras al-Din. Meanwhile, the Islamist government of Turkey controls several territorial enclaves in northern Syria, in partnership with Syrian fighters notorious for human-rights abuses and the persecution of religious and ethnic minorities. There is a concrete risk that they will once again attack the US-backed Syrian Democratic Forces (SDF) and the affiliated autonomous administration of north and east Syria.

With US support, the SDF liberated much of eastern Syria from the grip of the Islamic State, but they are now struggling to hold back an Islamic State resurgence and to stave off new Turkish-led offensives. Assad, supported by Hizbullah, Iran and Russia, remains ready to exploit US irresoluteness and Turkish aggression. This explosive situation fuels regional instability, feeding the growth of the most radical strains of political Islam and the long-term challenge of accommodating refugees and migrants. Without negating

Federico Manfredi Firmian is on the faculty of Political Science at Sciences Po in Paris.

Survival | vol. 63 no. 6 | December 2021–January 2022 | pp. 159–182 https://doi.org/10.1080/00396338.2021.2006456

the United States' broad strategic intent to avoid over-commitment to the Middle East, the Biden administration could chart a more effective Syria policy that could help stabilise much of Syria and improve the security outlook for the region.

Reckoning with past policy blunders

When the Arab Spring first rocked Syria in 2011, the Obama administration understandably sought to bring about a democratic transition. Assad refused to comply and instead cracked down on the protests. Initially, they were broadly representative of Syria's ethnic and confessional diversity, and included Sunni Arabs, which constitute a majority, as well as Christians, Alawites, Druze and Kurds. The crisis, however, devolved into a confrontation mainly between Syria's Sunni majority and the predominantly Alawite regime, which – although several Sunni Muslims held influential positions in the security apparatus until 2011 – has generally oppressed and politically marginalised Sunnis for decades. The United States and its European allies imposed sanctions on leading regime figures. That was a reasonable course of action, but could not stop the bloodshed or usher in meaningful political change. As the repression intensified, and as Syria's peaceful uprisings gave way to armed insurgency, Qatar, Saudi Arabia and Turkey began to support armed opposition groups, with US coordination.[2]

Foreign governments had different reasons for backing the insurgency. Turkish President Recep Tayyip Erdogan hoped the Syrian revolution would empower the Muslim Brotherhood or a like-minded organisation, which would have presumably looked up to him as a patron and ally. Qatar's monarchy backed the opposition due to an unwavering commitment to Islamist causes. Saudi Arabia's aim was to contain Iran and weaken Hizbullah. The Obama administration likewise calculated that a democratic transition in Syria would diminish both Iran's and Hizbullah's influence in the region, and seemingly believed that radical Sunni Islamists could be sidelined in a post-Assad political transition.[3] Instead, foreign support for the insurgency opened the way for a vicious civil war that killed hundreds of thousands and displaced more than half of Syria's population, internally and in a vast refugee diaspora.

The Obama administration's first major mistake was failing to understand that arming the Syrian opposition would only exacerbate violence and tear apart Syrian society. From the early stages of the war, it was clear that Islamist organisations were acquiring undue influence. The Syrian branch of the Muslim Brotherhood had a history of violence, most notably by virtue of its 1976–82 insurgency.[4] Its involvement in the post-Arab Spring uprisings was controversial from the start, even within the Syrian opposition. The Brotherhood nonetheless managed to secure the largest share of seats in the Istanbul-based Syrian National Congress and came to control its 'Assistance Committee', the body responsible for both extending humanitarian aid and funding the armed opposition.[5] Salafi-jihadist organisations also acquired new leverage, as they ran weapons-smuggling operations across Syria's porous borders with Iraq, Lebanon and Turkey.[6]

As the war intensified, the Syrian military's scorched-earth tactics led the United States to step up its support for opposition groups. The first reports that the CIA was active in Turkey and Jordan to help US allies decide which rebel groups to arm emerged in June 2012.[7] At that time, the weapons in question already included automatic rifles, rocket-propelled grenade launchers (RPGs) and anti-tank missiles, funnelled into Syria by way of shadowy intermediaries, including the Muslim Brotherhood.[8] Supposedly the CIA's 'vetting' of the rebels was a way for the US to prevent the weapons from falling into the hands of radicals. But most of the arms Qatar, Saudi Arabia and Turkey smuggled into Syria were going to groups with links to the Brotherhood or salafi-jihadist networks.[9]

Reports that several cargo planes loaded with old Yugoslav weapons had travelled from Croatia to Jordan between late 2012 and early 2013 provided further evidence of foreign-state support for the rebels. The Saudi monarchy had paid for the materiel, which included heavy artillery, mortars, recoil-less rifles and RPGs, and was secretly transferring it to opposition forces in Syria with the help of the CIA.[10] Meanwhile, Qatar alone spent some $3 billion to support the insurgency in Syria between 2011 and 2013.[11] Qatar even shipped Chinese-made FN-6 man-portable air-defence missile launchers to Syria, via Turkey.[12] Salafi-jihadist armed groups such as Liwa al-Islam and Ahrar al-Sham thus continued to receive direct support from the Gulf states and Turkey, with US knowledge and support.[13]

In 2012 and 2013, foreign-state support for the insurgency enabled it to control ever-larger pockets of territory. In March 2013, Raqqa became the first provincial capital to fall under rebel rule as a result of a joint offensive involving the Free Syrian Army, Ahrar al-Sham and Jabhat al-Nusra. Later that same month, leaked US National Security Agency documents revealed that Saudi Arabia had supplied 120 tonnes of explosives and other weapons to rebel forces, alongside directives to 'burn Damascus' and 'raze to the ground' its international airport.[14] (The leaks also indicated that the US government was aware of these exchanges.) Coordinated attacks on the Syrian capital involving the Free Syrian Army, Ahrar al-Sham, Liwa al-Islam and Jabhat al-Nusra unfolded throughout early 2013, resulting in new rebel gains. In response, Assad's military stepped up its use of chemical weapons, leading to the August 2013 Ghouta chemical attack. Much has been said about Obama's failure to enforce his self-imposed 'red line'.[15] Yet the least appreciated consequence of his restraint was that it led the United States to intensify its support for the Syrian rebels and its efforts to punish Assad.

Jordanian operatives stole CIA-supplied weapons

In this context, the US launched 'Timber Sycamore', an extensive CIA programme to arm and train Syrian rebels fighting Assad.[16] A separate programme, called 'Train and Equip', reportedly cost $500 million and wound up benefitting Jabhat al-Nusra, which seized weapons and other assets from hapless US-backed fighters.[17] Several other scandals eventually beset US support for the rebels. The *New York Times* and Al-Jazeera reported that rogue Jordanian intelligence operatives had stolen CIA-supplied weapons and sold them on the black market, and that investigators believed a Jordanian police captain had used some of the weapons to kill two American contractors, two Jordanians and a South African in Amman.[18] A Jordanian soldier killed three American soldiers involved in the training of Syrian fighters.[19] And some of the factions the CIA had vetted and deemed worthy of US support came under the international spotlight for ghastly war crimes.[20] In one of the most gruesome episodes, Nour al-Din al-Zenki fighters were caught on video beheading a teenage boy in Aleppo.[21] A three-year study funded by the European Union and the German government later found that efforts by the US and its allies to supply arms to Syrian rebels 'dramatically increased the quantity and quality of weapons' held by the Islamic State.[22]

In time, US policymakers understood that supporting Islamist rebels in Syria had been a tremendous mistake. Timber Sycamore cost the US government well over $1bn over the life of the programme.[23] It failed to unseat Assad. Beyond that, it undoubtedly inflicted untold misery on the Syrian people. A US official boasted that CIA-backed fighters had killed or injured approximately 100,000 Syrian soldiers and their allies.[24] Yet the Vietnam War had long ago exposed the fallacy of body counts as a metric of success. Furthermore, military service is mandatory in government-controlled parts of Syria, so not all Syrian soldiers were supporters of the regime. There is no sure way to determine how many Syrian civilians were killed or maimed as a result of violence and counter-violence involving CIA-backed fighters but, given the scale of the war, even a conservative estimate would have to be in the thousands. Timber Sycamore may well have been one of the United States' most ill-conceived and deadly covert-action programmes.

Not all US policies in Syria had such disastrous repercussions. One bright spot was the burgeoning partnership that emerged between the US military and Syrian Kurdish forces. At first glance, the Democratic Union Party (Partiya Yekîtiya Demokrat or PYD) may not have appeared to be an obvious US ally. Founded in 2003, it was ideologically and organisationally close to the Kurdistan Workers' Party (Partiya Karkerên Kurdistan or PKK), which the US has long designated a terrorist organisation. The People's Defence Units (Yekîneyên Parastina Gel or YPG) were the PYD's armed wing, constituted in 2011 to defend Syrian-Kurdish communities from the ravages of war. It is undeniable that the most prominent figures in the PYD and YPG had all received PKK training and that they ascribed to its idiosyncratic 'democratic confederalism' ideology.[25] Still, from the outset of the war in Syria, PYD and YPG cadres were primarily concerned with safeguarding vulnerable Syrian civilians from the violence of Islamist rebels.[26]

In 2012, soon after holding official meetings with US officials in Washington on the possibility of opening a new front against Assad, the PYD and YPG took over several towns in northern Syria, establishing an autonomous administration officially espousing secular, democratic socialism.[27] In the following years, the rise of the Islamic State and its takeover of Raqqa and Mosul set the stage for closer ties between the US military and Syrian-Kurdish fighters. In summer 2014, as the Obama administration mustered a broad international coalition to fight the Islamic State, the YPG was already engaged in gruelling battles against genocidal jihadists in northeast Syria as well as in the borderlands of Iraq. Indeed, while Iraqi prime minister Nuri al-Maliki and Masoud Barzani, president of the Kurdish Region of Iraq, bickered over military strategy, the YPG fought strenuously to save the tens of thousands of besieged Yazidis. Alongside its all-women sister militia, the Women's Protection Units (Yekîneyên Parastina Jin or YPJ), the YPG breached Islamic State positions in Iraq, enabling thousands of Yazidis to escape from the barren slopes of Mount Sinjar, across the desert and into Syrian territory. US airstrikes against the Islamic State then provided the YPG and the YPJ with much-needed respite. Thereafter, intelligence-sharing and joint military efforts became more frequent and exhaustive. The United States also secretly deployed a small number of special-operations forces to Syria to fight alongside the YPG.[28] US support for Kurdish fighters later proved decisive in the battle for Kobani, preventing the fall of the city to the Islamic State and averting yet more bloodshed.[29]

The US Department of Defense came to understand that Kurdish fighters in Syria were more committed to democratic values than any Islamist force. The Pentagon thereafter deepened its ties with the YPG and helped it evolve into a broader and more inclusive force, under the banner of the SDF.[30] Formally established in October 2015, the SDF comprised the YPG and YPJ, several Arab militias (including those from the Shammar confederation and other tribes) and minority self-defence groups such as the Assyrian Military Council and Yazidi units. With the backing of the US military, these diverse forces went on to liberate much of northeast Syria from the Islamic State, including Raqqa, in October 2017. Subsequent advances in the Deir ez-Zor governorate brought about one-third of Syria under the control of the SDF, marking the high point of US influence in Syria.

Meanwhile, Russia's military intervention in Syria and the partnership between the United States and the SDF resulted in major setbacks for the armed opposition and the Islamic State. Erdogan was incensed. From the earliest stages of the conflict, Turkey had supported the rebels, hoping to bring about an Islamist government in Damascus. Once it became clear the opposition would not succeed in overthrowing Assad, Erdogan refocused Turkish policy on consolidating rebel-held enclaves in northern Syria to eke out what gains he could and to stymie Kurdish autonomy. Erdogan apparently had no problem with jihadists on Turkey's southern border but was greatly concerned about the YPG's ties to the PKK. In summer 2016, Turkey's first direct military forays in Syria enabled the beleaguered rebels to take over new territories, initially at the expense of the Islamic State. The Turkish government then formalised a new rebel coalition to combat both the Islamic State and the YPG-led SDF. The Turkish military presence on Syrian soil thereafter fundamentally altered the conflict's dynamics: if the Syrian government and Kurdish fighters could defeat Islamist rebels, they would ultimately have to yield to Turkey's superior military force.

In October 2017, the Turkish president announced a new military deployment in Syria. Formally, the goal was to ensure compliance with the Idlib de-escalation zone, which Erdogan had just brokered with Russian President Vladimir Putin to establish a buffer between government-held Syria and the parts of Idlib under rebel control. In reality, Turkish forces were angling to seize the Kurdish-majority district of Afrin. In cooperation with Hayat Tahrir al-Sham (formerly known as Jabhat al-Nusra), they set up positions in Idlib, just south of Afrin.[31] Although the YPG had controlled Afrin since 2012, there was little it could do to forestall the impending attack.

In early 2018, Turkey launched the enigmatically named *Olive Branch* operation, seizing Afrin in partnership with rebel forces and forcing thousands of Kurds and other minorities to flee.[32] The Turkish-backed rebels then occupied abandoned houses and shops or otherwise coerced residents to flee through threats, extortion, abduction, torture and murder.[33]

Mao Zedong had theorised that guerrillas should move among the people as fish swim in the sea; Erdogan's military was employing the counter-insurgency doctrine known as 'draining the sea'.[34] Turkey's strategy was to thoroughly eradicate the YPG presence in Afrin through the forced displacement of supportive civilian populations – primarily Kurds, Yazidis, Christians and other minorities.[35]

Soon thereafter, Erdogan redoubled diplomatic pressure to coax then-president Trump into allowing Turkey to take over a 30-kilometre-wide strip all along the Syria–Turkey border, allegedly to prevent the PKK from using the area as a rear base. Though publicly characterised as a 'buffer zone', Turkey had other purposes in mind for this land. Controlling it would have provided Turkey with a readily accessible area for the resettlement of Syrian refugees, whom Erdogan had long exploited to consolidate Turkey's hegemony over northern Syria and to dilute the Kurdish population in strategic borderlands. Syrian Kurds and other minorities, including those from the Armenian, Assyrian, Syriac and Chaldean communities, understood that Turkey's military intervention in their homelands would entail ethnic cleansing. While Erdogan's government couched its intentions in the rhetoric of counter-terrorism, Syrian opposition groups aligned with Turkey had no qualms about expressing their eagerness to massacre Kurds and other minorities, whom they labelled 'infidels'.[36] A well-known Syrian analyst once sympathetic to the cause of the opposition described the Syrian fighters backing the Turkish incursion into northern Syria as 'misfits of the conflict, the worst of the worst', who were 'notorious for extortion, theft, and banditry, more like thugs than rebels'.[37]

The partial US withdrawal from northern Syria in October 2019 was so sudden and unexpected that it caused an immediate wave of panic and fear among borderland residents. Some 200,000 fled southward with whatever they could carry, as Turkey occupied the areas between Tell Abyad and Ras al-Ayn with the support of Syrian jihadist fighters.[38] Among their numerous war crimes was the torture and murder of the Kurdish-Syrian politician Hevrin Khalaf, who dedicated much of her life to peacebuilding, feminism and democracy.[39] As she was driving home, Ahrar Al-Sharqiya militants dragged her out of her car so violently they tore the hair from her head.[40]

They then shot her and watched her die. Trump manifested no interest in the fate of US allies and vulnerable civilian populations. Having ordered the withdrawal of hundreds of US troops from the borderlands abutting Turkey against the best judgement of leading US policymakers and military commanders, Trump brushed off the ensuing violence as irrelevant to US interests. 'Let someone else fight over this long-bloodstained sand', he said.[41]

US forces had first arrived in Syria to prosecute the war against the Islamic State. Locals had then greeted them with flowers and ululations of joy. When they pulled back from the northern borderlands in October 2019, effectively allowing Turkish aggression, they were showered with insults and pelted with rotten vegetables and old shoes. Many US soldiers who served alongside the SDF were deeply upset by Trump's decision and reckoned that their abrupt departure constituted a betrayal. 'They trusted us and we broke that trust', said one US Army officer who had worked alongside the SDF. 'It's a stain on the American conscience.'[42]

Trump manifested no interest in the fate of allies

As much as the SDF had cherished their partnership with the United States, the US pullback meant that only a swift return of the Syrian state could spare Kurds and other minorities from forced displacement and new onslaughts of salafi-jihadist violence.[43] The SDF thus negotiated a redeployment of Syrian and Russian forces to Kobani, Qamishli and other border towns, to halt the advances of the Turkish military and its extremist Syrian proxies. Putin then brokered a ceasefire with Erdogan. Under its terms, Russian military police and the Syrian army were to patrol the border, while the SDF were to retreat further south.[44] Turkey held on to a 32 km-wide strip of territory between Tell Abyad and Ras al-Ayn, comprising some 3,000 km² of Syrian territory. The consequences have been far-reaching. According to the United Nations, the rebels have since 'engaged in widespread and organized looting and property appropriation' and subjected civilians to torture, sexual violence and other war crimes.[45] Assad's forces returned to Manbij, Kobani, Qamishli, Hasakah and Raqqa. Russia enjoyed new leverage in north and east Syria, as did Iran. On this record, the partial US withdrawal from northern Syria was unequivocally a blunder.

Against all odds: the survival of the autonomous administration

Despite Turkey's territorial takeovers and the redeployment of Syrian and Russian forces to the northern borderlands, the autonomous administration did not collapse. To this day it still controls approximately 45,000 km² (about a quarter of Syria) and is home to more than 3m people. How did it manage to survive?

One important reason is that the SDF maintained a unified command structure and a steadfast commitment to regional autonomy. With a total fighting force of approximately 100,000, including both military and police, the SDF remain a force to be reckoned with.[46] Assad and Russia may want them to disband, give way to the Syrian Arab Army and join local police or paramilitary forces, but SDF commander Mazloum Abdi is not inclined to subordinate his force. In addition, notwithstanding Trump's directives, the United States still maintains troops in parts of northeast Syria, albeit at some distance from the border. If the US did not fully withdraw, it was largely thanks to the discreet manoeuvrings of prescient US officials, who concealed the true size of the US footprint in Syria from the Trump White House.[47] Because of the enduring if diminished US presence in Syria, and the SDF's grit and resilience, Assad and his allies do not have the ability to take over the northeast by force.[48] For the time being, they are playing a waiting game and engaging in divide-and-rule tactics, trying to set Arab tribes against Kurdish fighters.

In addition to being a formidable security asset, the autonomous administration of north and east Syria has shown signs of real diversity and inclusivity. While powerful state actors long exploited sectarian and ethnic identities as vectors of influence, the SDF's military coalition includes both Kurds and Arabs. Though primarily Muslim, it also has Christian and Yazidi representation. In 2017, the YPJ announced the establishment of the first all-women Arab battalion, the Martyr Amara Brigade.[49] Although enlistment is voluntary, an appreciable number of Arab women have since joined the SDF. Of course, many socialist groups champion egalitarianism during their formative stages only to backslide into more authoritarian rule once they consolidate power. Nevertheless, the autonomous administration's conduct so far seems more than merely decorative.

Political developments in northeast Syria also reflect a firm commitment to diversity and equal representation of men and women in key decision-making bodies. A man and a woman co-chair all leadership positions in public administration. In March 2016, when the three self-styled 'cantons' of Afrin, Kobani and al-Jazeera agreed to establish a federal democratic system for Rojava-Syria, its co-leaders were Mansour Saloum, an Arab man from Tell Abyad, and Hediya Yousef, a Kurdish woman from the Jazeera canton. In December 2016, they agreed on a new draft constitution and dropped the Kurdish term 'Rojava' altogether to highlight their commitment to a truly multi-ethnic administration.[50] Commune elections took place in September 2017. Municipal and provincial elections followed only weeks later. In both, approximately 70% of eligible voters took to the polls, electing candidates for offices in male–female pairs.[51] A commitment to diversity and inclusivity was also evident in the 2018 decision to transfer the capital of the autonomous administration from the Kurdish-majority city of Qamishli to Ayn al-Issa, an Arab town.[52]

This is not to say that political processes in north and east Syria are without exception consistent with democratic principles. Among the shortcomings of the autonomous administration is the preponderance of PYD figures in positions of authority and their failure to accommodate legitimate opposition parties, such as the Kurdish National Council (KNC). The KNC boycotted the 2017 vote, citing PYD intimidation and repression.[53] Region-wide legislative elections, originally scheduled to take place in January 2018, were postponed indefinitely, and thus far the PYD-led administration has appointed all members of the legislature, known as the Democratic People's Congress. However imperfectly, though, the autonomous administration has taken important steps towards the establishment of proto-democratic institutions. Ongoing unity talks aimed at reconciling the PYD and the KNC are under way with political support from the United States, offering some hope for deeper democratisation.

It is also worth underscoring how substantially the autonomous administration ameliorated the legal rights and status of minorities and women. For decades, Ba'athist Syria outlawed the teaching of the Kurdish language in public schools and its use in workplaces. Syrian authorities also prevented families from giving Kurdish names to their children and banned printed materials in Kurdish.[54] Yazidis likewise suffered from systematic Ba'athist discrimination. Because Syrian law did not recognise their faith as a distinct religion, Yazidi pupils in public schools were forced to study Islam. Yazidis could not apply their own rules in personal-status matters such as marriage, divorce and paternity, and often found themselves in a legal grey zone.[55] Syrian women, meanwhile, suffered from institutionalised discrimination on the basis of legal principles derived from sharia law. Today, gender equality, freedom of religion and language, and cultural rights are all enshrined in the laws of the autonomous administration. New laws also mandate equal inheritance shares for males and females.[56] Polygamy, child marriage and unilateral divorce are forbidden. Legislation even promotes environmentalism and conservation – for example, by requiring agricultural cooperatives to pursue environmental sustainability.[57] Such progressive policies are the result of the grassroots initiatives of local populations, and thus represent a positive example not only for Syria but for the entire region.

The autonomous administration also shows that large numbers of Syrian Muslims have little taste for Islamist rule and support the equal treatment of men and women, the protection of minorities and other democratic principles. Arabs from across Syria are still joining the SDF in large numbers and presently constitute a majority in the ranks of the organisation.[58] The American sociologist Amy Austin Holmes conducted multiple visits to northeast Syria in 2019 and interviewed some 300 fighters, from all ethnic and religious backgrounds. She found that many Arabs joined because they supported decentralisation and grassroots political organisation; social harmony between different ethnic and religious groups; women's rights and gender equality; or rejection of religious fundamentalism.[59]

The way forward

The United States' indecisiveness is largely the result of an understandable tendency towards restraint that has developed in response to the failures of the US occupations of Afghanistan and Iraq. Nation-building and democratisation efforts in conflict-torn countries rarely go well, and the United States must grapple with numerous other pressing challenges, from the COVID-19 pandemic to the rise of China to global climate change. Yet turning a blind eye to Syria would be problematic on multiple levels. Most critically, it would afford Erdogan and Assad the freedom to make even more aggressive moves than they have so far, and would ultimately empower some of the most destabilising forces in the Middle East, ranging from the Islamic State and al-Qaeda to Hizbullah and Iran. In a world as deeply interconnected as the present one, responsible international actors ought to recognise that political violence, conflict spillovers and related humanitarian and refugee crises are bound to have far-reaching international implications. To hope that the problems of Syria will somehow remain confined to the Middle East would be naive, callous and outright dangerous.

Syria also differs from Afghanistan and Iraq in that the security and incipient democratisation processes of its autonomous administration did not result from foreign occupation but rather from grassroots initiatives. Accordingly, the United States does not need to try to export democracy or engage in nation-building in Syria. It simply ought to defend and consolidate the achievements of local allies. This would not require the deployment of large numbers of troops. A light military footprint would suffice.

In terms of formulating policy, the first step would be to recognise that Turkey constitutes an existential threat to the autonomous administration and an obstacle to peace in Syria. In the first year following the October 2019 ceasefire agreement, Turkey committed more than 800 ceasefire violations to test SDF defences and lay the groundwork for future military offensives.[60] In addition, Turkey's reliance on the remnants of the salafist groups Ahrar al-Sham and Nour al-Din al-Zenki, now reorganised under the command of the so-called Syrian National Army, should be a source of concern for the United States and its partners. Also troubling is Erdogan's inclination to offer diplomatic and military cover for the Salvation government in Idlib, as it serves as a facade for the salafist group Hayet Tahrir Al-Sham's rule. Turkey's belligerent foreign policy has also antagonised Greece and Cyprus, and stirred conflict in Libya and Nagorno-Karabakh.

As disruptive as Erdogan has become, however, talk of suspending or expelling Turkey from NATO is counterproductive. The North Atlantic treaty provides no mechanism for doing so, and pursuing ad hoc measures would risk undermining the cohesion of the organisation. Moreover, such a move would have adverse effects on international security: the United States and its NATO allies would lose the Incirlik air base, the Kürecik radar base and the Allied Land Command in Izmir, while Erdogan would likely realign Turkey with Russia, destabilising the regional balance of power. A better strategy for curbing Erdogan's bellicose foreign policy would be for the United States to simply stand strong in the face of specific threats and hostile actions. Even a thin US military presence would deter new Turkish offensives as long as the United States clearly communicated its position on Turkish aggression. In 2017, for example, when Erdogan threatened to attack Manbij, the United States dispatched special-operations forces in armoured vehicles with clearly visible US insignia to patrol the area, and Turkey backed down.[61]

On the more difficult question of Turkey's future as a democracy and NATO member, the United States, the United Kingdom, France and other like-minded democracies should act in concert to hold back Erdogan through a combination of military firmness and economic incentives until Turkey returns to an international alignment that is more in tune with liberal-democratic values. This may or may not come to pass. But, in the meantime, constraining Turkey and thus reducing the risk of Turkish aggression would enable the SDF to bolster the autonomous administration against the Assad regime, Iran and Russia in northeast Syria.[62]

Washington also should remain vigilant in the struggle against the Islamic State. Thousands of its fighters remain active in the Syrian desert, awaiting an opportunity to revive the caliphate. In recent months they have perpetrated several high-profile assassinations, including those of female activists Seda al-Faysal and Hend Latif al-Kidr. Al-Hol and other detention camps in northeast Syria remain serious and intractable problems. Al-Hol alone holds more than 60,000 Islamic State sympathisers, for the most part wives, widows and children of fighters. Many hold foreign passports, but their countries of origin usually refuse to take them back out of security concerns. Within the detainee population, hardened militants continue to enforce Islamic State rules of conduct, killing those who cooperate with the camp's authorities. General Frank McKenzie, commander of US Central Command, has noted that 'unless the international community finds a way to repatriate, reintegrate into home communities, and support locally grown reconciliation … we are buying ourselves a strategic problem 10 years down the road when these children grow up radicalized'.[63] The SDF remain a vital partner for securing these goals, as they not only run detention camps but also manage ongoing reconciliation programmes.[64] Furthermore, the SDF is an important partner in wider US counter-terrorism efforts. For instance, they provided crucial intelligence in the US-led hunt for Abu Bakr al-Baghdadi, leading to his death in Idlib in late 2019.[65]

Beyond security imperatives, the autonomous administration is in dire need of economic development. Historically, the areas it controls have been some of Syria's poorest. Yet they have potential, containing approximately 95% of Syria's oil reserves and about 50% of its natural gas.[66] Syria's largest oilfield, Al-Omar,

The administration is in dire need of development

and its largest gas field, Conoco, are both in administration territory. (That said, Syria's oil fields are operating well below capacity due to war damage and lack of investment.[67]) Agriculture is also promising. Despite poor water systems, droughts and desertification, the autonomous administration encompasses what was once Syria's breadbasket, producing most of its wheat, barley, cotton and livestock. Lack of investor confidence and insufficient public funds are holding back development.

The United States could spur investment and development in north and east Syria by protecting the autonomous administration against external aggression. While an explicit security guarantee would unnecessarily agitate Turkey and discomfit American restrainers, robust US interaction with the autonomous administration on the ground and general US diplomatic statements of support would send a message that Washington will backstop the administration against local challenges. This would enable the authority to reallocate part of its budget away from security and towards healthcare, education and much-needed infrastructure repairs and upgrades. It would also undoubtedly boost private investment, remittances and overall economic activity. In partnership with the European Union and European national governments, the US Department of State and the US Agency for International Development could also provide development aid to assist in restoring roads, rehabilitating damaged water systems and rejuvenating the energy sector. The US could also help marshal foreign aid and technical expertise through international non-governmental organisations.

Finally, the Biden administration could do more to foster democratisation. The US should continue to support the ongoing unity talks among the PYD, the KNC and other Kurdish parties. Abdi was instrumental in initiating and promoting them, and believes the Biden administration could play a constructive role in smoothing out differences among rival parties and supporting confidence-building mechanisms.[68] Successful unity talks could encourage freer and fairer elections in north and east Syria. That eventuality could ease tensions between the autonomous administration and Turkey, with the KNC playing a key role by engaging Turkish authorities on mutual security guarantees alongside the United States. It would not be easy to achieve stability and harmony, of course, but neither would it be impossible.

*　　*　　*

Restoring local trust in the United States is important for countering the Islamic State and other potentially transnational jihadist groups, and may have become more urgent in the wake of the United States' fraught withdrawal from Afghanistan. As a result, there may be a somewhat greater appetite for a calibrated upshift in US Syria policy at the White House, among US agencies and in Congress.[69] Implicitly securing the autonomous administration against Turkish attacks would be the best means for the US to forestall attempts by the Syrian government and its allies to reimpose central-government rule over northeast Syria, and would go a long way towards rebuilding trust. Together with European partners – in particular, the UK and France – the US would need to provide economic support as well as military protection for the autonomous administration to ensure the relative stability of northeast Syria. The effort could produce genuine strategic dividends. An autonomous administration reliably supported and nurtured by the United States and its partners could help inoculate poor and marginalised communities against the spread of salafi jihadism and other radical ideologies, and serve as a model of democracy and multiculturalism for all Syrians.

Notes

1 See Anchal Vohra, 'Assad's Syria Is Starting to Starve like Saddam's Iraq', *Foreign Policy*, 2 December 2020, https://foreignpolicy.com/2020/12/02/bashars-assads-syria-is-starving-like-saddams-iraq/.

2 See Karen DeYoung and Liz Sly, 'Syrian Rebels Get Influx of Arms with Gulf Neighbors' Money, US Coordination', *Washington Post*, 15 May 2012, https://www.washingtonpost.com/world/national-security/syrian-rebels-get-influx-of-arms-with-gulf-neighbors-money-us-coordination/2012/05/15/gIQAds2TSU_story.html; Jonathan Schanzer, 'Saudi Arabia Is Arming the Syrian Opposition', *Foreign Policy*, 27 February 2012, https://foreignpolicy.com/2012/02/27/saudi-arabia-is-arming-the-syrian-opposition/; Liam Stack, 'In Slap at Syria, Turkey Shelters Anti-Assad Fighters', *New York Times*, 27 October 2011, https://www.nytimes.com/2011/10/28/world/europe/turkey-is-sheltering-antigovernment-syrian-militia.html; and Michael Weiss, 'Turkey's Hand in the Syrian Opposition', *Atlantic*, 26 October 2011, https://www.theatlantic.com/international/archive/2011/10/turkeys-hand-in-the-syrian-opposition/247330/.

3 There is a vast body of literature on how participation in democratic political processes could moderate Islamist movements and parties. See Stathis Kalyvas, 'Commitment Problems in Emerging Democracies: The Case of Religious Parties', *Comparative Politics*, vol. 32, no. 4, July 2000, pp. 379–98; Vali Nasr, *The Rise of Islamic Capitalism: Why the New Muslim Middle Class is the Key to Defeating Extremism* (New York: Free Press, 2009); Kasper Ly Netterstrøm, 'After the Arab Spring: The Islamists' Compromise in Tunisia', *Journal of Democracy*, vol. 26, no. 4, October 2015, pp. 110–24; Jillian Schwedler, *Faith in Moderation: Islamist Parties in Jordan and Yemen* (Cambridge: Cambridge University Press, 2006); and Fareed Zakaria, 'Islam, Democracy and Constitutional Liberalism', in James Demetrios Caraley (ed.), *American Hegemony: Preventive War, Iraq and Imposing Democracy* (New York: Academy of Political Science, 2004).

4 See, for instance, Hanna Batatu, *Syria's Peasantry, the Descendants of Its Lesser Rural Notables, and Their Politics* (Princeton, NJ: Princeton University Press, 1999), pp. 260–78.

5 See Yezid Sayigh, 'The Coming Tests of the Syrian Opposition', Carnegie

Endowment for International Peace, 19 April 2012, https://carnegie-mec.org/2012/04/19/coming-tests-of-syrian-opposition-pub-47877; and Liz Sly, 'Syria's Muslim Brotherhood Is Gaining in Influence over Anti-Assad Revolt', *Washington Post,* 12 May 2012, https://www.washingtonpost.com/world/syrias-muslim-brotherhood-is-gaining-influence-over-anti-assad-revolt/2012/05/12/gIQAtIoJLU_story.html.

6   See 'Jihadists, Weapons Moving from Iraq to Syria', Agence France-Presse, 11 February 2012, https://eng-archive.aawsat.com/theaawsat/news-middle-east/jihadists-weapons-moving-from-iraq-to-syria; and Erika Solomon, 'Rebel Rivalry and Suspicion Threaten Syria Revolt', Reuters, 27 April 2012, https://uk.reuters.com/article/us-syria-rebels/rebel-rivalry-and-suspicions-threaten-syria-revolt-idUSBRE83Q0S120120427.

7   See David Cloud and Raja Abdulrahim, 'US Has Secretly Provided Arms Training to Syria Rebels Since 2012', *Los Angeles Times*, 21 June 2013, https://www.latimes.com/world/middleeast/la-xpm-2013-jun-21-la-fg-cia-syria-20130622-story.html; and Eric Schmitt, 'CIA Said to Aid in Steering Arms to Syrian Opposition', *New York Times*, 21 June 2012, https://www.nytimes.com/2012/06/21/world/middleeast/cia-said-to-aid-in-steering-arms-to-syrian-rebels.html.

8   See Schmitt, 'CIA Said to Aid in Steering Arms to Syrian Opposition'.

9   See David Sanger, 'Rebel Arms Flow Is Said to Benefit Jihadists in Syria', *New York Times*, 14 October 2012, https://www.nytimes.com/2012/10/15/world/middleeast/jihadists-receiving-most-arms-sent-to-syrian-rebels.html.

10   See C.J. Chivers and Eric Schmitt, 'Arms Airlift to Syria Rebels Expands, with Aid from CIA', *New York Times*, 24 March 2013, https://www.nytimes.com/2013/03/25/world/middleeast/arms-airlift-to-syrian-rebels-expands-with-cia-aid.html; Eliot Higgins, 'Evidence of Multiple Foreign Weapon Systems Smuggled to the Syrian Opposition in Daraa', Brown Moses Blog, 25 January 2013, http://brown-moses.blogspot.com/2013/01/evidence-of-multiple-foreign-weapon.html; Nour Malas, 'Syrian Rebels Get Missiles', *Wall Street Journal*, 17 October 2012, https://www.wsj.com/articles/SB10000872396390443684104578062842929673074; and Sergio Peçanha, 'An Arms Pipeline to the Syrian Rebels', *New York Times*, 24 March 2013, https://archive.nytimes.com/www.nytimes.com/interactive/2013/03/25/world/middleeast/an-arms-pipeline-to-the-syrian-rebels.html.

11   See Roula Khalaf and Abigail Fielding Smith, 'Qatar Bankrolls Syrian Revolt with Cash and Arms', *Financial Times*, 16 May 2013, http://ig-legacy.ft.com/content/86e3f28e-be3a-11e2-bb35-00144feab7de#axzz6ezG2x9nz.

12   See Elliot Higgins, 'Chinese MANPADS in Syria', Brown Moses Blog, 3 March 2013, http://brown-moses.blogspot.com/2013/03/chinese-manpads-in-syria-does-2-2-fn-6.html; and Mark Mazzetti, C.J. Chivers and Eric Schmitt, 'Taking Outsize Role in Syria, Qatar Funnels Arms to Rebels', *New York Times*,

30 June 2013, https://www.nytimes.com/2013/06/30/world/middleeast/sending-missiles-to-syrian-rebels-qatar-muscles-in.html.

13 See Hassan Hassan, 'The Army of Islam Is Winning in Syria', *Foreign Policy*, 1 October 2013, https://foreignpolicy.com/2013/10/01/the-army-of-islam-is-winning-in-syria/; and Khaled Yacoub Oweis, 'Insight: Saudi Arabia Boosts Salafist Rivals to al-Qaeda in Syria', Reuters, 1 October 2013, https://www.reuters.com/article/us-syria-crisis-jihadists-insight-idUSBRE9900RO20131001.

14 Quoted in Hussein Murtaza, 'NSA Document Says Saudi Prince Directly Ordered Coordinated Attack by Syrian Rebels on Damascus', *Intercept*, 24 October 2017, https://theintercept.com/2017/10/24/syria-rebels-nsa-saudi-prince-assad/.

15 See Jeffrey Lewis and Bruno Tertrais, 'The Thick Red Line: Implications of the 2013 Chemical-weapons Crisis for Deterrence and Transatlantic Relations', *Survival*, vol. 59, no. 6, December 2017–January 2018, pp. 77–108.

16 See Anne Barnard and Karam Shoumali, 'US Weaponry Is Turning Syria into a Proxy War with Russia', *New York Times*, 12 October 2015, https://www.nytimes.com/2015/10/13/world/middleeast/syria-russia-airstrikes.html?_r=0; and Ernesto Londoño and Greg Miller, 'CIA Begins Weapons Delivery to Syrian Rebels', *Washington Post*, 11 September 2013, https://www.washingtonpost.com/world/national-security/cia-begins-weapons-delivery-to-syrian-rebels/2013/09/11/9fcf2ed8-1b0c-11e3-a628-7e6dde8f889d_story.html.

17 On the Syria 'Train and Equip' programme and how Jabhat al-Nusra seized weapons and other assets from US-backed rebels, see Michael D. Shear, Helene Cooper and Eric Schmitt, 'Obama Administration Ends Efforts to Train Syrians to Combat ISIS', *New York Times*, 9 October 2015, https://www.nytimes.com/2015/10/10/world/middleeast/pentagon-program-islamic-state-syria.html.

18 See Mark Mazzetti and Ali Younes, 'C.I.A. Arms for Syrian Rebels Supplied Black Market, Officials Say', *New York Times*, 26 June 2021, https://www.nytimes.com/2016/06/27/world/middleeast/cia-arms-for-syrian-rebels-supplied-black-market-officials-say.html; and Ali Younes and Mark Mazzetti, 'Weapons for Syrian Rebels Sold on Jordan's Black Market', Al-Jazeera, 27 June 2016, https://www.aljazeera.com/news/2016/6/26/weapons-for-syrian-rebels-sold-on-jordans-black-market.

19 See Rana Sweis, 'Jordanian Sentenced to Life in Prison for Killing 3 US Soldiers', *New York Times*, 17 July 2017, https://www.nytimes.com/2017/07/17/world/middleeast/jordan-killing-us-soldiers.html.

20 Amnesty International, 'Torture Was My Punishment: Abductions, Torture and Summary Killings Under Armed Group Rule in Aleppo and Idlib, Syria', 5 July 2016, https://www.amnesty.org/download/Documents/MDE2442272016ENGLISH.PDF.

21 See Nabih Bulos, 'Syrian Rebels Once Supported by US Appear to Behead Child in Video', *Los Angeles Times*, 19 July 2016, https://www.latimes.com/world/middleeast/la-fg-syria-behead-

ing-video-20160719-snap-story.html.

22 Conflict Armament Research, 'Weapons of the Islamic State', 4 December 2017, https://www.conflictarm.com/reports/weapons-of-the-islamic-state/.

23 Mark Mazzetti, Adam Goldman and Michael S. Schmidt, 'Behind the Sudden Death of a $1 Billion Secret CIA War in Syria', New York Times, 2 August 2017, https://www.nytimes.com/2017/08/02/world/middleeast/cia-syria-rebel-arm-train-trump.html.

24 The unnamed US official is quoted in David Ignatius, 'What the Demise of the CIA's Anti-Assad Program Means', Washington Post, 20 July 2017, https://www.washingtonpost.com/opinions/what-the-demise-of-the-cias-anti-assad-program-means/2017/07/20/f6467240-6d87-11e7-b9e2-2056e768a7e5_story.html. On the Vietnam War body-count controversy, see Lewis Sorley, A Better War: The Unexamined Victories and Final Tragedy of America's Last Years in Vietnam (New York: Harcourt Brace, 1999), pp. 21–2, 42.

25 On the early ideological development of the PKK, see its founding manifesto: Abdullah Öcalan, Kürdistan Devriminin Yolu [The Way of Kurdish Revolution] (Cologne: Weşanen Serxwebun, 1978). On the PKK's ideological shift away from Marxism–Leninism and towards democratic confederalism, see Abdullah Öcalan, Democratic Confederalism (London: Transmedia Publishing, 2011).

26 For greater detail on relations between the PYD, the YPG and the PKK, see 'Syria's Kurds: A Struggle Within a Struggle', International Crisis Group, Middle East Report no. 136, 22 January 2013, https://d2071andvip0wj.cloudfront.net/syrias-kurds-a-struggle-within-a-struggle.pdf.

27 Ibid. See also DeYoung and Sly, 'Syrian Rebels Get Influx of Arms with Gulf Neighbors' Money, US Coordination'.

28 See Adam Entous, Joe Parkinson and Julian E. Barnes, 'US Cooperated Secretly with Syrian Kurds in Battle Against Islamic State', Wall Street Journal, 21 October 2014, https://www.wsj.com/articles/u-s-cooperated-secretly-with-syrian-kurds-in-battle-against-islamic-state-1413939876.

29 See Julian E. Barnes, 'B-1 Pilots Describe Bombing Campaign Against ISIS in Kobani', Wall Street Journal, 17 February 2015, https://blogs.wsj.com/washwire/2015/02/17/b-1-pilots-describe-bombing-campaign-against-isis-in-kobani/.

30 See John Davison, 'New US-backed Syrian Rebel Alliance Launches Offensive Against Islamic State', Reuters, 31 October 2015, https://www.reuters.com/article/us-mideast-crisis-syria-idUSKCN-0SP0EA20151031; Tom Perry and Naline Malla, 'Western States Train Kurdish Force in Syria, Force's Leader Says', Reuters, 10 September 2015, https://www.reuters.com/article/us-mideast-crisis-syria-kurds-idUSKCN0RA1NE20150910; and 'US General Told Syria YPG: You Have Got to Change Your Brand', Reuters, 22 July 2017, https://www.reuters.com/article/us-mideast-crisis-usa-ypg-idUSKBN1A62SS.

31 See 'Averting Disaster in Syria's Idlib Province', International Crisis Group, Middle East Briefing no. 56, 9 February 2018, https://d2071andvip0wj.cloudfront.net/

b056-averting-disaster-in-syrias-idlib-province_0.pdf; and 'First Turkish Military Convoy Enters Syria's Idlib', Reuters, 12 October 2017, https://www.reuters.com/article/us-mideast-crisis-syria-turkey-idUSKBN1CH31K.

32 See Amnesty International, 'Syria: Turkish Occupation of Afrin Has Led to Widespread Human Rights Violations – New Findings', 1 August 2018, https://www.amnesty.org.uk/press-releases/syria-turkish-occupation-afrin-has-led-widespread-human-rights-violations-new.

33 See United Nations General Assembly, 'Report of the Independent International Commission of Inquiry on the Syrian Arab Republic', A/HRC/45/31, 14 August 2020, https://reliefweb.int/sites/reliefweb.int/files/resources/A-HRC-45-31-en.pdf.

34 See, respectively, US Marine Corps, *Mao Tse-Tung on Guerrilla Warfare* (Washington DC: US Marine Corps, 1961), pp. 8, 93; Alexander B. Downes, 'Draining the Sea by Filling the Graves: Investigating the Effectiveness of Indiscriminate Violence as a Counterinsurgency Strategy', *Civil Wars*, vol. 9, no. 4, December 2007, pp. 420–44; and Benjamin Valentino, Paul Huth and Dylan Balch-Lindsay, 'Draining the Sea: Mass Killing and Guerrilla Warfare', *International Organization*, vol. 58, no. 2, April 2004, pp. 375–407.

35 On Turkey's actions in Afrin, see Rachel Hagan, 'How Syria's Afrin Became Hell for Kurds', Open Democracy, 11 November 2020, https://www.opendemocracy.net/en/north-africa-west-asia/how-syrias-afrin-became-hell-for-kurds/?fbclid=IwAR19a71hC7QO8

EAhanx3qwEDcNImYiiMDmA YNG-W0GLD6-L7Pd4C41Y8BnY.

36 See Sarah El Deeb and Joseph Krauss, 'Money, Hatred for the Kurds Drives Turkey's Syrian Fighters', Associated Press, 15 October 2019, https://apnews.com/article/7386b1149d2642afb3258e3d07d167dc.

37 The analyst is Hassan Hassan, quoted in Ben Hubbard and David Kirkpatrick, 'Kurds' Sense of Betrayal Compounded by Empowerment of Unsavory Rivals', *New York Times*, 18 October 2019, https://www.nytimes.com/2019/10/18/world/middleeast/kurds-sense-of-betrayal-compounded-by-empowerment-of-unsavory-rivals.html.

38 See Laura Seligman, 'Turkey Begins Resettling Refugees in Northeastern Syria', *Foreign Policy*, 9 December 2019, https://foreignpolicy.com/2019/12/09/turkey-resettling-refugees-northeastern-syria/.

39 See Nader Ibrahim et al., 'Hevrin Khalaf: Death of a Peacemaker', BBC, 13 January 2020, https://www.bbc.com/news/av/world-middle-east-51068522. See also Amnesty International, 'Syria: Damning Evidence of War Crimes and Other Violations by Turkish Forces and Their Allies', 18 October 2019, https://www.amnesty.org/en/latest/news/2019/10/syria-damning-evidence-of-war-crimes-and-other-violations-by-turkish-forces-and-their-allies/.

40 See Hagan, 'How Syria's Afrin Became Hell for Kurds'.

41 White House, 'Remarks by President Trump on the Situation in Northern Syria', 23 October 2019, https://trumpwhitehouse.archives.gov/

briefings-statements/remarks-president-trump-situation-northern-syria/.

42   Quoted in Eric Schmitt et al., 'Pullback Leaves Green Berets Feeling "Ashamed", and Kurdish Allies Describing "Betrayal"', *New York Times*, 13 October 2019, https://www.nytimes.com/2019/10/13/world/middleeast/kurds-syria-turkey-trump.html.

43   See Mazloum Abdi, 'If We Have to Choose Between Compromise and Genocide, We Will Choose Our People', *Foreign Policy*, 13 October 2019, https://foreignpolicy.com/2019/10/13/kurds-assad-syria-russia-putin-turkey-genocide/.

44   See 'Full Text of Turkey, Russia Agreement on Northeast Syria', Al-Jazeera, 22 October 2019, https://www.aljazeera.com/news/2019/10/22/full-text-of-turkey-russia-agreement-on-northeast-syria.

45   UN General Assembly, 'Report of the Independent International Commission of Inquiry on the Syrian Arab Republic'.

46   Amy Austin Holmes, 'The United States Can Counter Putin and Assad with Light Footprint in Syria', *Foreign Policy*, 21 October 2020, https://foreignpolicy.com/2020/10/21/the-united-states-can-counter-putin-and-assad-with-a-light-footprint-in-syria/. See also 'Operation Inherent Resolve: Lead Inspector General Report to the US Congress', 1 April–30 June 2019, pp. 29–30, https://media.defense.gov/2019/Aug/09/2002169448/-1/-1/1/Q3FY2019_LEADIG_OIR_REPORT.PDF.

47   See Katie B. Williams, 'Outgoing Syria Envoy Admits Hiding US Troop Numbers', *Defense One*, 12 November 2020, https://www.defenseone.com/threats/2020/11/outgoing-syria-envoy-admits-hiding-us-troop-numbers-praises-trumps-mideast-record/170012/.

48   See Fabrice Balanche, 'The Fragile Status Quo in Northeast Syria', PolicyWatch 3,343, Washington Institute for Near East Policy, 1 July 2020, https://www.washingtoninstitute.org/policy-analysis/view/the-fragile-status-quo-in-northeast-syria.

49   See Amy Austin Holmes, 'Arabs Across Syria Join the Kurdish-led Syrian Democratic Forces', Middle East Research and Information Project, 28 July 2020, https://merip.org/2020/07/arabs-across-syria-join-the-kurdish-led-syrian-democratic-forces/.

50   'Rojava' is the name Syrian Kurds use to designate the Kurdish-majority areas of Syria. The term stems from the word *roj*, meaning sun, and denotes the place of sunset, or the 'west' of Kurdistan. As the term is strongly associated with Kurdish identity and aspirations for political independence, the new political authorities have deemed it inflammatory and divisive, and decided to drop it, despite pushback from Kurdish nationalists.

51   Kayla Koontz, 'Borders Beyond Borders: The Many (Many) Kurdish Political Parties of Syria', Policy Paper 2019–21, Middle East Institute, https://www.mei.edu/sites/default/files/2019-10/Borders%20Beyond%20Borders_Oct.%2025%2C%202019.pdf.

52   Wladimir van Wilgenburg, 'New Administration Formed for Northeastern Syria', Kurdistan 24, 6 September 2018, https://www.kurdistan24.net/en/news/c9e03dab-

6265-4a9a-91ee-ea8d2a93c657.

53 On the long-standing tensions between the PYD and the KNC, see International Crisis Group, 'Syria's Kurds: A Struggle Within a Struggle'. On the 2017 elections and the KNC boycott, see Koontz, 'Borders Beyond Borders'.

54 See Jordi Tejel, *Syria's Kurds: History, Politics and Society* (Abingdon: Routledge, 2008).

55 See Office of the United Nations High Commissioner for Human Rights, 'Persecution and Discrimination Against Kurdish Citizens in Syria', September 2009, http://lib.ohchr.org/ HRBodies/UPR/Documents/session12/ SY/KIS-KurdsinSyria-eng.pdf. The Syrian state allows recognised religious communities, such as Sunni Muslims, Greek Orthodox and Druze, to follow their own religious teachings and apply their own rules in personal-status matters.

56 See Ofra Bengio, 'Game Changers: Kurdish Women in Peace and War', *Middle East Journal*, vol. 70, no. 1, Winter 2016, pp. 30–46.

57 On social ecology, see Murray Bookchin, *The Ecology of Freedom* (Naperville, IL: New Dimensions Foundation, 1982). On environmentalism in north and east Syria, see Wes Enzinna, 'A Dream of Secular Utopia in ISIS' Backyard', *New York Times Magazine*, 29 November 2015, https://www.nytimes.com/2015/11/29/ magazine/a-dream-of-utopia-in-hell.html; and Dor Shilton, 'In the Heart of Syria's Darkness, a Democratic, Egalitarian, and Feminist Society Emerges', *Haaretz*, 8 June 2019, https://www.haaretz. com/middle-east-news/.premium.

MAGAZINE-amid-syria-s-darkness-a-democratic-egalitarian-and-feminist-society-emerges-1.7339983. On agricultural cooperatives in north and east Syria, see Sinan Hatahet, 'The Political Economy of the Autonomous Administration of North and East Syria', Research Project Report 2019/16, Middle East Directions, 29 November 2019, http:// medirections.com/images/dox/MED_ WPCS_2019_16.pdf.

58 See Holmes, 'Arabs Across Syria Join the Kurdish-led Syrian Democratic Forces'.

59 While the sample is rather small, survey design and sampling methods ensured representation of geographic, gender and ethnic diversity, making inferences more reliable. See Holmes, 'Arabs Across Syria Join the Kurdish-led Syrian Democratic Forces'; and Amy Austin Holmes, 'SDF's Arab Majority Rank Turkey as the Biggest Threat to NE Syria: Survey Data on American Partner Forces', Wilson Center, October 2019, https://www. wilsoncenter.org/sites/default/files/ media/documents/publication/ sdf_arab_majority_rank_turkey_as_ biggest_threat.pdf.

60 Amy Austin Holmes, 'Despite Ceasefire Agreement, Turkey Implicated in More than Eight Hundred Violations', Council on Foreign Relations, 13 October 2020, https://www.cfr.org/blog/despite-ceasefire-agreement-turkey-implicated-more-eight-hundred-violations.

61 See Liz Sly, 'With a Show of Stars and Stripes, US forces in Syria Try to Keep Warring Parties Apart', *Washington Post*, 8 March 2017, https:// www.washingtonpost.com/world/

middle_east/with-a-show-of-stars-and-stripes-us-forces-in-syria-try-to-keep-warring-allies-apart/2017/03/08/c77671a8-0352-11e7-9d14-9724d48f5666_story.html.

62 See the statements of Mazloum Abdi in Holmes, 'The United States Can Counter Putin and Assad with Light Footprint in Syria'.

63 Quoted in Robert Burns, 'US General Says IS in Iraq and Syria Still Long-term Threat', Associated Press, 19 November 2020, https://apnews.com/article/politics-islamic-state-group-syria-iraq-c15ed37959f39e7d40f7c613fc8cb5e8.

64 See the statements of Mazloum Abdi on the release of low-level Islamic State prisoners, in Amberin Zaman, 'Syrian Kurdish Commander Sees Chance to Ease Tensions with Turkey Under Biden', Al-Monitor, 9 November 2020, https://www.al-monitor.com/pulse/originals/2020/11/syria-mazlum-kobane-sdf-mediate-pkk-us-election-biden-trump.html. See also Jeff Seldin, 'US Backs Release of "Low-level" Islamic State Prisoners in Syria', Voice of America, https://www.voanews.com/middle-east/us-backs-release-low-level-islamic-state-prisoners-syria.

65 Tamara Qiblawi, 'A Spy Stole ISIS Leader Baghdadi's Underwear for DNA Test, Kurds Say', CNN, 29 October 2019, https://edition.cnn.com/2019/10/29/middleeast/baghdadi-sdf-underwear-syria-intl/index.html; and Eric Schmitt, Helene Cooper and Julian E. Barnes, 'Trump's Syria Troop Withdrawal Complicated Plans for al-Baghdadi Raid', New York Times, 27 October 2019, https://www.nytimes.com/2019/10/27/us/politics/baghdadi-isis-leader-trump.html. Regarding ongoing US counter-terrorism efforts in Idlib, see Eric Schmitt, 'Al-Qaeda Feels Losses in Afghanistan and Syria but Stays Resilient', New York Times, 28 October 2020, https://www.nytimes.com/2020/10/27/world/middleeast/al-qaeda-afghanistan-syria-somalia.html.

66 International Crisis Group, 'Squaring the Circles in Syria's North East', Middle East Report no. 204, 31 July 2019, https://d2071andvip0wj.cloudfront.net/204%20squaring-the-circles_0.pdf.

67 Hatahet, 'The Political Economy of the Autonomous Administration of North and East Syria'. See also Seth J. Frantzman, 'Will Oil Deal for Eastern Syria Help or Hurt Those Fighting ISIS?', Jerusalem Post, 2 August 2020, https://www.jpost.com/middle-east/will-oil-deal-for-eastern-syria-help-or-hurt-those-fighting-isis-637187.

68 Mazlum is quoted in Zaman, 'Syrian Kurdish Commander Sees Chance to Ease Tensions with Turkey Under Biden'.

69 See, for example, Reem Salahi, 'Afghanistan Demonstrates Why It's Time for a Clear Syria Policy, Starting with Northeast Syria', Atlantic Council, 3 September 2021, https://www.atlanticcouncil.org/blogs/menasource/afghanistan-demonstrates-why-its-time-for-a-clear-syria-policy-starting-with-northeast-syria/.

Copyright © 2021 The International Institute for Strategic Studies

Disarming Arguments: Public Opinion and Nuclear Abolition

Ondrej Rosendorf, Michal Smetana and Marek Vranka

On Easter weekend 1962, the United Kingdom's Campaign for Nuclear Disarmament drew a record 150,000 people for the final part of an annual four-day march from Aldermaston to London's Trafalgar Square. Twenty years later, New York's Central Park saw up to one million people protesting nuclear weapons in one of the largest political demonstrations in US history. Lawrence Wittner, a historian of peace movements, estimates that in October 1983 alone, some 5m people participated in nuclear-disarmament rallies around the world.[1]

Today, such high levels of public interest in nuclear disarmament are hardly imaginable. After the Cold War ended, the need to control, reduce and eventually abolish nuclear weapons lost prominence as a matter for public debate, and is now confined to what Nina Tannenwald has described as 'largely an inside-the-beltway, elite-driven process'.[2] While post-Cold War opinion polls indicate that nuclear abolition is not something that global publics oppose, there has been a steep decline in public involvement in and support for pro-disarmament activities.[3] Meanwhile, the nuclear threat, far from disappearing, may be greater than ever thanks to continuing nuclear proliferation and rising mistrust between nuclear-armed states.[4]

Ondrej Rosendorf is a PhD student in the International Relations programme of the Faculty of Social Sciences, Charles University, and a Junior Researcher at the Peace Research Center Prague. **Michal Smetana** is a Researcher and Lecturer at the Faculty of Social Sciences, Charles University, Coordinator of the Peace Research Center Prague and Head of the Experimental Lab for International Security Studies (ELISS). He is the lead author on this study. **Marek Vranka** is a Lecturer in the Faculty of Social Sciences, Charles University, Head Researcher at the Prague Laboratory for Experimental Social Sciences and Researcher at the Peace Research Center Prague.

Survival | vol. 63 no. 6 | December 2021–January 2022 | pp. 183–200 https://doi.org/10.1080/00396338.2021.2006454

To invigorate public support for a nuclear-weapons-free world, disarmament advocates have framed their arguments in favour of nuclear abolition in a variety of ways. For example, in their famous op-ed published in the *Wall Street Journal* in 2007, Cold War veterans George Shultz, William Perry, Henry Kissinger and Sam Nunn called for global disarmament to prevent nuclear proliferation among terrorist groups and 'dangerous states' such as North Korea and Iran.[5] The International Campaign to Abolish Nuclear Weapons (ICAN), which was awarded the 2017 Nobel Peace Prize, frames its own disarmament advocacy in terms of human rights and human security, foregrounding the humanitarian consequences of any use of nuclear weapons.[6]

Among scholars interested in nuclear disarmament, there have been some limited attempts to disaggregate individual pro-disarmament arguments and discuss their pros and cons.[7] However, rigorous studies that examine how the public perceives these arguments and that identify which of them are considered the most persuasive have been lacking. To fill this gap and empirically test the strength of the various cases for nuclear disarmament, we surveyed a large, representative sample of American citizens. In the survey, we asked the participants about their general attitudes towards global nuclear disarmament, as well as their views on the six arguments that are commonly used by disarmament advocates to justify nuclear abolition: the risk of nuclear terrorism; the behaviour of nuclear-armed 'rogue states'; the prospect of catastrophic nuclear war; the potential humanitarian impact of nuclear use; the danger of nuclear accidents; and the economic costs of nuclear arsenals.[8]

Before we present our findings, however, it is worth considering the critical role of public engagement in achieving nuclear arms control and disarmament during the Cold War and afterwards. A key theme emerges: throughout our nuclear history, public pressure has significantly shaped states', and particularly US, policies. To be effective, however, advocates of disarmament need to engage the public with arguments that resonate.

Nuclear disarmament and public engagement

Even in democratic countries, nuclear-weapons programmes are often shrouded in secrecy and controlled by a small group of elite political stakeholders without much public scrutiny.[9] Nevertheless, during the Cold War, public activism was frequently a key force driving the emergence of anti-nuclear norms, as well as more formal international cooperation in nuclear arms control and disarmament.[10]

After the atomic bombings of Hiroshima and Nagasaki, a popular movement against nuclear weapons gradually emerged in the United States and elsewhere.[11] This early anti-nuclear activism gained strength throughout the 1950s and seemed to be instrumental in the stigmatisation of nuclear weapons as an unacceptable instrument of warfare, and in the gradual establishment of the 'nuclear taboo' – the norm of nuclear non-use.[12] As Tannenwald notes in her seminal 2007 book *The Nuclear Taboo*:

> domestic public opinion was an important factor both in constraining US leaders' resort to use of nuclear weapons and in forming the taboo itself. US leaders were sensitive to public attitudes toward nuclear weapons because they perceived that domestic support for US security policies was essential to waging the Cold War against the Soviet Union.[13]

The invention and atmospheric testing of the 'H-bomb' incited another powerful wave of worldwide protests against nuclear armaments.[14] Mounting public pressure was a key reason why the United States and the Soviet Union declared unilateral testing moratoria in 1958 and started negotiating a formal non-testing agreement. This process, given added impetus by the near miss of the 1962 Cuban Missile Crisis, eventually culminated in 1963 with the signature of the Partial Test Ban Treaty, which prohibits all but underground nuclear tests. This treaty was the first formal arms-control instrument to regulate the arms race between the nuclear powers.[15]

Popular resistance to nuclear weapons slowed somewhat through the mid-1970s, only to be revived in the second half of the decade.[16] One of the anti-nuclear movement's tangible successes of that period was the cancellation of the Carter administration's plan to develop and deploy a neutron bomb, a decision taken primarily in response to both domestic and allied public pressure.[17] Plans to deploy intermediate-range *Pershing* II nuclear missiles in Europe and the continuation of the nuclear arms race under the Reagan administration led to massive anti-nuclear demonstrations in the

Western bloc and the consolidation of the grassroots 'Nuclear Freeze' movement in the United States. In its heyday in the first half of the 1980s, Nuclear Freeze managed to gain the support of a wide array of peace organisations, politicians, religious bodies, and academic, professional and women's associations, exerting considerable influence on American politics.[18]

Moved in part by public pressure, but also in part by his own personal aversion to nuclear weapons, US president Ronald Reagan eventually reversed what had been a hawkish approach to nuclear issues. In his November 1983 speech to the Japanese parliament, he called for significant reductions in the US and Soviet nuclear arsenals, and declared that 'our dream is to see the day when nuclear weapons will be banished from the face of the earth'.[19] This alteration of Washington's position, which was strongly influenced by the demands of the freeze movement, led to the resumption of talks with the Soviets on the control of intermediate-range nuclear weapons. These negotiations resulted in the adoption of the Intermediate-Range Nuclear Forces (INF) Treaty of 1987, the first arms-control treaty to eliminate a whole class of nuclear weapons.[20]

Since the end of the Cold War, nuclear disarmament has lost urgency in the eyes of the general public. Despite the Obama administration's support for nuclear abolition and the adoption of the Treaty on the Prohibition of Nuclear Weapons (TPNW) in 2017, disarmament advocates have struggled to attract public attention.[21] Yet public support has clearly been a key factor in changes to the global nuclear order. As noted by American philosopher Jacob Nebel, 'the support of the American people is essential to disarm the US nuclear arsenal. This power may not be a sufficient factor, but it is a necessary one. Disarmament advocates should try to persuade the president, legislators, and international leaders, but most fundamentally, they must persuade other people.'[22]

Six arguments for nuclear abolition

To promote nuclear disarmament as a worthy policy goal, pro-abolition advocates have put forward a range of arguments about its desirability. The six broad arguments identified earlier were first suggested by Anne Harrington, Eliza Gheorghe and Anya Loukianova Fink in their 2017 article for the *Bulletin of the Atomic Scientists*.[23]

The nuclear-terrorism argument relates to the threat of non-state actors acquiring and detonating a nuclear device. While speculation about this threat was present during the Cold War, after the events of 9/11 fears grew that a crude nuclear device might be detonated in a populated area.[24] The argument that nuclear disarmament makes sense in the context of terrorist activities builds on the premises that terrorists are actively seeking nuclear weapons and are willing to use them against the civilian population; that, so long as there are nuclear weapons in the world, they can be stolen and misused by terrorists; and that terrorists, because they have no territory of their own, cannot be deterred by a threat of nuclear retaliation as state actors can.[25] In other words, the existence of nuclear weapons makes their use by terrorist groups a possibility, but nuclear weapons cannot be used to counter this threat.

The 'rogue states' argument centres on a similar problem: there are state actors that do not play by the rules of international order. These states are governed by leaders who do not make decisions based on rational calculations of utility cost and therefore are 'undeterrable' according to the logic of deterrence theory. So long as there are nuclear weapons in the world, these actors can acquire and use them.[26] The problem of 'rogue states' took on great importance in post-Cold War American politics – particularly under the George W. Bush administration – and was frequently connected with the proliferation of nuclear and other weapons of mass destruction.[27] As Kissinger, Shultz, Perry and Nunn noted in their call for a nuclear-weapons-free world, 'North Korea's recent nuclear test and Iran's refusal to stop its program to enrich uranium … highlight the fact that the world is now on the precipice of a new and dangerous nuclear era'.[28]

The nuclear-war argument seriously questions the notion of 'eternal stability' in the strategic relationship between nuclear powers. Proponents of this argument suggest that as long as there are nuclear weapons, there is also the possibility of their use, and any use of nuclear weapons in a conflict between nuclear-armed actors could escalate to the level of nuclear war. Such a war could destroy human civilisation as we know it. Moreover, mutual deterrence always involves some probability of failure. This problem has been exacerbated by the gradual disintegration of the world's arms-control architecture, which has caused some analysts to suggest that the world is currently closer to an extinction-level nuclear war than at any time since 1945.[29]

The humanitarian argument approaches the problem of nuclear disarmament from a human-security perspective, following a similar logic to that employed by the successful campaigns to ban landmines and cluster munitions.[30] Proponents of this argument suggest that any use of nuclear weapons would have catastrophic humanitarian consequences, resulting in untold human suffering and the violation of fundamental human rights. Moreover, since there are no circumstances in which the use of nuclear weapons would be legitimate, the weapons themselves are immoral and should be abolished. Such humanitarian framing has been employed by many disarmament actors in recent years, most notably by ICAN and its 'Humanitarian Initiative' campaign that culminated in the adoption of the TPNW.[31]

The accidents argument suggests that the complex systems used for the management of states' nuclear arsenals are prone to accidents with potentially catastrophic consequences, even when highly supervised. Indeed, it is their very complexity that makes accidents inevitable.[32] Some have pointed out that the history of nuclear-weapons programmes is full of technical malfunctions, human errors and 'close calls', in which nuclear weapons were almost used by mistake.[33] Given the inevitability and potentially severe consequences of such accidents, the only sure way to prevent an accidental catastrophe is to abolish all nuclear weapons.

The costs argument highlights the economic trade-offs that societies must make to develop and maintain nuclear arsenals. Given that such arsenals are exceedingly expensive, their dismantlement would free up resources that could be used elsewhere, such as in healthcare, education or domestic infrastructure projects. This argument has been particularly prominent in recent years as all nine nuclear-armed countries have pursued nuclear-modernisation programmes.[34]

Disarmament advocates frequently use several arguments simultaneously. However, the persuasiveness of each argument may vary in the eyes of different audiences, and even some analysts have suggested that certain arguments are inefficient, counterproductive or otherwise problematic, while expressing a preference for others. For example, Zia Mian argues that 'it is possible to overcome some of the potential problems over nuclear weapon abolition that result from arguments based purely on national security and national interest by broadening the frame to include normative, moral, and legal considerations'.[35] A report of the US in the World Initiative, on the other hand, argues that 'the fact that nuclear weapons are a source of risk – not the fact that they are morally wrong – should be presented as the underlying reason why the issue of nuclear weapons matters'.[36] Nebel proposes that 'the risk-reduction framework, combined with moral and legal arguments that appeal to people's basic beliefs, should be the baseline strategy'.[37] Finally, in their original piece, Harrington, Gheorghe and Fink suggest that the costs argument has relatively fewer downsides and 'stands out for its potential to spark a more informed debate and greater public engagement on the issue'.[38] Yet there has been little empirical data on public attitudes to support such conclusions.

Surveying public attitudes

To examine public attitudes towards specific pro-disarmament arguments, we worked with Ipsos, a prominent polling company, to survey a representative sample of 1,000 American adults in April 2021.[39] As shown in Figure 1, we found that 76% of Americans agreed that the United States 'should now take the lead and start negotiating with other nuclear-armed countries to make immediate steps to achieve global nuclear disarmament', whereas 24% disagreed with this statement. This result corresponds to the 2008 World Public Opinion poll, in which 77% of American respondents agreed and 20% disagreed with a proposed plan to completely eliminate nuclear weapons according to a specific timeline, as well as the Simons Foundation's 2007 poll, in which 73% of respondents supported and 14% opposed the elimination of all nuclear weapons through an enforceable agreement.[40]

In Figure 1, we also show that taking the initiative towards disarmament was more supported by people identifying as Democrats (83%) than as Independents (74%) or Republicans (68%). Women and those reporting a yearly household income above $90,000 were slightly more likely to express support. The age and education of respondents were not found to be significant in determining respondents' attitudes.

Figure 1: **Percentage of 1,000 survey respondents who agreed the US should lead negotiations to achieve global nuclear disarmament**

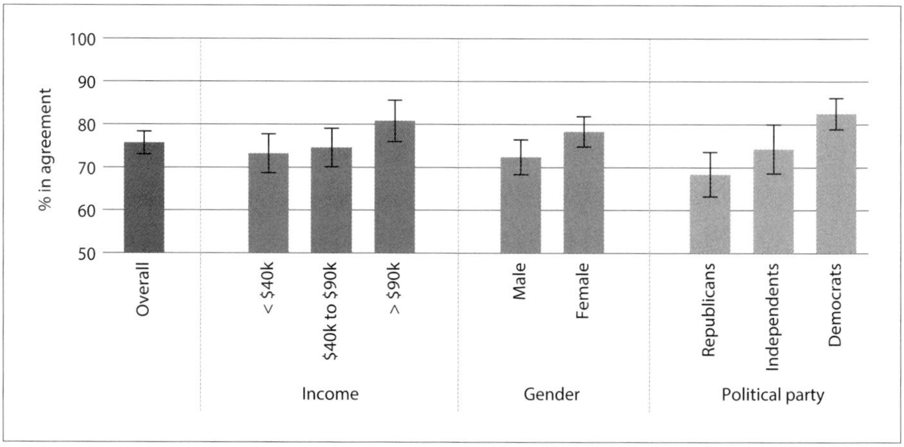

Error bars represent 95% confidence intervals.

To examine the relative effectiveness of various pro-disarmament arguments, we asked our respondents about their attitudes towards the six most common ones (nuclear terrorism, nuclear-armed 'rogue states', catastrophic nuclear war, humanitarian impact, nuclear accidents and economic costs). Contrary to the expectations of Harrington and her colleagues, however, American citizens seem to find the costs argument to be the least persuasive (see Figure 2).[41] We found more support for the arguments about the threat of nuclear war, nuclear terrorism and the humanitarian impact of nuclear use.

The two arguments that performed the best were those related to the possibility of nuclear accidents and the threat of nuclear-armed rogue states. While another study would be required to rigorously explain why these two arguments stand out, we can offer some tentative propositions here. Firstly, recent scholarship shows that the 2011 Fukushima Daiichi disaster had an impact on public attitudes towards nuclear power in general and the prospect of nuclear accidents in particular.[42] Some anti-nuclear activists suggest that public perceptions might have been further influenced by the highly popular 2019 TV series *Chernobyl* that portrays the 1986 nuclear accident in the former Soviet Union.[43]

As for the 'rogue states' argument, our findings are in line with the Simons Foundation poll that indicated over 95% of Americans see the goal

Figure 2: **Percentage of 1,000 survey respondents who agreed with a given reason for the elimination of nuclear weapons**

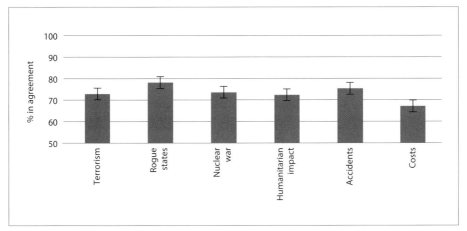

Error bars represent 95% confidence intervals.

of preventing the spread of nuclear weapons as important, while 82% agree that countries that do not possess nuclear weapons should be prevented from developing them.[44] The problem of foreign 'rogues' seeking weapons of mass destruction has been a prominent theme in US politics since the 1990s,[45] and has strongly influenced the development of the country's nuclear strategy since the end of the Cold War.[46] Iran's breaches of non-proliferation norms, and North Korea's clandestine development and testing of nuclear weapons and long-range ballistic missiles, have featured prominently in the foreign policies of several administrations since the early 2000s.[47] Yet diplomatic efforts have failed to resolve the issue, meaning there is still reason for Americans to perceive rogue states as a serious security threat, and even an existential threat in the case of North Korea, which has already acquired the capability to deliver its nuclear weapons on intercontinental ballistic missiles.[48]

Choosing the right argument

From the perspective of nuclear-disarmament advocates, it is useful to further disaggregate these findings in a way that allows campaigns to target their messaging to different subgroups. Figure 3 shows the relative persuasiveness of the six pro-disarmament arguments when survey respondents are broken down according to their party affiliation.

The data suggests that, for those who identify with the Democratic Party, all the arguments except for costs are similarly effective. In other words, Democrats seem responsive to five of the arguments about the desirability of nuclear disarmament and only slightly less so to the sixth.

Differences in the persuasiveness of individual arguments become much more prominent when we look at the Republican respondents. Among Republicans, the argument about nuclear-armed rogue states seems to be the most effective by far – perhaps not surprisingly, considering the prominence of the 'rogue state' narrative in the public discourse of Republican administrations since the Cold War.[49] Support drops for arguments about nuclear terrorism, accidents and nuclear war, and even more so for arguments about the humanitarian impact and costs of maintaining a nuclear arsenal.

These findings allow us to draw some tentative conclusions of potential use to disarmament campaigns. Importantly, the arguments about the possibility of nuclear accidents – frequently employed by ICAN and other pro-disarmament non-governmental organisations – can be safely used to target broad audiences irrespective of their political orientation. However, arguments about the humanitarian impact of nuclear-weapons use will likely resonate much less with Republican voters than with Democrats.

Figure 3: **Percentage of 1,000 survey respondents who agreed with a given reason for the elimination of nuclear weapons, by party affiliation**

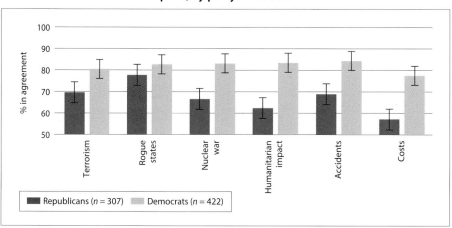

Error bars represent 95% confidence intervals.

To persuade more conservative Republicans, who are less supportive of nuclear abolition overall, disarmament campaigns should consider using the 'rogue states' argument, which appears the most likely to influence their attitudes. The argument about nuclear terrorism – as used by Kissinger, Shultz, Perry and Nunn – appears to be relatively less persuasive for both groups. Finally, the argument concerning the high costs of nuclear arsenals underperforms with both Republicans and Democrats.

Even though respondents found some arguments in our survey to be less persuasive, this does not necessarily imply that disarmament advocates should completely avoid using them. Research on framing strategies in the field of human rights shows that the use of multiple frames does not detract from the effects of the most persuasive frame.[50] To maximise their chances of success, it may thus prove beneficial for disarmament advocates to incorporate additional arguments to expand their support base. To that end, the combination of arguments about the possibility of nuclear accidents and nuclear-armed 'rogue states' seems to be the most promising.

*   *   *

Our research into the effectiveness of various arguments in favour of disarmament points to some promising avenues for further research. Firstly, while our data reveals some trends in attitudes towards specific arguments about the desirability of nuclear abolition, we currently do not have a clear answer as to *why* individuals hold these attitudes. Secondly, our research investigated only the most common arguments *in favour* of nuclear disarmament. Similar studies could be undertaken to examine why individuals *oppose* nuclear abolition – perhaps because they fear the instability that might result from the absence of nuclear deterrence, or because they worry about 'cheaters' who would maintain clandestine arsenals – and to devise specific counter-framing that could attempt to sway opponents in the other direction.[51]

Finally, our study shows that, as indicated in earlier polls, the American public in general is strongly supportive of global nuclear disarmament and would like to see the United States take the lead in bringing the world closer to this goal. This finding militates against the notion that nuclear disarmament is a utopian fantasy. It is also true, however, that the pro-disarmament majority appears not very likely to make political choices on that basis. Nuclear disarmament has not been a particularly salient issue in the United States. In recent years there has been little public pressure on elected officials to take steps in this direction – particularly in comparison with the Cold War era. One possible explanation for this might be that many Americans are sceptical of the notion that a world without nuclear weapons is attainable given the contemporary geopolitical climate. Some people may perceive nuclear disarmament as a noble yet hardly realisable idea, something akin to 'world peace'. Studies that might persuade the public about the *feasibility* of nuclear abolition may therefore be crucial for disarmament advocacy. As Margaret Beckett, then the UK's secretary of state for foreign and Commonwealth affairs, stated in a 2007 address, 'believing that the eventual abolition of nuclear weapons is possible can act as a spur for action on disarmament. Believing, at whatever level, that it is not, is the surest path to inaction.'[52]

Acknowledgements

The authors thankfully acknowledge funding by the Charles University Center of Excellence programme UNCE/HUM/28 (Faculty of Social Sciences/Peace Research Center Prague) and PROGRES Q18.

Notes

[1] Lawrence S. Wittner, 'Where Is the Nuclear Abolition Movement Today?', in Kerstin Vignard (ed.), *Civil Society and Nuclear Disarmament* (Geneva: UNIDIR, 2010), p. 7, http://unidir.org/files/publications/pdfs/civilsociety-and-nuclear-disarmament-en-321.pdf.

[2] Nina Tannenwald, 'Life Beyond Arms Control: Moving Toward a Global Regime of Nuclear Restraint and Responsibility', *Dædalus*, vol. 149, no. 2, 2020, p. 217. See also Thomas R. Rochon and Stephen P. Wood, 'Yodeling in the Echo Chamber: Public Opinion and the Nuclear Freeze', in Thomas R. Rochon and David S. Meyer (eds), *Coalitions and Political Movements: The Lessons of the Nuclear Freeze* (Boulder, CO: Lynne Rienner, 1997), pp. 25–46.

[3] See Simons Foundation, 'Global Public Opinion on Nuclear Weapons', 2007, http://www.thesimonsfoundation.ca/sites/default/files/2007 Poll on Global

Public Opinion on Attitudes Towards Nuclear Weapons_0.pdf; World Public Opinion, 'Publics Around the World Favor International Agreement to Eliminate All Nuclear Weapons', 9 December 2008, https://web.archive.org/web/20100106060557/http://www.worldpublicopinion.org/pipa/articles/international_security_bt/577.php?nid=&id=&pnt=577&lb=btis; Soka Gakkai International, 'Survey on Youth Attitudes Toward Nuclear Weapons and Their Humanitarian Consequences', 2013, https://www.peoplesdecade.org/pdf/npt2013/npt2013_01_text.pdf; and Wittner, 'Where Is the Nuclear Abolition Movement Today?', p. 7.

4   See Stewart Prager et al., 'Physicists Mobilize to Reduce the Nuclear Threat. Again', *Bulletin of the Atomic Scientists*, 24 January 2020, https://thebulletin.org/2020/01/physicists-mobilize-to-reduce-the-nuclear-threat-again/.

5   George P. Shultz et al., 'A World Free of Nuclear Weapons', *Wall Street Journal*, 4 January 2007, http://online.wsj.com/news/articles/SB116787515251566636.

6   International Campaign to Abolish Nuclear Weapons (ICAN), 'Humanitarian Case', https://www.icanw.org/humanitarian_case.

7   See Anne I. Harrington, Eliza Gheorghe and Anya Loukianova Fink, 'What Arguments Motivate Citizens to Demand Nuclear Disarmament?', *Bulletin of the Atomic Scientists*, vol. 73, no. 4, 2017, pp. 255–63; Jacob Nebel, 'The Nuclear Disarmament Movement: Politics, Potential, and Strategy', *Journal of*

Peace Education, vol. 9, no. 3, 2012, pp. 225–47; and Zia Mian, 'Beyond the Security Debate: The Moral and Legal Dimensions of Abolition', in George Perkovich and James M. Acton (eds), *Abolishing Nuclear Weapons: A Debate* (Washington DC: Carnegie Endowment for International Peace, 2009), pp. 295–306.

8   An appendix containing a comprehensive description of our data-collection method, text of individual survey questions and the detailed results of our survey is available online at https://prcprague.cz/s/SVO_Survival_2021_Appendix.zip.

9   For a more general discussion of civilian control and accountability with respect to domestic governance of nuclear-weapons programmes in nuclear-armed states, see Hans Born, Bates Gill and Heiner Hänggi (eds), *Governing the Bomb: Civilian Control and Democratic Accountability of Nuclear Weapons* (Oxford: Oxford University Press, 2010).

10   See Jeffrey W. Knopf, *Domestic Society and International Cooperation: The Impact of Protest on US Arms Control Policy* (Cambridge: Cambridge University Press, 1998).

11   For an excellent account of the early years of the nuclear-disarmament movement, see Lawrence S. Wittner, *One World or None: A History of the World Nuclear Disarmament Movement Through 1953* (Stanford, CA: Stanford University Press, 1993).

12   See Nina Tannenwald, 'Stigmatizing the Bomb: Origins of the Nuclear Taboo', *International Security*, vol. 29, no. 4, 2005, pp. 5–49; and Lawrence S. Wittner, *Confronting the Bomb: A*

Short History of the World Nuclear Disarmament Movement (Stanford, CA: Stanford University Press, 2009). For a theoretical discussion of the relationship between public opinion and elite decision-making concerning the use (or non-use) of nuclear weapons, see Daryl G. Press, Scott D. Sagan and Benjamin A. Valentino, 'Atomic Aversion: Experimental Evidence on Taboos, Traditions, and the Non-use of Nuclear Weapons', *American Political Science Review*, vol. 107, no. 1, 2013, pp. 193–4.

13 Nina Tannenwald, *The Nuclear Taboo: The United States and the Non-use of Nuclear Weapons Since 1945* (Cambridge: Cambridge University Press, 2007), p. 48.

14 See Lawrence S. Wittner, *Resisting the Bomb: A History of the World Nuclear Disarmament Movement, 1954–1970* (Stanford, CA: Stanford University Press, 1998).

15 See Daryl Kimball and Wade Boese, 'Limited Test Ban Treaty Turns 40', *Arms Control Today*, vol. 33, no. 8, 2003, pp. 37–8.

16 See Lawrence S. Wittner, 'The Forgotten Years of the World Nuclear Disarmament Movement, 1975–78', *Journal of Peace Research*, vol. 40, no. 4, 2003, pp. 435–56.

17 See Wittner, *Confronting the Bomb*, pp. 132–3; and Vincent A. Auger, *The Dynamics of Foreign Policy Analysis: The Carter Administration and the Neutron Bomb* (Lanham, MD: Rowman & Littlefield, 1996).

18 See David S. Meyer, *A Winter of Discontent: The Nuclear Freeze and American Politics* (New York: Praeger, 1990); L. Marvin Overby, 'Assessing Constituency Influence: Congressional Voting on the Nuclear Freeze, 1982–83', *Legislative Studies Quarterly*, vol. 16, no. 2, 1991, pp. 297–312; and J. Michael Hogan and Ted J. Smith, 'Polling on the Issues: Public Opinion and the Nuclear Freeze', *Public Opinion Quarterly*, vol. 55, no. 4, 1991, pp. 534–69.

19 Ronald Reagan, *Public Papers of the Presidents of the United States: Book 2* (Washington DC: Federal Register Division, National Archives and Records Service, General Services Administration, 1985), p. 1,576.

20 See Jeffrey Knopf, 'The Nuclear Freeze Movement's Effect on Policy', in Thomas R. Rochon and David S. Meyer (eds), *Coalitions and Political Movements: The Lessons of the Nuclear Freeze* (Boulder, CO: Lynne Rienner, 1997), pp. 127–61.

21 For a discussion of different approaches to nuclear-disarmament advocacy after the end of the Cold War, see Alyn Ware, 'Advocacy Networks and a World Free of Nuclear Weapons', in Nik Hynek and Michal Smetana (eds), *Global Nuclear Disarmament: Strategic, Political, and Regional Perspectives* (Abingdon: Routledge, 2015), pp. 122–44. For scholarly debate about the TPNW, see Laura Considine, 'Contests of Legitimacy and Value: The Treaty on the Prohibition of Nuclear Weapons and the Logic of Prohibition', *International Affairs*, vol. 95, no. 5, 2019, pp. 1,075–92; Heather Williams, 'Prohibition and Its Discontents', *Survival*, vol. 59, no. 3, June–July 2017, pp. 205–8; Scott Sagan and Benjamin A. Valentino, 'The Nuclear Weapons Ban Treaty:

Opportunities Lost', *Bulletin of the Atomic Scientists*, 16 July 2017, https://thebulletin.org/nuclear-weapons-ban-treaty-opportunities-lost10955; Michal Onderco, 'Why Nuclear Weapon Ban Treaty Is Unlikely to Fulfil Its Promise', *Global Affairs*, vol. 3, nos 4–5, 2017, pp. 391–404; Tilman Ruff, 'Negotiating the UN Treaty on the Prohibition of Nuclear Weapons and the Role of ICAN', *Global Change, Peace & Security*, vol. 30, no. 2, 2018, pp. 233–41; Rebecca Davis Gibbons, 'The Humanitarian Turn in Nuclear Disarmament and the Treaty on the Prohibition of Nuclear Weapons', *Nonproliferation Review*, vol. 25, nos 1–2, 2018, pp. 11–36; Harald Müller and Carmen Wunderlich, 'Nuclear Disarmament Without the Nuclear-weapon States: The Nuclear Weapon Ban Treaty', *Dædalus*, vol. 149, no. 2, 2020, pp. 171–89; and Michal Onderco et al., 'When Do the Dutch Want to Join the Nuclear Ban Treaty? Findings of a Public Opinion Survey in the Netherlands', forthcoming in *Nonproliferation Review*.

22 Nebel, 'The Nuclear Disarmament Movement', p. 227.

23 Harrington, Gheorghe and Fink, 'What Arguments Motivate Citizens to Demand Nuclear Disarmament?'

24 See Thomas C. Schelling, 'Thinking About Nuclear Terrorism', *International Security*, vol. 6, no. 4, 1982, pp. 61–77; Brian Michael Jenkins, *The Likelihood of Nuclear Terrorism* (Santa Monica, CA: RAND Corporation, 1985); Graham Allison, *Nuclear Terrorism: The Ultimate Preventable Catastrophe* (New York: Macmillan Press, 2004); Michael A. Levi, *On Nuclear Terrorism* (Cambridge, MA: Harvard University Press, 2009); and Charles D. Ferguson et al., *The Four Faces of Nuclear Terrorism* (Abingdon: Routledge, 2005).

25 See Shultz et al., 'A World Free of Nuclear Weapons'; Sam Nunn, 'Taking Steps Toward a World Free of Nuclear Weapons', *Dædalus*, vol. 138, no. 4, 2009, pp. 153–6; and Ban Ki-moon, 'Secretary-General's Remarks to Security Council Open Debate on the Non-proliferation of Weapons of Mass Destruction', 23 August 2016, https://www.un.org/sg/en/content/sg/statement/2016-08-23/secretary-generals-remarks-security-council-open-debate-non.

26 See Harrington, Gheorghe and Fink, 'What Arguments Motivate Citizens to Demand Nuclear Disarmament?', p. 257. The term 'rogue states' appears in quotation marks to highlight the highly politicised nature of the phrase. For some critical perspectives on the concept of 'rogue states', see Anna Geis and Carmen Wunderlich, 'The Good, the Bad, and the Ugly: Comparing the Notions of "Rogue" and "Evil" in International Politics', *International Politics*, vol. 51, no. 4, 2014, pp. 458–74; Wolfgang Wagner, Wouter Werner and Michal Onderco (eds), *Deviance in International Relations: 'Rogue States' and International Security* (London: Palgrave Macmillan, 2014); Alexandra Homolar, 'Rebels Without a Conscience: The Evolution of the Rogue States Narrative in US Security Policy', *European Journal of International Relations*, vol. 17, no. 4, 2011, pp. 705–27; Michal Smetana, *Nuclear Deviance: Stigma Politics and*

the Rules of the Nonproliferation Game (London: Palgrave Macmillan, 2019); and Carmen Wunderlich, *Rogue States as Norm Entrepreneurs: Black Sheep or Sheep in Wolves' Clothing?* (Cham: Springer, 2020).

27   See Tanya Ogilvie-White, 'The Defiant States: The Nuclear Diplomacy of North Korea and Iran', *Nonproliferation Review*, vol. 17, no. 1, 2010, pp. 115–38; Robert Litwak, *Outlier States: American Strategies to Change, Contain or Engage Regimes* (Washington and Baltimore, MD: Woodrow Wilson Center Press and Johns Hopkins University Press, 2012); and Michael Klare, *Rogue States and Nuclear Outlaws: America's Search for a New Foreign Policy* (New York: Hill and Wang, 1996).

28   Shultz et al., 'A World Free of Nuclear Weapons'.

29   See Bulletin of the Atomic Scientists, Science and Security Board, 'Closer than Ever: It Is 100 Seconds to Midnight', 2020 Doomsday Clock Statement, https://thebulletin.org/doomsday-clock/current-time/.

30   See John Borrie, 'Humanitarian Reframing of Nuclear Weapons and the Logic of a Ban', *International Affairs*, vol. 90, no. 3, 2014, pp. 625–46; and Matthew Bolton and Elizabeth Minor, 'The Humanitarian Initiative on Nuclear Weapons: An Introduction to Global Policy's Special Section', *Global Policy*, vol. 7, no. 3, September 2016, https://doi.org/10.1111/1758-5899.12326.

31   The humanitarian argument has also been used by the International Committee of the Red Cross (ICRC), Abolition 2000, Pax Christi, Women's International League for Peace and Freedom (WILPF), Mayors for Peace, International Physicians for the Prevention of Nuclear War (IPPNW) and even many pro-disarmament states, perhaps most prominently Austria. See, for example, 'Pledge Presented at the Vienna Conference on the Humanitarian Impact of Nuclear Weapons by Austrian Deputy Foreign Minister Michael Linhart', 8–9 December 2014, https://www.bmeia.gv.at/fileadmin/user_upload/Zentrale/Aussenpolitik/Abruestung/HINW14/HINW14_Austrian_Pledge.pdf.

32   See Scott Sagan, *The Limits of Safety: Organizations, Accidents, and Nuclear Weapons* (Princeton, NJ: Princeton University Press, 1995).

33   See Patricia Lewis, Heather Williams and Benoît Pelopidas, 'Too Close for Comfort: Cases of Near Nuclear Use and Options for Policy', Chatham House Report, April 2014.

34   See SIPRI, 'Sipri Yearbook 2019: Armaments, Disarmament and International Security', 2019, especially Part II, chapter 6, 'Overview', https://www.sipriyearbook.org/view/9780198839996/sipri-9780198839996-chapter-6.xml#sipri-9780198839996-chapter-6-div1-033. The costs argument has been frequently employed by ICAN, Greenpeace, the WILPF, the UK's Campaign for Nuclear Disarmament, the International Peace Bureau and more. See, for example, ICAN, 'Enough Is Enough: 2019 Global Nuclear Weapons Spending', May 2020, https://d3n8a8pro7vhmx.cloudfront.net/ican/pages/1549/attachments/original/1589365383/

ICAN-Enough-is-Enough-Global-Nuclear-Weapons-Spending-2020-published-13052020.pdf?1589365383.

35 Mian, 'Beyond the Security Debate: The Moral and Legal Dimensions of Abolition', p. 297.

36 US in the World Initiative, 'Talking About Nuclear Weapons with the Persuadable Middle', 2009, p. 2.

37 Nebel, 'The Nuclear Disarmament Movement: Politics, Potential, and Strategy', p. 239.

38 Harrington, Gheorghe and Fink, 'What Arguments Motivate Citizens to Demand Nuclear Disarmament?', p. 7.

39 See the appendix containing a comprehensive description of our data-collection method and the detailed results of our survey at https://prcprague.cz/s/SVO_Survival_2021_Appendix.zip.

40 World Public Opinion, 'Publics Around the World Favor International Agreement to Eliminate All Nuclear Weapons'; and Simons Foundation, 'Global Public Opinion on Nuclear Weapons', p. 15.

41 See Harrington, Gheorghe and Fink, 'What Arguments Motivate Citizens to Demand Nuclear Disarmament?', p. 7.

42 See Martin W. Bauer et al., 'The Fukushima Accident and Public Perceptions About Nuclear Power Around the Globe: A Challenge and Response Model', *Environmental Communication*, vol. 13, no. 4, 2019, pp. 505–26; and Michael Siegrist, Bernadette Sütterlin and Carmen Keller, 'Why Have Some People Changed Their Attitudes Toward Nuclear Power After the Accident in Fukushima?', *Energy Policy*, vol. 69, June 2014, pp. 356–63.

43 See, for example, Jessica R. Towhey, 'Will HBO's "Chernobyl" Miniseries Impact Perceptions of Nuclear Power?', Inside Sources, 23 June 2019, https://www.insidesources.com/will-hbos-chernobyl-miniseries-impact-perceptions-of-nuclear-power/.

44 Simons Foundation, 'Global Public Opinion on Nuclear Weapons', pp. 5, 6.

45 See Shereen Kotb and Gyung-ho Jeong, 'The US Congress and Rogue States', *Foreign Policy Analysis*, vol. 17, no. 3, July 2021, pp. 1–20.

46 See David S. McDonough, *Nuclear Superiority: The 'New Triad' and the Evolution of Nuclear Strategy*, Adelphi 383 (Abingdon: Routledge for the International Institute for Strategic Studies, 2006); and Michal Smetana, 'A Nuclear Posture Review for the Third Nuclear Age', *Washington Quarterly*, vol. 41, no. 3, 3 July 2018, pp. 137–57.

47 See Tanya Ogilvie-White, 'The Defiant States: The Nuclear Diplomacy of North Korea and Iran', *Nonproliferation Review*, vol. 17, no. 1, 2010, pp. 115–38; and Michal Smetana, *Nuclear Deviance: Stigma Politics and the Rules of the Nonproliferation Game* (London: Palgrave Macmillan, 2020).

48 On the threat from North Korea, see Michael Elleman, 'The Secret to North Korea's ICBM Success', *Survival*, vol. 59, no. 5, October–November 2017, pp. 25–36.

49 See Robert I. Rotberg (ed.), *Worst of the Worst: Dealing with Repressive and Rogue Nations* (Washington DC and Somerville, MA: Brookings Institution Press, 2007); Alexander T.J. Lennon and Camille Eiss, *Reshaping Rogue States: Preemption, Regime Change,*

and US Policy Toward Iran, Iraq, and North Korea (Cambridge, MA: MIT Press, 2004); Klare, *Rogue States and Nuclear Outlaws*; and Homolar, 'Rebels Without a Conscience'.

50 See Kyla J. McEntire, Michele Leiby and Matthew Krain, 'How Combining Framing Strategies Affects Human Rights Micromobilization', *Research & Politics*, vol. 4, no. 2, 2017, pp. 1–11.

51 For critical perspectives on nuclear abolition, see, for example, Thomas C. Schelling, 'A World Without Nuclear Weapons?', *Dædalus*, vol. 138, no. 4, 2009, pp. 124–9; Charles L. Glaser, 'The Flawed Case for Nuclear Disarmament', *Survival*, vol. 40, no. 1, Spring 1998, pp. 112–28; Kenneth N. Waltz, 'Thoughts About Virtual Nuclear Arsenals', *Washington Quarterly*, vol. 20, no. 3, 1997, pp. 153–61; and Nik Hynek and Michal Smetana (eds), *Nuclear Disarmament: Strategic, Political and Regional Perspectives* (Abingdon: Routledge, 2015).

52 Margaret Beckett, 'Keynote Address: A World Free of Nuclear Weapons?', remarks at the Carnegie International Nonproliferation Conference, 25 June 2007, https://carnegieendowment.org/2007/06/25/keynote-address-world-free-of-nuclear-weapons-event-1004.

Copyright © 2021 The International Institute for Strategic Studies

Review Essay

Stranger than Fiction: Imagining Our Climate Future

Ben Barry and Jeffrey Mazo

How to Avoid a Climate Disaster: The Solutions We Have and the Breakthroughs We Need
Bill Gates. London: Allen Lane, 2021. £20.00. 272 pp.

The Ministry for the Future
Kim Stanley Robinson. London and New York: Orbit, 2020. £20.00/$28.00. 576 pp.

> *'Tis strange, but true; for truth is always strange;*
> *Stranger than fiction; if it could be told,*
> *How much would novels gain by the exchange!*
> *How differently the world would men behold!*

> Lord Byron, 'Don Juan', canto 14, stanza 102

In August 2021, the United Nations Intergovernmental Panel on Climate Change (IPCC) issued its sixth and final report on the current and future state of the climate, concluding that the consequences of global warming were 'widespread, rapid and intensifying'.[1] Secretary-General António Guterres called the report a 'code red for humanity. The alarm bells are deafening.'[2] But people could see for themselves: the summer, like many others this century, had already brought unprecedented, sustained heatwaves in many parts of the world. The IPCC reported that such events would only increase in frequency and severity, even if net-zero carbon is achieved by 2050.

Ben Barry is Senior Fellow for Land Warfare at the IISS. **Jeffrey Mazo** is Associate Fellow for Conflict, Security and Development at the IISS.

Survival | vol. 63 no. 6 | December 2021–January 2022 | pp. 201–208 https://doi.org/10.1080/00396338.2021.2006460

In *How to Avoid a Climate Disaster,* American software engineer, business leader and philanthropist Bill Gates discusses why a net-zero world is necessary, and the various technological solutions that could achieve it. He is, by his own admission, late to the party; the philanthropic foundation he set up with his then-wife Melinda in 2000 focused both on education in the United States and on global health and development. But the latter issues intertwine with climate change, and by 2015 he was deeply involved in climate matters, mainly in the promotion of investment in low-carbon technologies.

Much of the book treads old ground. Gates is not an expert in these subjects, although he certainly has the pull to mobilise whatever expertise he needs to understand the issues and inform his quest for solutions. But if there is nothing here that hasn't been said many times before, it certainly needs to be repeated as many times as it takes to fully sink in. Gates's celebrity makes him a useful messenger, even if, as he puts it, 'the world is not exactly lacking in rich men with big ideas about what other people should do, or who think technology can fix every problem' (p. 14).

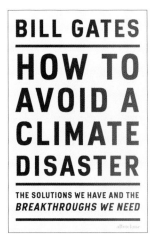

Innovation and disruption

Although the core of the book does deal with opportunities for technological solutions to the problem of reaching net zero, it is in the final three chapters on policymaking and process that Gates's unique background, perspective and insights really come to the fore. He notes that 'a big breakthrough like a new type of battery would be sexier than the policies that led some chemist to invent it' (p. 181). Only an engineer could call a new type of battery sexy, but he is right in arguing that how to innovate is as (or even more) important as what to innovate.

Gates argues that technology, policy and 'markets' (companies, investors, financial markets) work in complementary ways and must be shaped at the same time, and in the same direction, to achieve net zero. Through the historical trajectory of nuclear power, biofuels, and solar and wind power, he shows how failures stem from neglect of one or more of these 'levers', and how successful innovation is possible.

Achieving net zero will, he argues, involve both 'expanding the supply of innovations' and 'accelerating the demand for innovations' (p. 199), a conceptualisation that helps clarify the challenges. For the former, he calls for a fivefold increase in research and development investment over the next decade, going all-in on high-risk, high-reward projects, public–private partnerships and integration of basic and applied research. This is the 'Manhattan Project' model of technological innovation. It will require an effort of political will, but ramping up demand for innovation is even more difficult. Here, government purchasing power, tax and other financial incentives, infrastructure investment and regulatory reform come into their own, but must be integrated so as not to work at cross purposes.

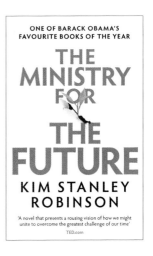

As a key player in the personal-computer revolution, Gates has a lifetime of experience in the transformational role of new technologies, as well as ways to foster innovation. He is thus surely aware that the technological innovations necessary to reach net zero will both entail and generate changes to personal behaviour, society and the economy such that the world in 2050 will be vastly different from today's. More different, in fact, than today's world is from that of 1991, even as that year (with the First Gulf War and the collapse of the Soviet Union) was one of the great post-war inflection points.

Gates admits that 'I think more like an engineer than a political scientist, and I don't have a solution to the politics of climate change' (p. 14). He acknowledges that political barriers need to be overcome – he just doesn't know how. But even the attempt will create tremendous social disruption and unintended consequences, possibly extending to political breakdown, civil unrest and inter-state violence. This is speculative, to be sure, but that is the point. There are a myriad of possible futures, even in a 'business as usual' world, but it is the role of analysts to constrain the range of possibilities.

Warning from the future

Among the many books about potential conflict are fictional portrayals of hypothetical wars. Notable examples include the 1978 novel *The Third World War: August 1985*, a future history of a war between the Warsaw Pact and NATO.[3] General Sir John Hackett and his fellow authors sought to warn that, without an increase in European defence spending, NATO might be defeated by a Soviet attack on Germany. The book was a bestseller, but its intended message on European defence spending was largely lost in the noise.

More recent examples of this small but respectable genre include General Sir Richard Shirreff's 2016 book *2017: War with Russia*, an account of an imaginary conflict between Russia and NATO.[4] Although the scenario involved NATO's new front line and modern military technology, including cyber, the message was much the same as Hackett's. Like its predecessor, it was a bestseller, but also like its predecessor, it had little discernible effect on European or British defence spending.

A notable addition to the genre, involving perhaps an even greater existential threat than a third world war, is Kim Stanley Robinson's *The Ministry for the Future*. Robinson is an American author whose work ranges from history (true or counterfactual) through future history to science fiction (the category into which his work is most frequently pigeonholed). But unlike Hackett and Shirreff, Robinson has the advantage of being a full-time author who writes mainly about the future. His characters are better realised and his plot more rounded, producing a much more readable book.

The novel opens with a graphic account of a severe heatwave in northwest India, with temperatures and humidity reaching levels that kill 20 million Indians too poor to have air conditioning. The harrowing impact on the Indian population is witnessed by a US aid worker. Given various weather events worldwide over the last two years, and the most recent assessment report of the IPCC, this is a highly plausible scenario.

The all-too-predictable climate catastrophe in India leads to the political, diplomatic and economic mandate for the UN to form an office that can take forward the implementation of the 2015 Paris agreement. This 'Ministry for the Future' is able to build on the sense of urgency imparted by the lethal Indian heatwave, as well as a second, even more lethal heatwave in the countries bordering the Persian Gulf that displaces tens of millions of people. It garners credibility and political authority as the representative of the interests of unborn generations. Through a combination of political and economic measures, including the implementation of a carbon currency, it persuades nations and industry to move faster towards net zero. By the end of the book, for example, ships are increasingly propelled by sails, which incorporate modern technology to generate electricity as another source of power. Robinson also portrays the potential strengths and weaknesses of various methods of geo-engineering carbon out of the atmosphere.

Use of force

As the ministry gains strength and impact, an insurgency simultaneously emerges against hydrocarbon consumption, beginning in India where the 'Sons of Kali' rapidly establish a global footprint. They use classic terrorist and guerrilla methods against individuals and industry they consider to be the greatest emitters and therefore climate villains. Many of their attacks make use of advanced technology. Swarms of armed civilian drones, for example, are used to attack executive jets and shipping, and for targeted killings against members of the 'carbon oligarchy', in order to drive away customers and depress share prices. Genetically engineered pathogens are used to attack cattle. This globalised, networked climate insurgency is realistically and credibly portrayed.

The rise of the insurgency is paralleled by the Ministry for the Future's own use of covert force. Early in the story, a deniable and highly secure secret wing for armed action is formed after a short conversation between the ministry head and her deputy. But after its foundation, this direct-action organisation, which uses assassination, sabotage and intimidation, becomes invisible to the reader, who is left to assume that some of the armed action against profligate hydrocarbon-burning individuals and businesses is committed by the ministry's 'black ops' division rather than the insurgents. Whether the two organisations are coordinating their activities is also left to the imagination.

This portrayal of how today's climate emergency might result in violence is one of the novel's most interesting threads. As a great deal of strategic analysis has already shown, the more climate change impacts the weather, resulting in an increasing number of extreme weather events worldwide, the more likely it becomes that intra- and inter-state violence will eventually result. Analysts at the International Institute for Strategic Studies (IISS) have already concluded that climate change is exacerbating conflict in the Sahel and Somalia.[5] What makes this fictional portrayal useful to strategists is the vivid example it offers of how a transnational insurgency against climate change itself might arise, and how it might act.

It also illustrates how a non-violent group might set up a deniable arm's-length organisation that uses violence to further its aims. Organisations have paired overt peaceful action with the covert use of lethal force to further their political aims before: a good example is the African National Congress's armed-action wing established by Nelson Mandela. Scenarios in which nations or international organisations consider themselves so threatened by climate change that they resort to armed action against carbon emitters are all too plausible. They might also occur more quickly than might be imagined. Among the many 'known unknowns' about climate change is the risk of high-impact tipping points that greatly accelerate global warming, such as rapidly warming permafrost releasing large volumes of methane, triggering a self-reinforcing positive-feedback loop, or the collapse of the Atlantic Ocean circulation system as a result of the melting Greenland ice cap, paradoxically leading to freezing conditions in Europe. In such cases, the triggering of violence by climate change would also be accelerated.

*   *   *

There is now a vast body of work about climate change and its potential as a threat multiplier or accelerant of conflict – a 'fifth horseman' of the apocalypse. But few authors present the big picture of how political action, economics and technology might be employed to arrest global warming and establish a sustainable industrial ecosystem for the planet better than Gates and Robinson, in their own ways. *The Ministry for the Future* offers further value through its unique combination of plot, readability, climate literature, and political, economic and technological imagination to illuminate how climate change might give rise to armed action by insurgencies, international organisations and even governments.

Authors of near-future history or science fiction face the risk that their work will be quickly overtaken by events and advances in technology, rendering them dated or even quaint. By 1982, three years before the events portrayed in Hackett's 1978 novel, he was already compelled to write a sequel making the narrative retroactively consistent with actual history – 'retconning', in the parlance of popular culture.[6] Forty years on, our modern geopolitical world is perhaps even stranger than he could have imagined. Robinson's novel is likely to suffer the same fate – whether or not its warning from the future is heeded. The physical course of climate change, not to mention the political, social and cultural responses to it, may resemble Robinson's portrayal in spirit, but not in detail. What the world will look like in 2050 is anybody's guess.

Notes

[1] Intergovernmental Panel on Climate Change, 'Climate Change Widespread, Rapid and Intensifying – IPCC', press release, 9 August 2021, https://www.ipcc.ch/2021/08/09/ar6-wg1-20210809-pr/.

[2] 'Secretary-General's Statement on the IPCC Working Group 1 Report on the Physical Science Basis of the Sixth Assessment', 9 August 2021, https://unfccc.int/news/secretary-general-s-statement-on-the-ipcc-working-group-1-report-on-the-physical-science-basis-of.

[3] John Hackett et al., *The Third World War: August 1985* (London: Sidgwick & Jackson, 1978).

[4] Richard Shirreff, *2017: War with Russia* (London: Coronet, 2016).

[5] See, for example, Shiloh Fetzek and Jeffrey Mazo, 'Climate Change, Scarcity and Conflict', *Survival*, vol. 56, no. 5, August–September 2014, pp. 143–70.

[6] John Hackett et al., *The Third World War: The Untold Story* (London: Sidgwick & Jackson, 1982).

Copyright © 2021 The International Institute for Strategic Studies

Review Essay

Colombia's River of Life and Death

Russell Crandall

Magdalena: River of Dreams
Wade Davis. London: Bodley Head, 2020. £25.00. 401 pp.

> Colombia as a nation is the gift of the river. The Magdalena is the story
> of Colombia.
>
> Wade Davis, *Magdalena*, p. xxii

The waters of the Magdalena River might be called the lifeblood of Colombia. Extending more than 1,500 kilometres from its source in the south of the country to the Caribbean Sea in the north, the river crosses the entire span of Colombia – not an easy feat in a nation twice the size of Texas. It has long been a critical enabler of the country's wealth and has shaped the fortunes of its people, 80% of whom live within the river's massive drainage area.

In his latest opus *Magdalena*, the rightfully storied Canadian travel writer Wade Davis traces the geography of this mighty river and its role in Colombia's history. For Davis, the Magdalena is not just the country's central artery but the reason Colombia 'exists as a nation', the 'lifeline' that permitted Colombians to begin to tame this geographically diverse land (p. xxii). Its significance runs deeper than mere geography, however: much

Russell Crandall is a professor of American foreign policy and international politics at Davidson College in North Carolina, and a contributing editor to *Survival*. His latest books are *Drugs and Thugs: The History and Future of America's War on Drugs* (Yale University Press, 2020) and, with Britta Crandall, *"Our Hemisphere"?: The United States in Latin America, from 1776 to the Twenty-first Century* (Yale University Press, 2021).

Survival | vol. 63 no. 6 | December 2021–January 2022 | pp. 209–220 https://doi.org/10.1080/00396338.2021.2006476

like the Mississippi River in the United States, the Magdalena is 'a corridor of commerce and a foundation of culture', having influenced and fostered Colombia's 'music, literature, poetry, and prayer' (p. xxii).

Magdalena is the result of the author's roughly half-dozen research trips, conducted over five years and in all seasons, in which he explored the river from its mouth on the Atlantic coast to its source way up in the Andes. These trips were not the author's first experience of Colombia: his lifelong love affair with the country began with a school trip in 1968, when Davis was only 14. 'For eight weeks,' he writes, 'I encountered the warmth and decency of a people charged with a strange intensity, a passion for life, and a quiet acceptance of the frailty of the human spirit. Several of the older Canadian students longed for home. I felt as if I had finally found it' (p. xiv).

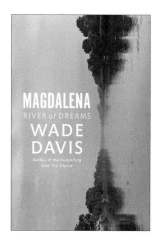

Best of times, worst of times

In 1974, the adventurer returned to Colombia, this time arriving with a one-way ticket, a tattered backpack and copies of George Lawrence's *Taxonomy of Vascular Plants* and, inevitably, Walt Whitman's *Leaves of Grass*. He would embark on an odyssey that was as soul-enlivening as it was body-wracking:

Both figuratively and literally I drank from every stream, even from tire tracks in the road. Naturally I was constantly sick, but even that seemed part of the process, malaria and dysentery fevers growing through the night before breaking with the dawn. Every adventure led to another. Once on a day's notice I set out to traverse the Darién Gap. After nearly a month on the trail, I became lost in the forest for a fortnight without food or shelter. When finally I found my way to safety, I stumbled off a small plane in Panama, drenched in vomit from my fellow passengers, with only the ragged clothes on my back and three dollars to my name. I had never felt so alive. (pp. xiv–xv)

In the ensuing years Davis became an acolyte of legendary botanist Richard Evans Schultes, eventually writing his biography, the seminal

One River, published in 1996. As Davis explains, the tome was meant not just as a tribute to Schultes but as a 'love letter to a nation scorned by the world' for its association with drugs and the crimes of Pablo Escobar (p. xv). When the Spanish translation, *El río*, hit Colombia in 2002, the nation was at one of its many historical nadirs, buckling under the violent conflict between Marxist guerrillas and rightist paramilitaries.

With an initial print run of 500, Davis did not have much hope that many Colombians would read the book. During a visit to Colombia in 2008, however, he was startled to discover that it had taken off, in large part through word of mouth. Far beyond the expected audience of anthropologists and biologists, the book was embraced by 'old and young, men and women, artists, musicians, corporate executives and priests, politicians from across the political spectrum' (p. xv). In the coastal city of Santa Marta, he saw an adolescent reading a beat-up copy, and in a meeting with former defence minister Rafael Pardo he spotted a copy on a desk. Even the sister of Fabio Ochoa Vásquez, a notorious member of the Medellín Cartel, asked if Davis would visit her brother in prison. 'The book, she said, meant a great deal to him' (p. xvi).

Davis concludes that his book resonated so deeply because it depicted Colombia and Colombians 'completely in defiance of the dark clichés' (p. xvi). *Magdalena* continues this work, but without neglecting the country's many struggles and challenges. Through the centuries, the Magdalena has borne witness to the best and worst of Colombia.

Like so much of the New World, what has become the modern country of Colombia has been scarred not just by the weaponry and deities wielded by Europeans, who started arriving in the sixteenth century, but by the dissemination of the 'concentrated essence of death itself': the microbes of diseases such as smallpox (p. 243). After a century and a half of European rule, the once 70-million-strong indigenous population in the Americas had dwindled to 3.5m – a genocide of unspeakable proportions. In the coastal region where the mighty Magdalena pours into the Atlantic, disease and violence slashed the local indigenous population (*los naturales*) from 70,000 to 800 by 1570.

Jumping forward two centuries, Davis shows that the wars for Latin American independence made for strange bedfellows, uniting secular and scientific revolutionaries with blue-blooded, New World-born aristocrats, who were anti-Enlightenment but nonetheless wanted to defeat the monarchy for 'the opportunity to displace the regal regime with themselves, a new privileged class anointed by God and destined to lead a national government faithful always to the clergy, tradition, and the past' (pp. 60–1).

After independence was consolidated in 1819, the insurmountable differences between these two groups became clear, leading to the creation of rival political parties. In the decades that followed, the Liberals and Conservatives – red and blue – each considered the other an existential threat, especially given their shared assumption that whichever party gained power would monopolise the state's capacity for violence. According to Davis, 'the weakness of the federal state, together with a tortuous mountain landscape that hindered transportation and communications, encouraged strong regional identities even as it empowered local strongmen only too willing to exploit this reciprocity of hatred' (p. 61).

Indeed, the Andean nation experienced eight civil wars and more than a dozen provincial rebellions in its first century of existence. In one fleeting but savage episode, the appointment of Conservatives to a top post at the National Library and as envoy to London resulted in a clash between the government and Liberal radicals that killed around 500 people on both sides. La Batalla de la Humareda, as the episode came to be known, took place on a single day in June 1885. The War of a Thousand Days, which commenced in 1899, involved both sides 'hacking each other to death', with 80,000 killed out of a population of only 4m. The conflict pushed the country to the brink of collapse as it destroyed the value of the national currency (the peso), brought about the loss of the province of Panama and caused damages valued at 500% more than the national budget (p. 61). A new era of internecine strife known as La Violencia would begin in 1948, sparked by the assassination of a populist Liberal politician, Jorge Eliécer Gaitán, in Bogotá. The ensuing decade of chaos would result in the deaths of hundreds of thousands of people.

Nation-building, Colombia-style

While the Magdalena and its communities may have been scarred by colonial-era violence, the river was also the primary means by which the colonists began building the 'new' nation – and how they began extracting wealth from it too.

Linking the river to the Colombian hinterland called for unorthodox methods, given the country's challenging terrain. For three centuries after the Spanish conquest, Colombia's imports and exports were carried along treacherous *caminos de arriería* (muleteer roads) 'cut through the forests and carved into the sides of mountains … [that] fell away from the Andean heights to link every town and city to the Río Magdalena' (p. 30). First laid out centuries before the Spanish landed, these roads featured many perils: 'precipitous exposures, mules buried chest-deep in mud, dead oxen along the edge of the trail, often with vultures perched on top' (p. 30). Outsiders wondered how the country could enter the modern era with such an unreliable and primitive transportation system.

Yet it worked. By the middle of the nineteenth century, Bogotá was a bona fide capital city, its museums, universities and bookstores giving it the deserved moniker of the 'Athens of South America'. (Today, Colombian book fairs are some of the largest and most prestigious in the Spanish-speaking world.) In the latter part of the nineteenth century, a huge range of imported items – French champagne and perfume, German construction equipment, English umbrellas – was carried on the backs of mules from Honda (where river navigation commenced) to the fog-shrouded capital city. Any items that were too large or heavy to carry were disassembled and loaded piece by piece. One intrepid *arriero* (muleteer) reportedly delivered a disassembled generator all the way to a remote high-Andean pueblo. 'He was greeted as a hero and toasted upon his arrival with *aguardiente* and cascades of blossoms as the entire community celebrated the arrival of light' (p. 31).

Carried in the other direction were exports destined for the furthest reaches of the globe: tobacco and coffee from the cities of Ambalema and Armenia, gold from the mines of Segovia and almost all of Medellín's industrial output (including the quarter-million Panama hats sent abroad in 1915). 'Everything moved thanks to the strength, skill, and endurance of the *arrieros* and their animals', writes Davis. 'It was a unique culture of the open sky, of men and boys whose home was the ground beneath their feet, and whose moods and passions set them completely apart from ordinary cowboys, or *vaqueros*' (p. 31). Even today the *arrieros* loathe horses: 'Who would want to work with horses, so often petulant, preening, and precious, when an uncomplaining mule is tougher, lives longer, is cheaper to feed, less vulnerable to disease, capable of carrying far greater loads, and, like the men themselves, as solid as the stones that mark the trails that define their lives?' (p. 31).

Love in the time of *vapores*

An especially fascinating aspect of Colombia's river-driven trajectory involves the country's storied *vapores* (steamboats). Alonso Restrepo of Cali – a long-standing acquaintance of Davis – started his job with the Naviera Colombia in the early 1940s, and has never forgotten the excitement of a *vapor* arriving at the port city of El Banco. Davis's imagination gives us a rich sense of what this might have looked like:

> On board might be an orchestra from Bogotá, a band of *costeños* playing *vallenato*, or jazz musicians riffing off the rhythms of Lucho Bermúdez, whose songs were the sound of romance on every journey along 'our mother river,' the Magdalena. On the jetty, there always stood a lone *zambo*, playing a drum or a flute. In the ravine running away from the shore would be dozens of men and women from the *palenques*, all dancing and singing. As long as a vessel was in port, there was a permanent party, with people gathering at all hours beneath the thatch of a great shelter mounted over the concrete slab at portside. There were no rules. The only constants were the rhythms of *vallenato*, *cumbia*, and *tambura* [domestic musical genres]. Sleep was optional. (p. 257)

Drawing upon this abundance of life and energy, Gabriel García Márquez – the magical-realist author described as the 'greatest Colombian who ever lived' by former president Juan Manuel Santos – gave the Magdalena a starring role in two of his greatest novels, *Love in the Time of Cholera* and *The General in His Labyrinth*. Davis explains the towering significance of the river to this genre-defining author: 'All of the themes that informed his work – forgetfulness and love, violence and hope, progress and decadence, fertility and death – are to be found in the eddies and back channels and currents of a river that literally carried him, as a boy, to his destiny, allowing him to enter a world of language and literature where he would discover just what words can do' (p. 330).

For García Márquez, riverboat life proved a treasure trove of stories and characters. He would take 11 extended round-trip voyages on the Magdalena from his home on the coast up to Bogotá. His maiden trip, at the age of 16 in 1943, was on the famously opulent *David Arango*. Davis sets the scene:

> As an orchestra welcomed the passengers and the ship made ready to sail, García Márquez rushed to the highest deck and watched as the lights of the town of Magangué slowly receded in the darkness. Tears filled his eyes, and he remained, as he later recalled, in a state of ecstasy throughout the entire night and, indeed, the entire journey. It took six days to reach Puerto Salgar, where he caught the train for Bogotá. A boy from the coast who had never stood higher than the hood of a truck found himself climbing into the Andes, whistling and wheezing like a struggling *arriero* gasping for air. (p. 332)

Damp, grey, cold – and, for him, lonely – Bogotá came as a shock to García Márquez. Davis writes that 'he longed for heat and home … In his yearning, the Magdalena, a river flowing for over three million years, became the antidote to Bogotá, his lifeline to the coast, where everything was awash in color and passion, where flirtations with parrots and sunbirds were the norm and daily life, as he would later write, was but a pretense for poetry' (p. 332).

García Márquez was to witness the re-emergence of violence in Colombia and the destruction of the riverboat life he so passionately loved. As an infant in 1928, he found himself but a stone's throw away from where the United Fruit Company machine-gunned scores of banana-plantation workers, 'leaving the plaza of Ciénaga blanketed with the dead' (p. 333). As a young man in Bogotá in 1948, his lodging was a block or two from the café where Gaitán was assassinated, plunging the capital into a round of Liberal–Conservative violence that would leave 'generations of Colombians looking over their shoulders in fear, waiting for the moment when death would find them' (p. 333).

In 1961, and now living in Mexico City, García Márquez received the bitter news that the *David Arango*, that venerable vessel of his maiden river trip, had been destroyed in a fire. 'That day', he later wrote, 'ended my youth' (p. 333). The novelist had given up on the Magdalena, which by then had been despoiled by pollution. In his memoir *Living to Tell the Tale*, García Márquez tells the story of two leftist guerrillas on the run from the army who jumped into the river for safety, only to die from its poisons.

River of death

The story of how the Magdalena became polluted is illustrated by Davis's account of his visit to the river city of Barrancabermeja, the petroleum capital of Colombia. In 'Barranca' (as Colombians call it), Davis found a city where pipelines extended in all directions, refineries defined the skyline and 'active wellheads seemed to outnumber the cattle' (p. 223).

Oil had first been discovered locally in 1904, and a refinery was built roughly two decades later. Before that, Barranca's main purpose had been to serve as a refuelling stop for the *vapores* on the way up or down the river. Things would change dramatically after 1920, when the Tropical Oil Company defeated some foreign competitors in a dubious process to gain dominion over more than 1m acres in and around Barranca.

Much like elsewhere in the world, the riches generated by the region's natural resources were a mixed blessing. According to Davis, 'wealth and easy money fomented vice – prostitution, gambling, and drinking – as surely as the concentration and exploitation of labor spun into being a whirlwind of political activism' (p. 224). The situation would only worsen after the discovery of a massive oilfield in 1983, making Barrancabermeja an 'irresistible target' for illicit actors seeking to 'cripple or destroy the nation-state' (p. 224). According to Davis:

> Paramilitaries stalked union leaders and human rights activists in the back alleys of the city, while in distant fields and forests, cadres of the [pro-Cuban guerrilla group] ELN, utterly unconcerned about the implications for the environment and the land, sought ways to damage or destroy the pipelines, which have always been the focus of their revolutionary

zeal. The only traffic on the river were the barges that carried the refined petroleum products to the sea, and the bodies of the dead. (p. 225)

Davis's experience of Barranca reminded me of my own time in the city. In 1997–98, having just completed a master's programme in international relations, I served as a human-rights worker with Catholic Relief Services, an assignment that took me to Barrancabermeja at the very height of its terror. While I spent less than a week there, I will never forget what I saw – and smelled. Months later, having returned to graduate school in the US, I awoke to the news that there had been yet another massacre in Barrancabermeja. I would go on to write for the *Wall Street Journal* that

> such violence has become all too common in Colombia. With over half of the nation's territory believed to be in the hands of either paramilitary groups or left-wing guerrillas, it is no exaggeration to say the country has become ungovernable.
>
> [...]
>
> Over the past year, I worked with a human-rights team in Barrancabermeja and as of today I still do not know if any of my acquaintances were among those killed in last month's massacre. I do, however, remember the words of one local resident when we were visiting a community that had just suffered a paramilitary attack. 'Where is the state? The military? Without them, we live in the wild west and there are many bandits but no sheriff.'[1]

I would later discover that my colleagues had not been killed in the massacre, news which brought only a limited form of relief given that this did not mean any fewer people had been killed. My stay in Barranca may have been brief, but my admiration for the courage of the local activists I met there has lasted a lifetime.

Dealing with drugs

Since the mid-1960s, Colombia's internal war has claimed the lives of 220,000 soldiers, guerrillas and non-combatants, with another 100,000 having simply disappeared. The carnage has only been compounded by Colombia's long association with one of its most famous exports: drugs. From 1996 to 2000, eight Colombians were kidnapped each day; upwards of 5m fled their native land; and 7m people were internally displaced – numbers that have rarely been equalled.

Davis acknowledges that Colombia's drug cartels are a home-grown phenomenon, but writes in *Magdalena*'s preface that the blame for the country's drug violence ultimately rests with 'every person who has ever bought street cocaine and every foreign nation that has made possible the illicit market by prohibiting the drug without curbing its use in any serious way' (p. xvii):

> Imagine how differently the people of the United States would feel about their War on Drugs, not to mention their casual consumption of cocaine in bars and board rooms across the nation, if they knew that as a consequence of both obsessions, no fewer than eighty million fellow Americans would be driven from their homes or forced into exile. (p. xvi)

For Davis, there is no question that insatiable global demand for cocaine fanned the flames of war in Colombia. 'Without the black money, readily taxed, stolen, or siphoned away, the struggle of the leftist guerrillas would have fizzled out decades ago, and the blood-soaked paramilitary forces might never have come into being' (p. xvii).

*   *   *

After 2000, Colombia's military (with US assistance) managed to gain some control, and security improved. The 2016 peace deal between the left-wing Revolutionary Armed Forces of Colombia (FARC) and Bogotá represented a major step towards bringing the internal conflict to an end, although the smaller ELN did not sign the deal, and there have still been episodes of violence.

Nevertheless, many are optimistic about Colombia's future. Davis is especially excited about the legions of well-educated and industrious Colombians once resident in New York, Charlotte, Miami and Madrid who are returning to *la patria* to help rebuild. Colombian exiles aren't the only ones fired up: in 2016, upwards of half the Colombian population took an internal trip – something that had been unimaginable just a few years before. And if Colombia's violent history might be said to have had a silver lining, it could be the way it helped ensure that the country's vast virgin territories were not marred by development, as was the case in Ecuador's Amazon basin, which was 'utterly transformed by oil and gas exploration, colonization, and deforestation', according to Davis (p. xix). He suggests that this accidental conservation may prove to be the country's 'real peace dividend, the opportunity for the nation to consciously and deliberately decide the fate of its greatest asset: the land itself, along with the forests, rivers, lakes, mountains, and streams' (p. xix). Given that the author describes Colombia as 'the repository of fully 10 percent of the terrestrial biological wealth of the entire planet', this is no small asset (p. 227).

At the heart of it all flows the Magdalena, about which Davis is also optimistic. While the river may have experienced some dark times, 'through all the years of the worst of the violence, the Magdalena never abandoned the people. It always flowed. Perhaps … it may finally be time to give back to the river, allowing the Magdalena to be cleansed of all that has soiled its waters' (p. xxii). Colombia's river of life may yet be reborn.

Notes

[1] Russell Crandall, 'Colombia Needs a Stronger Military', *Wall Street Journal*, 12 June 1998.

Copyright © 2021 The International Institute for Strategic Studies

Book Reviews

Counter-terrorism and Intelligence
Jonathan Stevenson

Damascus Station: A Novel
David McCloskey. New York: W. W. Norton & Co., 2021.
$27.95. 419 pp.

There are two basic reasons for someone to read a good spy novel: to enjoy vicarious thrills without risk and to learn about the espionage trade. A third reason is to glean something halfway profound about human nature, but only the rare book that transcends the genre and vaults into the realm of genuine literature – penned by the likes of John le Carré, Graham Greene or Charles McCarry, who have no evident successors – can fulfil that objective. There is a fourth reason: to become smarter about a real-world situation than reading newspapers, magazines or non-fiction books allows. *Damascus Station*, David McCloskey's estimable debut novel, makes that happen with respect to Syria's ongoing civil war. McCloskey knows so much about it because he was a gifted CIA analyst who covered Syria during the critical years of the uprising there that the novel spans: 2011–13, when the Arab Spring was in full flourish.

In essence, the book is about a small cadre of CIA case officers, not quite rogue but getting there, whose primary vocation of collecting intelligence and, if possible, changing facts on the ground becomes intertwined with the occupational hazards of human loss and vengeance. Perhaps the most remarkable aspect of the author's multifaceted effort to tell this story is the penetrating gaze it provides into the dynamics of Syrian President Bashar al-Assad's ruthlessness and the war's political complexity, while evading sanitising redaction by CIA reviewers charged with vetting the manuscript for any impermissible disclosure of sources, methods, tradecraft or sensitive substantive intelligence. Only a

Survival | vol. 63 no. 6 | December 2021–January 2022 | pp. 221–228 https://doi.org/10.1080/00396338.2021.2006470

savvy and judicious insider could have drilled down so deeply and at the same time revealed sufficiently little.

The principal players are Sam Joseph, a CIA case officer, and Mariam Haddad, the Syrian official he recruits as an agent. From a literary standpoint, it is unfortunate that McCloskey employs so many clichés to flesh them out: Joseph is whip-smart and something of a cowboy, Haddad beautiful and passionate. They both know martial arts. They fall in love and grow predictably conflicted in their motivations as a quirky, mission-driven supervisor tries to steer them right. Such unsubtle embellishment only makes the characters two-dimensional, offering readers less to care about. Redeeming dubious writing about personalities, romance and sex, however, is McCloskey's extraordinarily deft integration of the craft of intelligence – including the interplay of human intelligence and ultra-modern technical means, such as satellites and artificial intelligence – with the geopolitics of an extended moment in recent history.

McCloskey draws on several real-life events: Hizbullah's torture and murder of CIA officer William Buckley in 1984; the assassination by car bomb of Imad Mughniyah, Hizbullah's chief of staff, in 2008; Assad's use of chemical weapons on his own people in 2012 and 2013; and the kidnapping of journalist Austin Tice near Damascus in 2012. Compressing the timing of the corresponding notional events into months rather than decades conjures a Syria even more roiling and scabrous than the real one, yet one still grounded in essential truth. Presiding over it is an Assad laser-focused on staying in power and carrying on the minority rule of the Alawites and the suppression of the Sunni majority, answerable not so much to the Russians, Iranians and Hizbullah fighters who have enabled him to remain in power – the main Russian liaison is a blustery drunk – as to the memory of his equally vicious but far courtlier father, Hafez al-Assad. This depiction nicely captures the twisted and imperviously narcissistic sense of destiny that seems to drive many authoritarian rulers, and to inspire terrorism both for and against them. And McCloskey drives home another underappreciated truth: even if the United States has officially disengaged from Syria, agents recruited by the CIA continue to operate there, invisibly and thanklessly, for complicated and often private reasons.

The Happy Traitor: Spies, Lies and Exile in Russia –
The Extraordinary Story of George Blake
Simon Kuper. London: Profile Books, 2021. £14.99. 270 pp.

Traitors are an unavoidable preoccupation of intelligence services, and some stand out more than others for various reasons. For Kim Philby it was his effortless duplicity, for Aldrich Ames his bloodless venality. What set apart

George Blake – the Secret Intelligence Service (SIS) officer who turned while a captive of North Korea in 1953, revealed the CIA's Berlin communications-intercept tunnel to the KGB, burned hundreds of agents of whom some were executed, was imprisoned in the United Kingdom for treason and escaped to the Soviet Union – was the exasperating opacity about his psychological motivations, which he took to his grave last year at age 98. If Simon Kuper had hoped for valedictory candour when he wrangled a three-hour interview with Blake in 2012, Blake essentially reiterated that Marxism made political sense to him and that US military brutality had offended him, eliding Josef Stalin's nearly unsurpassed savagery. Nevertheless, Kuper has written a smooth, substantive and pithy biography that draws judicious but still interesting inferences.

Blake (originally Behar) was born in Rotterdam to a Calvinist mother and a Jewish father, shipped off to relatives in Egypt at age 13 when times were tough, then back to the Netherlands at 16, in 1939. A year later, the Nazis invaded the country. Separated from his family, who had fled to England, he joined the Dutch resistance, evading his German pursuers and finding his way to Scotland. Rating his multivalent and itinerant background assets for a spy, the SIS enlisted him and in time had him recruiting agents to penetrate Soviet and satellite intelligence services. Of course, aspects of the very qualities that made Blake an effective intelligence officer – in particular, an unsteady sense of a homeland – also seemed to make him more susceptible to treason. When held by the North Koreans, 'he was a failed SIS officer, an ex-Dutchman and an ex-Calvinist, a cosmopolitan adrift. He was making up his identity as he went along' (p. 52). It is telling that Philby – a consummate upper-crust Englishman like the rest of the Cambridge Four – never adapted to Soviet life, whereas Blake did, disdaining Philby's self-pitying insularity.

Among Blake's other intriguing revelations, as told by Kuper, is that, despite their ruthlessness and notoriety, the Soviet intelligence services were largely ignored by Soviet leaders. Echoing le Carré – of whom Blake was a fan (pp. 200–1) – Kuper lodges the point with typical wryness: 'We are conditioned to think of the world of espionage as a treasure chest of great secrets. In fact, it is more like a junk shop whose proprietor has lost track of his stock' (p. 119). We are also accustomed to think of traitors and defectors as diabolical and calculating, yet they tend to be just as confused about their motivations as anyone else. Blake himself had a strain of fatuous egotism, and it showed in his conveniently exculpatory 'appeals to determinism' (p. 214). He was, says Kuper, a 'gentle, fascinating, cerebral, cosmopolitan and baffling old man' (p. 218) – and one whom Vladimir Putin eulogised.

Errand into the Wilderness of Mirrors: Religion and the History of the CIA
Michael Graziano. Chicago, IL: University of Chicago Press, 2021. $45.00. 251 pp.

The CIA is sometimes portrayed as a blandly white Anglo-Saxon Protestant (WASP) institution that has largely subordinated religious considerations to more palpable American strategic interests, such as military and economic power. In his sophisticated, fascinating and well-written application of scholarship to practical matters of state, Michael Graziano, an assistant professor of history at the University of Northern Iowa, corrects this view.

His keynote observation is that the agency sprang from the wartime Office of Strategic Services (OSS), which was led by the charismatic William 'Wild Bill' Donovan – an observant and self-identified Catholic war hero and Wall Street lawyer who trained and influenced many of the CIA's first-generation officers. The Catholic Church's permeating mode of social and political influence informed what he called a 'religious approach' to intelligence work (p. 15). During the Second World War, he cultivated operational OSS relationships with American Catholic leaders and with the Vatican itself (including Pope Pius XII). For him – and for the CIA at its inception – religion was a pervasive, cost-free strategic weapon, and its mastery by the intelligence community was essential. Believers of any powerful religion or sect – Christians, Jews, Muslims, Hindus or Buddhists; Catholics or Protestants, Sunnis or Shi'ites – could and should be manipulated in the service of American strategic objectives.

Thus, Donovan embraced a 'generalizable theory of religion, something that could be applied to a variety of people and places around the world' (p. 28) – in other words, the world-religions paradigm. In an important chapter, Graziano notes that, as president, Dwight D. Eisenhower believed that a 'religious factor' in American foreign policy lent American democracy ideological depth and cohesion that was useful in the Cold War. In the mid-1950s, Admiral Arthur Radford, chairman of the Joint Chiefs of Staff, whom Eisenhower respected, proposed an ambitious plan known as 'Militant Liberty' that cast religion and individual freedom as key elements of an expeditionary – and what would now be called 'whole-of-government' – US foreign policy that would mobilise religious forces worldwide to counter Soviet communism and revitalise Western cultural values. Senior CIA officials dismissed Militant Liberty as simplistic, myopic and 'untenable', reflecting 'a protestant evangelical emphasis' that was 'meaningless if not repugnant' in many non-Christian societies. Allen Dulles, then the director of central intelligence, formally rejected the plan, noting that many foreigners would 'deeply resent' the 'implication that our particular formulations of "liberty" constituted universal values' (pp. 88–9).

Somehow this sophistication was lost. During much of the Cold War, the CIA cynically co-opted anti-communist Catholic and other religious institutions and leaders in oppressing left-wing revolutionaries – notably in Latin America, where it sought to suppress the burgeoning 'liberation theology' movement, and in Southeast Asia, where Edward Lansdale advocated 'spiritual aid' (p. 137) to fuel counter-insurgency. These efforts had the weakness of 'rendering foreign cultures understandable only through the terms of your own' (p. 151), producing a blinkered brand of Orientalism that backfired emphatically with respect to Iran in 1979. This prompted a more nuanced CIA appreciation of religion, including the different sects of Islam and liberation theology versus Catholic orthodoxy. Graziano's fine study stops at the end of the Cold War. But given the US intelligence community's chequered record in the campaign against Islamic extremism and jihadist terrorism, the cycles of insight and obtuseness illuminated in his study may have continued over the past 20 years.

Hate in the Homeland: The New Global Far Right
Cynthia Miller-Idriss. Princeton, NJ: Princeton University Press, 2020. £25.00/$29.95. 263 pp.

American Zealots: Inside Right-wing Domestic Terrorism
Arie Perliger. New York: Columbia University Press, 2020. £22.00/$28.00. 225 pp.

Alt-right Gangs: A Hazy Shade of White
Shannon E. Reid and Matthew Valasik. Oakland, CA: University of California Press, 2020. £24.00/$29.95. 201 pp.

Kathleen Belew's *Bring the War Home: The White Power Movement and Paramilitary America*, published in 2018, remains the leading work on right-wing extremism in America. But in light of the 6 January 2021 insurrection at the US Capitol and the apparent persistence of Trumpism and right-wing groups, she could use help.

In *Hate in the Homeland*, Cynthia Miller-Idriss answers where and when, as well as why and how, radicalisation occurs. This takes her pacey, fact-rich inquiry to 'cultural spaces like far-right coffee shops, pop and country music, clothing brands, fight and fitness clubs and the mixed martial arts (MMA) scene, schools and college campuses, social media and online spaces, clubs and soccer stadiums, and spaces and places specific to microcommunities that overlap with far-right extremist groups, from evangelical churches to doomsday prepper communities and gun shows' (pp. 2–3). She details how the message is mainstreamed and normalised – that is, projected from those spaces, most powerfully via the internet and transnationally into larger society, through political speech about immigration and globalisation, conspiracy theories such as 'Pizzagate' and the George Soros-funded migrant caravan, and the retailing of extremist aesthetics. The latter have become subtler, as ostensibly typical accessories such as hoodies and T-shirts, but with coded references, have replaced the traditional neo-Nazi markers of shaved heads, high-top black combat boots and bomber jackets. Indeed, the far-right, anti-government 'Boogaloo Bois' have co-opted the Hawaiian shirt, once merely associated with plain-vanilla American leisure.

In the final chapter of her galvanisingly urgent book, Miller-Idriss asks a daunting but vital question: 'What would it take to ensure that everyone feels at home in the country where they live?' (p. 161). She is too wise to issue a pat answer, but sensibly points out that 'innovative, flexible, and youth-driven ideas' (p. 166) need to be planted precisely where far-right ideologies are now proliferating, and that such an effort – undertaken with considerable success in Germany since the Nazi era – calls for an integrated national approach extending well beyond traditional law enforcement.

Complementing Miller-Idriss's systemic treatment, Shannon Reid and Matthew Valasik's *Alt-right Gangs* and Arie Perliger's *American Zealots* scrutinise particular groups and types of groups, respectively. Charts, tables and graphs abound in Perliger's book – he is a criminologist – but he does not substitute them for analysis, providing lucid explanations of their significance. He offers a useful ideological typology of the American far right, noting that the differences are key to countering extremism insofar as they correspond to 'distinct organizational structures and modi operandi' (p. 29). He also takes a granular look, informed by statistics, at right-wing group composition and tactics. One particularly discomfiting observation is that the involvement of veterans and law-enforcement personnel in extremist groups affords them apparent legitimacy and mitigates public hostility towards them, even if they attack high-value symbolic targets. Another is that the democratic process, customarily considered a mechanism for discouraging political violence, has lately encouraged it. Perliger too ends his cogent dissection with the admonition that there is 'no silver bullet' to the right-wing terrorism problem, and that 'a multitude of measures on the state, communal, and individual levels' are required (pp. 159–60).

Reid and Valasik focus on the street-level youth groups that sometimes feed larger extremist organisations but that they consider a distinct phenomenon. While their study can be densely academic, it is also well organised and tightly conceptualised – presenting, for example, clarifying myth-versus-reality analyses and a trenchant 'focus box' on the Proud Boys. The authors echo Miller-Idriss and Perliger in calling for counter-extremism strategies that 'extend beyond suppression-based efforts' into the realm of proactive intervention (p. 131). On this crucial point, at least, there appears to be scholarly consensus.

The Bureau (French TV series)
Éric Rochant, writer and director (with others). Originally
released on Canal+. Distributed by Federation Entertainment
and Kino Lorber.

Credible spy stories are subtle and protracted, so it is difficult to spin them out in discrete episodes. As a result, there have been few dramatic TV series of high quality concerning espionage. For decades, the gold standard has been the BBC's 1979 miniseries of le Carré's novel *Tinker Tailor Soldier Spy*. The French series *The Bureau*, comprising 50 episodes, has arguably equalled it. Based on accounts of actual intelligence officers, it involves a small, elite unit within France's Directorate-General for External Security known as the 'Bureau of Legends', which out of its Paris headquarters runs long-term operations of potentially strategic significance through deep-cover agents-in-place. Over the course of the series' five seasons, the locales visited by bureau officers include Syria, Algeria, Georgia, Iran, Mali, Iraq, Turkey, Azerbaijan, Libya, Egypt, Ukraine, Yemen, Saudi Arabia, Jordan, Cambodia and, momentously, Russia, in roughly that order.

As this itinerary might hint, the show is a dazzling feat of narrative flow and integration. It revolves around a crack operative named Guillaume Debailly, played with preternatural comprehension by the vulpine Mathieu Kassovitz. In line with the anti-heroic cast of the cloak-and-dagger set, 'Malotru' – the codename of this nonpareil spy – means 'the lout'. He is indeed a beguiling figure, alternately seductive and repellent, devoted and treacherous, judicious and reckless, yet always stoical, brave and calculatedly enigmatic. He returns to Paris from Damascus after six years undercover, still in love with a Syrian woman, and triggers the effective cleavage of the bureau between the ethically rigid followers of director Henri Duflot (the marvellous Jean-Pierre Darroussin), a noble mensch who seems a little out of place, and more flexible types enamoured with Debailly, who better fits the spymaster profile precisely because he is shady and duplicitous. Suffice it to say that it takes a while for the unit to find equilibrium, if it ever does. A persistent if understated thrum of institutional jeopardy runs through it, reflecting the psychic toll of deception and risk as a way of life. The bureau's director, Mathieu Amalric's toxically paranoid Jean-Jacques Angel – reportedly based on the infamous CIA counter-intelligence chief James Jesus Angleton – nearly runs it aground.

Seamlessly reflected in bureau operations, and never clunkily framed in exposition, are France's geopolitical self-image and its essentially Gaullist way of being a great power. The organisation seeks to keep its own counsel and operate with substantial independence, but it is aware of its finite resources compared with, say, the CIA's. So it channels what it has into strategically ambitious efforts. These do attract the interest of other services, ensuring that the bureau will not be free from the CIA's insinuations, whether through double agents or more direct approaches. This is a very different kind of relationship than the one the British SIS has had with the United States, but it is still special in its own way – one of many substantially real-world subtleties magisterially registered by this superior television series.

United States
David C. Unger

The Walls Within: The Politics of Immigration in Modern America
Sarah R. Coleman. Princeton, NJ: Princeton University Press, 2021. £28.00/$35.00. 248 pp.

American attitudes towards immigration have changed greatly over the past half-century, with profound consequences for the legally recognised rights of all immigrants, including those who are authorised to be in the United States and those who are not. The ways in which changing attitudes were translated into new legislation and court precedents were shaped by both the Republican and Democratic parties and all three branches of government, and affected a wide range of public-services entitlements – from schools to Medicaid to social-security disability payments. These legal changes reduced benefits and narrowed eligibility not just for immigrants but also for native-born citizens through the workings of 'welfare reform'.

Because the changes have taken place incrementally over decades, with short-lived detours in one direction or the other, it has been hard even for those who lived through the process to gain a clear sense of the larger picture. In *The Walls Within,* Sarah R. Coleman, who teaches American history at Texas State University, documents the details in ways that clarify the larger whole. This painstaking methodology can at times seem a bit tedious. Despite, or more likely thanks to, these stretches of hard slogging, the reader gains a much fuller understanding of what has been happening, and is still happening today.

Coleman begins her history with the landmark immigration reform of 1965 (the Hart–Celler Act), which replaced the restrictive national-origin quota system enacted in the 1920s – a system that aimed to sharply reduce the massive Southern and Eastern European immigration that characterised the decades before the First World War, and to encourage immigration from Northwestern Europe instead. The Act promised a more generous, egalitarian system. But while it provided new opportunities for legal immigration from Asia and Africa, it capped, for the first time, the number of legal immigrants from the Western Hemisphere. Intentionally or not, this liberally minded legislative change fuelled decades of public controversy over the rights, status and fiscal burdens of what soon became millions of unauthorised immigrants, mainly of Mexican and Central American origin.

Coleman's book guides the reader through the presidencies of Jimmy Carter, Ronald Reagan, George H.W. Bush and Bill Clinton, showing how each tried to manage shifting political pressures from below, including court victories won by pro-immigrant groups but especially pressures from key constituencies in their respective political parties. In the case of the Democrats, that meant satisfying both unions and Hispanic voters, even though these two constituencies often pushed in opposite directions. For Republicans, the competing pressures came from employers of immigrant labour on the one side and rank-and-file conservative voters on the other, who saw immigration as a cultural, economic and criminal threat to the United States. The worsening economic, employment and income-distribution environment of recent decades significantly heightened these fears. In this context, immigrants were increasingly perceived as low-wage job-stealers.

Nevertheless, as Coleman's narrative shows, it was not simply a question of pro-immigration Democrats versus anti-immigration Republicans, at least not during the late twentieth century. Thus, while Reagan's immigration policies were more restrictive than Carter's, they were less so than Clinton's. Each president was, in turn, more focused on what his pollsters told him would play best in the next midterm or presidential election than on any ideological belief about the pros and cons of immigration.

Cry Havoc: Charlottesville and American Democracy Under Siege
Michael Signer. New York: PublicAffairs, 2020. $17.99. 400 pp.

Michael Signer was mayor of Charlottesville, Virginia, during the violent 'Unite the Right' rally that took place there in August 2017. In this book, he gives a month-by-month account of his two-year mayoral term, which began in January 2016. Preparations for and fallout from the Unite the Right rally dominate the narrative, especially for 2017. But there is enough discussion of other local issues such as housing, redevelopment and interactions among full-time city officials, elected city-council members and the general public to provide useful perspective.

Signer believes that the deadly clashes in 2017 could have been avoided, or at least better contained. He sees plenty of blame to go around. As he tells it, right-wing militias, the primary instigators, and left-wing counter-protesters might have been successfully kept apart had not perverse court decisions, poor policing strategies, inept political decision-making and inappropriate governance structures paralysed the Charlottesville city government's response. Signer accepts a share of the blame himself, though he fails to appreciate how much his own self-righteous pronouncements and go-it-alone political style contributed to the overall failure.

The chief villains of Signer's story are the white-nationalist leader (and University of Virginia graduate) Richard Spencer and the Charlottesville native who founded Unite the Right, Jason Kessler. Counter-protesters determined to answer alt-right violence with 'antifa' violence added to the combustible atmosphere, especially when the police failed to keep the two groups well separated. Signer also assigns a large share of the blame to the city-manager form of government, a Progressive Era reform that, in this case, left Charlottesville's elected officials powerless to supervise policing strategies or to decide on whether to grant Spencer and Kessler permits for their rallies.

Another major factor, according to Signer, is the current state of First Amendment law as defined by the Supreme Court, which prohibits any 'content-related' restrictions on speech or demonstrations, even if the content in question includes preparations for or incitements to violence. The issue of where to draw the line between respecting controversial political speech and protecting public order has divided Supreme Court justices for at least the past 70 years. Signer, a practising attorney, knows exactly where he stands on this issue: with Justice Robert Jackson, who argued in a famous 1949 dissent that the Bill of Rights should not be converted into a 'suicide pact'. The author has no patience with civil-liberties groups that take the other side. His arguments on this issue are well grounded and deserve respect.

More problematic is Signer's demonstrated lack of the basic skills elected officials normally need to successfully navigate crises and sharp political differences among their constituents, such as coalition-building and an instinct for give and take. While many of his ideas for improving the city had merit, Signer frequently sabotaged their chances through his impetuousness, self-righteousness or defensiveness. Stellar academics and lawyers do not necessarily make stellar mayors.

Our Founders' Warning: The Age of Reason Meets the Age of Trump
Strobe Talbott. Washington DC: Brookings Institution Press, 2020. $24.99. 240 pp.

Strobe Talbott sets out to demonstrate that Donald Trump's presidency represented the antithesis of the Enlightenment ideals expounded by America's Founding Fathers. He is surely right. Talbott also points out that Trump's political style exemplifies the kind of demagogic threat some of those founders explicitly warned against. Right again. But, to put it bluntly, so what?

Talbott is a noted journalist, diplomat and public intellectual. Though not a professional historian, he is well versed in America's founding traditions. His account of the intellectual lineage behind the founders' ideas is well grounded, gracefully written and illuminating. But readers of *Our Founders' Warning* may well ask how relevant eighteenth-century ideals are to the twenty-first-century configurations of American power.

Trump was scarcely the first American president to defiantly cast aside Enlightenment ideals. Talbott's catalogue of founders, like those of most historians, ends with John Quincy Adams, America's sixth president. His successor, Andrew Jackson, represented a clear, deliberate rupture with Enlightenment traditions, marked by his open championing of 'spoils system' patronage, his proud defiance of constitutional checks and balances, his willingness to fan sectionalist divisions and his blatant contempt for the good opinion of other nations. That was almost two centuries ago.

Trump's outlandish ways represent a clear rupture with the more recent past. But any attempt to situate Trumpism in American history needs a broader frame than that of Enlightenment lost. The angry public disaffection with liberal governance that Trump rode to power has its own historical lineage, reaching back at least as far as the social turmoil and policy failures of the 1960s and 1970s, and the resulting popular backlash against technocratic liberalism. Trumpism draws on much deeper roots in American history, such as the white-supremacist reaction that has shaped and deformed Southern, and to a lesser extent national, politics since the end of Reconstruction. It also draws on a long-standing strain of popular anti-immigrant attitudes that emerged during the Know Nothing politics of the 1840s and 1850s.

Talbott's warning that Trumpism poses an urgent, serious challenge to liberal-democratic and constitutional governance in America is timely and compelling, but Trumpism cannot fairly be portrayed as a singular phenomenon that stands in contradiction to the whole of American history. It is not so much an exotic ideology that has come from nowhere to distort contemporary American politics, but the latest recurrence of a long-standing, malevolent counter-tradition. Arguments based on Trump's contrast with the Founding Fathers will not be enough to exorcise this dangerous and home-grown spectre.

Post-Cold War Revelations and the American Communist Party: Citizens, Revolutionaries, and Spies
Vernon L. Pedersen, James G. Ryan and Katherine A.S. Sibley, eds. London: Bloomsbury Academic, 2021. £85.00. 272 pp.

Histories of American communism have generally fallen into one of two broad schools. Anti-communist histories focus on the Kremlin's countless manipulations of the American Communist Party to serve the unsavoury ends of Soviet foreign policy, Soviet espionage and Josef Stalin's intra-party vendettas. This ugly story certainly warrants repeated retelling in all its repellent details, but anti-communist histories often ignore another relevant consideration: many, if not most, party members joined to advance sincerely held pro-labour, anti-racist and anti-fascist convictions, and in a great many cases they succeeded in advancing these progressive causes through their party work. This story too is an integral part of the history of American communism. Neither this second story nor the first, nor the implicit tension between them, is adequately explained by histories that belong to the other main school of American communist historiography, which typically limits itself to hagiographic celebrations and memoirs of heroic struggles and anti-communist persecutions.

In other words, neither school does justice to the real-life contradictions and complexities of the subject matter. The animating narrative of Soviet manipulations, crimes and abrupt ideological flip-flops needs to be retold in ways that account for the genuine pro-labour, anti-racist and anti-fascist convictions and activities that made up the daily political life of party members. The inspirational stories of Congress of Industrial Organizations (CIO) organisers, Scottsboro Boys defenders and Abraham Lincoln Brigade volunteers need to be retold in ways that do not airbrush Soviet deviousness and the bloody Stalinist crimes for which individual party members allowed themselves to become shameless agents and apologists.

The ten essays in this cumbersomely titled book were written by participants in a 2018 conference at Williams College, MA, hosted by members of the Historians of American Communism to mark the 25th anniversary of the opening of the Soviet archives. Because the US Communist Party repeatedly destroyed its own archives or sent them to Moscow for safekeeping, these archives are essential to historians seeking a complete understanding of American communism.

Some of the essays in this volume, such as Edward P. Johanningsmeier's chapter on the radicalism of William Z. Foster and William C. Pratt's on the history of communist relations with American farmers, come close to achieving a balanced retelling. Others, such as Vernon L. Pedersen's chapter on the deliberate mythification of the Abraham Lincoln Brigade's role in the Spanish Civil War and Erik S. McDuffie's on the black left feminism of Claudia Jones, fall into familiar pitfalls of the two old schools. Denise Lynn's feminist analysis of the friendships of a disappeared communist, Juliet Stuart Poyntz, experiments with a newer, more promising approach, but produces few new insights.

Further archival research and greater historical perspective may yet produce a more satisfying treatment of this still incompletely understood chapter of twentieth-century American history.

After Nationalism: Being American in an Age of Division
Samuel Goldman. Philadelphia, PA: University of Pennsylvania
Press, 2021. $24.95. 148 pp.

Writers have formulated American nationalist narratives since the earliest days of the republic. One early version sought to portray latter-day Americans as spiritual heirs of the Pilgrim Fathers. Even today, children are taught familiar fictions about that first Thanksgiving in Massachusetts Bay Colony, while politicians win plaudits by invoking John Winthrop's Puritan-inspired vision of a 'shining city on a hill'. Such narratives seem to imply that white Anglo-Saxon Protestant (WASP) New Englanders exemplify 'real' Americans, while other groups can only qualify by emulating them. This is, of course, factually preposterous in a diverse land settled by immigrants, and culturally insulting to most contemporary Americans.

Later narratives have sought to acknowledge the reality of ethnic diversity by replacing normative religious and ethnic conformity with a new ideological conformity built around the idea of a supposed 'American Creed' dating back to the inspiring words of Thomas Jefferson and other Founding Fathers. Belatedly acknowledged truths of American history have made this narrative untenable as well. Inspiring quotations about universal, God-given rights to equality, liberty and justice cannot wipe away decades of forced removals of the continent's original inhabitants before and after independence; the slave-labour-based fortunes of the 'Virginia dynasty' that ruled and shaped the United States for most of its first 50 years; or the political dispossession of women for 150 years prior to the adoption of the 19th Amendment, and the economic and social discrimination they continue to endure.

Undaunted, nationalists have kept trying. Early-twentieth-century writers celebrated the so-called 'melting pot', in which immigrants from diverse foreign lands were supposedly fused into a newly homogenised race of Americans. This at least acknowledged America's immigrant roots, if not the legitimacy of the cultural heritages those immigrants brought with them. The melting pot was supposed to dissolve immigrant 'otherness' and assimilate the newly arrived to what amounted to an enhanced version of the pre-existing WASP culture. The later, pluralist narrative of the Cold War years went further towards acknowledging and accepting immigrant diversity, at least for white Americans, while the twenty-first-century narrative of multiculturalism actively celebrated almost all forms of diversity and otherness. But the multiculturalist narrative is arguably not nationalist at all.

None of these successive constructs adequately describes today's diverse and divided America. So it is no surprise that Samuel Goldman, who teaches political science at the George Washington University, sets out in this short book to imagine what might come after nationalism. His quest seems even more relevant after four years of the comic-book parody of nationalism that shaped Donald Trump's rhetoric of 'America First' and 'Make America Great Again'.

Goldman is content to muse and analyse rather than propose any post-nationalist synthesis of his own. Perhaps, at this fraught moment in American history, any such proposal would seem forced. By forgoing one, Goldman leaves readers enlightened and stimulated, but perhaps also disappointed. Surveying and critiquing the long history of American nationalism will have to suffice. That in itself is no small achievement.

Europe
Hanns W. Maull

Future War and the Defence of Europe
John R. Allen, Frederick Ben Hodges and Julian Lindley-French. Oxford: Oxford University Press, 2021. £25.00. 326 pp.

Coalition of the unWilling and unAble: European Realignment and the Future of American Geopolitics
John R. Deni. Ann Arbor, MI: University of Michigan Press, 2021. $75.00. 274 pp.

The European Union and the Use of Force
Julia Schmidt. Leiden: Brill, 2020. €160.00/$192.00. 360 pp.

Future War and the Defence of Europe is a hard-hitting, compelling analysis that relentlessly hammers home its central message: contrary to what the vast majority of European elites and citizens seem to think, war in Europe is no longer inconceivable, and will become even less so if Europe and the United States continue to sleepwalk away from NATO's commitment to collective defence in Europe. The authors – Julian Lindley-French, one of Europe's leading strategists, and two American ex-generals, one of them (John Allen) a former commander of American and NATO forces in Afghanistan and now president of the Brookings Institution, the other (Frederick Ben Hodges) the former commanding general of the US Army Europe – bookend their argument with two scenarios for a 2030 war in Europe. The first scenario sees NATO fail dramatically to meet the challenge to European security. The optimistic variant of the same scenario at the end of the book postulates sustained (and rather heroic) political efforts by European and American governments to catch up with the massive military build-ups and innovations of their potential adversaries, Russia and China, and with the risks accumulating in the continent's fragile southern neighbourhood.

The argument builds on a sophisticated analysis of technological developments in warfare, and of the threats and risks facing Europe on its northern and eastern flanks (Russia) and to the south (fragile states, Islamist terrorism, migration). On that basis, it then spells out in considerable detail what would need to happen within NATO to close the gap between security needs and security postures, in the US but above all in Europe. The authors are particularly worried about the impact of COVID-19 on European efforts to defend themselves against not only human-security threats but also military ones, as well as the implications of the pandemic for an already tense and shifting global balance of power. In their analysis of the future of warfare, they paint a vivid picture of how technological innovation is rapidly transforming the characteristics of war to produce what they call 'hyperwar' – a form of warfare that will prioritise speed and information management over destructive power, and even offer weaker powers opportunities to coerce bigger ones. NATO must prepare itself for hyperwar contingencies across the whole spectrum of threats and risks, from subversive hybrid-warfare activities within allied countries to military attacks from outside, including possible nuclear strikes.

To defend themselves effectively, according to the authors, NATO members need to 'enable a new and effective model of comprehensive security' (p. 270), 'strike a new balance between military power projection ... [and] enhanced people protection' (p. 271) and 'engage Russia with both defensive strength ... and sustained dialogue' (p. 271). They quote Edward Hallet Carr's *The Twenty Years' Crisis, 1919–1939* to sum up their position: 'we know that peaceful change can only be achieved through a compromise between the utopian concept of a common feeling of right and the realist conception of a mechanical adjustment to a changed equilibrium of force' (p. 271). That equilibrium is again changing rapidly, in Europe and East Asia. Europeans, in particular, will need to take a long, hard look at their defence, fundamentally rethink their optimistic assumptions about their security, and be prepared to spend much more not only on their military forces, but also on infrastructure resilience and efforts to encourage innovations in military technology within Europe. Europeans in particular, but also NATO governments overall, will also have to organise and integrate their forces much more effectively than they do today. If they fail to do so, American security guarantees for European allies will look increasingly shaky, and the ability of NATO members' national forces to cooperate effectively will be undermined by a growing gap in deployed technologies. The 'ultimate paradox' (p. 273) of an effective NATO defence of Europe is that the Europeans will need to become much more strategically autonomous to support America's ability to ensure the viability of NATO's collective-defence efforts in the future. This book, which would have benefitted from tighter editing to avoid redundancies and reduce excess text, is nevertheless an important wake-up call for Europeans that should be read widely and closely.

John R. Deni's *Coalition of the unWilling and unAble* also starts with a scenario, though one focused on turmoil in South Asia. A nuclear war with India leads to the break-up of Pakistan, an event that produces a vast humanitarian catastrophe requiring a major international military intervention under the auspices of the United Nations. This force is led and largely manned by the United States. As in the past, Washington looks for support from its European allies in this contingency, but as the book's title suggests, by 2030 Deni expects that those allies will no longer be willing or able to offer succour.

Deni's choice of scenario is unfortunate: his real message is not only about power projection in NATO's periphery, but also about its central mission of collective defence, two strands that are entangled throughout the argument. Yet the message is clear, and it corroborates that of Allen, Hodges and Lindley-French. As Deni's detailed assessment of extant trends in France, Germany, Italy, Poland and the UK shows, in all these major European allies, underlying economic and demographic trends are likely to hollow out military capabilities or, where this is less of a problem (as in Germany and Poland), defence postures may preclude the deployment of significant capabilities to support US missions beyond the NATO realm.

Deni is rather optimistic about Germany, however, where he sees not only solid foundations for future economic growth, but also, in the longer run, a shift towards a more permissive strategic culture that by 2030 could make Germany America's most important ally in missions requiring power projection beyond the geographic confines of the Alliance. France and Britain, on the other hand, are, in the author's view, likely to lose their erstwhile importance as US allies as a consequence of their persistent (France) or mounting (post-Brexit Britain) domestic economic and social problems. Italy seems to be even worse placed than Britain or France to prove a reliable US ally, while Deni is relatively optimistic about the economic prospects of Poland. Nevertheless, he assumes, plausibly, that Poland's military posture will remain firmly focused on the Russian threat and thus on territorial defence. This would preclude the development of significant capabilities for power projection.

Deni's inquiry into the ability and willingness of America's European allies to step up tends to concentrate on what used to be called out-of-area missions, while Allen, Hodges and Lindley-French focus on the central challenges to NATO's collective-defence function. The findings of the two studies are very similar, however: both conclude that the Alliance, and in particular its core European members, are badly prepared to meet future security challenges. The books arrive at this worrying conclusion from somewhat different directions – whereas Allen, Hodges and Lindley-French emphasise policy deficiencies that in their view can and should be corrected, Deni focuses on underlying economic and demographic trends that sometimes assume an almost tragic inevitability in his narrative. For him, the lessons of, and solutions to, the declining ability and willingness of European allies to support the United States in the pursuit of common purposes need to be drawn and implemented mostly by Washington. The book makes a number of useful suggestions concerning what the Americans could do to encourage and empower their European allies.

The title of Julia Schmidt's book, *The European Union and the Use of Force*, could suggest that it too might help us to understand Europe's security predicament. In fact, her study serves a rather different purpose by assessing the European Union's Common Security and Defence Policy (CSDP) from a legal perspective. More specifically, the author seeks to clarify two aspects of the CSDP's legal context: firstly, the policy's gradual but persistent progress towards political integration; and secondly, the opportunities and constraints faced by the CSDP under international law. The 'emerging signs of European integration in the CSDP' (p. 100) that Schmidt meticulously documents nevertheless remain quite limited; member states so far have resolutely blocked any serious efforts to allow the CSDP to constrain them 'in the conduct of their remaining foreign policy competences' (p. 312), according to the author. Whenever member states have been divided, the EU therefore has been bad at crisis management – but, one might add, even where they have been united, there has often been a lack of ambition. As Schmidt notes, while the EU claims the right to conduct military operations for purposes related to the United Nations' 'Responsibility to Protect' (R2P) doctrine, it has yet to do so.

International law constrains the EU's use of force. It is not an actor recognised by the UN Charter (though it is nevertheless bound by the charter's interdiction of the use of force), nor does it qualify under the charter as a regional organisation. Yet the CSDP can, under certain circumstances, also assume a role in implementing UN peacekeeping, or even peacemaking, decisions. Here, Schmidt's conclusion is that the EU 'seems to have established itself as a confident but not always as a reliable partner of the UN' (p. 310) – one of the rather few instances in her analysis where the deficiencies of the CSDP in terms of its capabilities, ambitions and performance become apparent.

Germany's Role in European Russia Policy: A New German Power?
Liana Fix. Cham: Palgrave Macmillan, 2021. £79.99. 246 pp.

In August 2021, German chancellor Angela Merkel undertook two trips, to Moscow and Kyiv. Undertaken in the run-up to her departure from office later that year, the separate journeys, which occurred within three days of each other, underlined the ambivalences in Germany's policies towards Eastern Europe – policies that try to straddle the increasingly tense and conflictual relationship not only between Russia and Ukraine, but between Russia and the EU over what the former calls its 'near abroad' and the latter its 'Eastern neighbourhood'. Not coincidentally, EU policies towards Russia are marked by a similar ambivalence. As Liana Fix shows in her excellent study of Germany's role in Europe's Russia policy during the period from EU enlargement in 2004 to 2019, Berlin dominated and significantly shaped those policies throughout that period, 'partly along, partly against the interests of new Eastern member states' (p. 158). This dominance built on Germany's traditionally close relationship with Russia, and thus on old bonds that survived and transcended, but also were profoundly shaped by, the horrors of the Second World War and the decades of Soviet occupation and control of East Germany.

So how exactly should one describe the role of Germany in European policies towards Russia – is 'leadership' a fitting term, or perhaps even 'hegemony'? On the basis of her four carefully researched case studies (EU policies towards the Russian–Georgian war in 2008; the 2010 EU–Russia Partnership for Modernisation; the 2010 Meseberg Initiative; and the EU reaction to the Russia–Ukraine conflict in 2014), Fix argues that Berlin's influence on Europe's Russia policies falls somewhere in between these labels. While Germany persistently attempted to shape the EU's policies towards Russia in line with its own preferences, and was able to do so more than any other member state, it did so in different ways (as junior partner in 2008, as agenda-setter and deal-maker in 2010, and as the leading power in 2014) and with varying degrees of success. Thus, Berlin, while providing steadfast leadership throughout, could not dominate Europe's Russia policies.

While Germany usually strove to embed its policies towards Russia in a European context, this was, as Fix shows, less the 'Europeanization' of Germany's Russia policy than the 'Germanification' of the EU's relationship with Russia (p. 159). At the same time, Berlin tried to keep its economic relations with Russia strictly bilateral, with the profoundly problematic and heavily contested Nord Stream 2 pipeline deal serving as a powerful manifestation and symbol of this German bilateralism. Efforts to keep Europe out of Nord Stream 2 ultimately failed, with the European Commission weighing in to bring the pipeline under its regulatory authority – the only instance, as Fix notes, where Germany experienced the Europeanisation of its relationship with Russia against its own wishes. Yet the pipeline will be completed, despite the objections of Eastern European member states and the US, thus extending the ambiguity at the heart of Germany's policies towards Russia into the future.

Project Europe: A History
Kiran Klaus Patel. Meredith Dale, trans. Cambridge: Cambridge
University Press, 2020. £19.99. 379 pp.

In 2012, the EU received the Nobel Peace Prize. The Nobel committee awarded the prize because the EU had 'over six decades contributed to the advancement of peace and reconciliation, democracy and human rights in Europe'. In his critical history of 'Project Europe', originally published in German in 2018, Kiran Klaus Patel begs to differ, if not to disagree, with the committee's view. As he shows in this important book, the conventional wisdom on European integration suffers from an 'exaggerated self-image' and several foundational myths that obscure a more complicated reality. Thus, Patel concludes that the European Community's/European Union's contribution to international peace was rather marginal during the 1950s and 1960s, but began to assume some importance from the 1970s onward.

Patel readily admits that European integration contributed to European reconciliation, but its contribution to what John Lewis Gaddis has called the 'Long Peace' between East and West was significant only during the 1970s and 1980s, and was overshadowed by the contribution of European integration to social peace within the member countries, notably through the much-maligned Common Agricultural Policy. The time frame of Patel's analysis ends with the Treaty of Maastricht in the early 1990s, but he notes that the issue of international peace, which seemed to have faded away with the end of the Cold War, is once again confronting Europeans 'with shocking urgency' (p. 273).

The author also finds it remarkably difficult to establish the contribution made by European integration to Europe's decades of growth and prosperity during *Les Trente Glorieuses* from 1945 to 1975. After sifting through the evidence, he concludes that this contribution was 'rather modest … at well below half of one percent of additional GDP growth per annum' (p. 112), but this again became more significant during the 1970s and 1980s, when European integration first ensured a modicum of economic stability during the crisis years of the 1970s and then facilitated the recovery during the 1980s.

Nor is the record of European integration in terms of democracy promotion and human rights quite as unblemished as the conventional narrative would have it, as Patel shows. The 'consolidation and protection of civil and human rights and democracy in the European Community proceeded in fits and starts', he writes (p. 171), moving in lockstep with broader advances in democracy and human rights in world affairs, rather than displaying any obvious European leadership. Moreover, it took a long time for European integration to focus on democracy and human rights *within* its member countries, an issue that has recently garnered much attention with signs of illiberal, authoritarian tendencies in Hungary, Poland and other member states. This is perhaps not all that surprising, given that integration traditionally has been a technocratic elite project that 'remained a blank on the radar of political attention and projection for most citizens' (p. 145). Yet integration's remarkable resilience and steady advances enabled the European Community from the 1980s onward to 'quasi-monopolize' European cooperation (p. 272), whereas, for a long time after its foundation in the early 1950s, it had been no more than one among several institutional frameworks for such cooperation. Progress on integration has, however, been a mixed blessing: while it has elevated the importance of the EU, the fact that the Union is now influential in truly important matters has also, in the author's view, made it vulnerable.

Patel concludes that a confluence of upheavals is threatening to overwhelm the 'inertia of established institutions, the diverse interests contained within them, and the general momentum of the integration process', and thus spell 'the end of the [European] project' (p. 273). His incisive study has lost nothing of its relevance since its original publication and deserves a wide readership.

Copyright © 2021 The International Institute for Strategic Studies

Closing Argument

Domestic Politics and the Global Balance

Erik Jones

I

When two Democratic senators can hold the Biden administration hostage, it is easy to start thinking about American decline. But the reality is that Joe Biden's is not the first American administration to find itself dependent upon the political whims of a small number of legislators, and it is not the only government to suffer from this kind of dysfunction.[1] We are not witnessing the birth of a new international system, at least not in any organised, purposive sense. Instead, we are seeing how the breakdown in domestic politics leads to world disorder. The more political leaders are forced to focus on reconciling domestic divisions, the more they tend to turn away from or even reject the multilateral relationships and institutions that give structure to global politics. The results of this shift are bad for policymaking both at home and abroad.

Governments obtain three main benefits from working across national boundaries. Firstly, they learn more about what each government is doing domestically and how the effects of national policies spill over from one country into the next. Such information makes it easier for governments to coordinate with one another to make their policies more effective.[2] Consider climate change. Every government will need to reduce carbon emissions for

Erik Jones is Director of the Robert Schuman Centre for Advanced Studies at the European University Institute in Florence and a Contributing Editor to *Survival*.

Survival | vol. 63 no. 6 | December 2021–January 2022 | pp. 243–252 https://doi.org/10.1080/00396338.2021.2006474

international efforts to succeed. If some governments cut back on the production of greenhouse gases but others increase it, all will suffer.[3]

Secondly, a multilateral system promotes common values, regulations and standards. The protection of human rights is possible only when there is a consensus about what those rights are and what it means to safeguard them. Recognition of this kind emerges through dialogue that includes not only governments but also non-state actors such as churches, advocacy groups and communities.[4] The development of common regulations for protecting workers, consumers and the environment likewise requires the involvement of trade unions, firms, employers' associations and non-governmental organisations.[5] Agreement on common standards makes trade more efficient, creating new opportunities for entrepreneurship and expanding access to the global economy.

Thirdly, multilateralism lends legitimacy to joint action, enabling governments and communities to respond to injustice or tragedy collectively rather than individually or through ad hoc coalitions. The heroic work done by the United Nations High Commissioner for Refugees in aiding refugees and displaced persons is a good example.[6] No one country or group of countries in isolation can effectively combat problems such as human trafficking, protecting endangered species, preventing deforestation or removing plastic from the sea.

These advantages of multilateralism are in many ways self-evident. Individuals form communities for the same reasons. No person and no state is truly self-sufficient. But there are daunting hurdles involved in facilitating multilateral cooperation at the global level, and not only in the form of expensive buildings to construct, large bureaucracies to maintain or an abundance of meetings to attend. They derive from the fact that states are not individuals, governments do not have single identities or coherent personalities, and nations are not really 'actors' with recognisable 'national interests' as clinically portrayed in theoretical models of the nation-state.

The messier reality is that dealing with state governments means dealing with their domestic politics. It is in that space that the reconciliation of competing interests within society occurs. Such reconciliation is never permanent; it is always a work in progress.

As a result, governments change, and their commitments to international agreements – in terms of coordination, values, regulations, standards and joint activity – change as well.[7]

The huge costs involved in multilateral cooperation arise from the need for governments to enforce agreements at the international level and to accept the constraints implied by such enforcement at home. The operation of the European Union illuminates the problem.[8]

Consider what happened when Italy adopted the euro as a shared currency with other EU member states. That decision emerged from a centre-left government that believed in the coordination of national fiscal policies, embraced a shared European understanding of the value of price stability, accepted common rules and standards for managing government accounts and governing the financial system, and agreed that monetary policy should be decided jointly within the Governing Council of the European Central Bank (ECB). For that government, participating in the euro was an expression of Italy's commitment to multilateralism and its appreciation of its advantages.

Successive centre-right governments, however, have questioned whether the costs of that commitment are worth the benefits. They have complained about the impact that replacing the lira with the euro had on prices across the country, worried about what would happen to Italian manufacturing if Italy could not depreciate its currency against that of major trading partners, and challenged the merits of yielding control over monetary policy to a central bank that was not focused on the needs of the Italian economy.

Italy's European partners fretted about the costs of sharing the euro with Italy as well. They challenged successive Italian governments to do more to pay down the national debt and to shore up the stability of the banking system. They refused to accept the risks of having the ECB purchase large volumes of Italian sovereign debt, compelling the Bank of Italy to assume those risks. And they demanded that Italy do more to improve the competitiveness of Italian manufacturing for fear that otherwise some future Italian government could try to abandon the euro as a common currency, creating turmoil in European financial markets.

Domestic populations throughout Europe have questioned the value of national commitments to the EU. Participation in the EU as a multilateral arrangement can impose high costs on individual member states. Tensions between national governments and Brussels have arisen over labour mobility and migration in Denmark, judicial reform in Poland, press freedom in Hungary, corporate taxation in Ireland and fiscal policy in Germany.

The point here is not to exaggerate the fragility of Europe. Most governments have muddled through and sustained their commitment to multilateralism. The British decision to leave the EU, however, reveals that that commitment cannot be taken for granted. It also underscores the fact that even like-minded governments can end multilateral relationships when they face powerful domestic forces.[9]

II

The Atlantic community is another manifestation of multilateralism, with the United States and Canada on one side and a host of European countries on the other. Some of these countries are in NATO; some are in the EU; all have committed to working together to promote peace and security, foster trade and investment, stimulate research and innovation, and tackle global problems associated with development, human rights and climate change. This community is strong because the two sides of the Atlantic share common values and have a long history of working together. They also share bonds of kinship that trace back to successive waves of migration, usually from Europe to North America but also movements – in much smaller numbers – in the other direction.

Despite what they have in common, however, the transatlantic relationship has become increasingly complicated. Tensions that built both during and after the Cold War were not limited to American military intervention. Many European governments supported US president George H.W. Bush when the United States liberated Kuwait in 1991, and even more supported Bill Clinton when his administration forced the Bosnian Serbs to the negotiating table at Dayton in 1995 and bombed Serbia to liberate Kosovo four years later. Most of the tensions have been over trade negotiations, capital-market liberalisation and the rise of global finance, and they have increased since the start of the twenty-first century. The last successful multilateral trade talks were held in the 1990s, an effort to promote another round having failed in the early 2000s.

Trade talks have continued on a bilateral basis, but due to their limited scope they have not significantly alleviated disputes. When the Americans and the Europeans tried to form a transatlantic trade and investment partnership during the Obama administration, they started with clear goals to promote growth and employment. They also identified areas in which they could find relatively easy agreement. What they did not expect, however, was how little patience people in the United States and many European countries would have with complex, secret bargains. Trade negotiators might protest that such deals are the bread and butter of any multilateral negotiation. Nevertheless, domestic groups in Europe started to worry that their representatives might give away something worth keeping.

Specifically, Europeans questioned whether negotiations with the United States might result in less protection of workers' rights, greater degradation of the environment or fewer safeguards on the quality of food. Importantly, these threats did not have to materialise for people to mobilise against an agreement. The mere possibility that something bad could happen that was beyond national control and oversight was enough.[10] As a result, while the Europeans and Americans came close to an agreement, neither side believed that domestic legislatures on either side of the Atlantic would ratify any accord. What started with a transatlantic bang ended in a whimper.

Popular outbursts over transatlantic trade negotiations did not prevent the Atlantic community from consolidating its position as the world's wealthiest and most integrated advanced industrial economy. But they did help foreclose crucial avenues of cooperation on macroeconomic policy and the regulation of financial institutions in the early 2000s, even before talk of a transatlantic trade and investment partnership. Thus, when American real-estate markets collapsed, the shock waves spread quickly across the Atlantic, precipitating not just a global economic and financial crisis but also a European sovereign-debt crisis.[11]

European and American differences over foreign and security policy certainly destabilised the economic partnership. The first major rift came soon after the United States invaded Afghanistan, when it became obvious that George W. Bush was preparing to attack Iraq.[12] Serious geopolitical disruptions ensued. The Iraq War created turmoil across the Middle East. Despite the advantages of the NATO Alliance, many Europeans began to worry that their close association with the United States impeded their unavoidable dealings with Russia, constrained their economic opportunities with China and put them at greater risk for transnational terrorism.

Again, it is worth stressing that the United States and Europe did not come into conflict. The transatlantic partnership has remained a cornerstone of global engagement for both sides of the Atlantic. Nevertheless, the multilateral effectiveness of the transatlantic relationship clearly diminished. Neither side proved able to coordinate policies across national boundaries as well as expected; they failed to establish robust shared regulations and standards; and they did not act jointly on issues of common significance. Moreover, other actors exploited their lack of coordination, as reflected in Russia's invasion of Georgia in 2008 and its annexation of Crimea in 2014. China was also able to successfully promote the Asian Infrastructure Investment Bank against the wishes of the Obama administration, and its Belt and Road Initiative has to an extent divided the EU.

In light of transatlantic weakness, successive US administrations have also behaved more unilaterally. They have taken advantage of the United States' unique digital capabilities to eavesdrop on sensitive communications.[13] They have exploited the US dollar's dominance in world commerce to enforce economic sanctions on trade between third countries. Henry Farrell and Abraham Newman call this the 'weaponization of interdependence'.[14] While Europe and North America depend upon each other for their prosperity, the United States uses that dependence to force Europeans to cooperate with American foreign policy.

An especially good illustration of this practice was the US decision to exclude Iran from the SWIFT financial-communications network in

2012.[15] SWIFT is a European company headquartered in Belgium, but it is owned by banks located across the globe, including in the United States. The Obama administration threatened to sanction American bankers who sat on SWIFT's board if that company did not stop providing services to Iranian banks. Eventually, European governments (including the European Parliament) acquiesced. Without access to interbank messaging, the Iranian financial system could not participate in the world economy. This was a major reason that Iran agreed to the Joint Comprehensive Plan of Action (JCPOA), which was intended to reintegrate Iran into the world economy in exchange for its agreement not to develop nuclear weapons.

While the Obama administration's leveraging of transatlantic interdependence was thus effective, the Trump administration used the same tactic to force the Europeans to stop doing business with Iran and undermine the JCPOA. The implications were not lost on America's European allies. SWIFT is an important multilateral forum through which banks work together to create standards for secure financial communication. Yet the United States' manipulation of the institution to pressure Iran has generated fears that Washington could also use it to undermine European interests. The same is true for the internet, where Europeans do not want to lose control over private information, and for financial markets, which Europeans worry could be destabilised. These concerns have prompted the European Commission to emphasise the importance of 'European sovereignty' in areas such as information and communications technology, and 'strategic autonomy' with respect to digital commerce.[16]

While the weaponisation of interdependence has not turned Europe and the United States into adversaries, it has reduced the attractiveness of transatlantic collaboration. The lesson is that multilateralism has advantages but creates vulnerabilities. That lesson comes on top of pre-existing scepticism about multilateral trade negotiations. The result is less transatlantic cooperation and order.

III

The tensions within the transatlantic partnership should not be overstated. The West may be less cohesive than it was in the past, but it is still united. The difference now is that adversaries like Russia and China are more assertive. They have less interest in promoting multilateralism at the global level than in carving out more freedom of manoeuvre for their national governments. They, particularly China, also have substantial resources they can bring to bear on great-power competition. In using these resources, they make it more urgent for Europeans and Americans to work together. Their cohesiveness is diminishing when it has never been more important.

Multilateral distortions are having a greater impact on the global balance of power than any early foreign-policy blunders by the Biden administration. They are also more significant than Europe's failure to assert itself as a unified actor in foreign affairs. A more steady-handed US administration would obviously be welcome, as would a more cohesive EU. Given domestic politics on both sides of the Atlantic, however, it is more reasonable to expect continued inconsistency in American governance and ongoing differences among EU member states.[17]

The challenge for leaders on both sides of the Atlantic is to rebuild their commitments to multilateralism. Meeting that challenge depends critically on their being able to build strong domestic constituencies to support constructive external engagement, even when that means making concessions in terms of domestic policy. The prospects are genuine if limited. The Biden administration's domestic agenda is pointing in that direction, as is the EU recovery and resilience programme known as 'Next Generation EU'. If these projects are moderately successful, they could do more than just invigorate domestic economic performance and ameliorate the deep divisions in American and European societies. They could also help reduce concerns among political leaders on both sides of the Atlantic that international engagement will come at too high a price.

It would be too much to expect the degree of deference to elites that prevailed after the Second World War, when today's international system was created, to arise now. But it is plausible to hope for domestic politics that are focused less tightly on the parochial interests of specific constituencies and more broadly on the national interest in world order.

Notes

1   See Erik Jones and Matthias Matthijs, 'Democracy Without Solidarity: Political Dysfunction in Hard Times', *Government and Opposition*, vol. 52, no. 2, April 2017, pp. 185–210.

2   The classic reference is Richard N. Cooper, *The Economics of Interdependence: Economic Policy in the Atlantic Community* (New York: Columbia University Press, 1968). Cooper wrote the book to explain the advantages of multilateralism to the American foreign-policy establishment.

3   See Anatol Lieven, 'Climate Change and the State: A Case for Environmental Realism', *Survival*, vol. 62, no. 2, April–May 2020, pp. 7–26.

4   See Daniel C. Thomas, *The Helsinki Effect: International Norms, Human Rights, and the Demise of Communism* (Princeton, NJ: Princeton University Press, 2001).

5   This is an area where the EU has exercised substantial influence. See, for example, Walter Mattli and Tim Büthe, 'Global Private Governance: Lessons from a National Model of Setting Standards in Accounting', *Law and Contemporary Problems*, vol. 68, no. 4, Summer 2005, pp. 225–62.

6   See Alexander Betts, Gil Loescher and James Milner (eds), *The United Nations High Commissioner for Refugees (UNHCR): The Politics and Practice of Refugee Protection*, 2nd edition (Abingdon: Routledge, 2011).

7   This dynamic helps explain why even governments that can afford to 'go it alone' will make concessions to bring more reticent governments into multilateral arrangements. See Lloyd Gruber, *Ruling the World: Power Politics and the Rise of Supranational Institutions* (Princeton, NJ: Princeton University Press, 2000).

8   The illustration here focuses on Europe, but applies elsewhere too. See Erik Jones, 'Idiosyncrasy and Integration: Suggestions from Comparative Political Economy', *Journal of European Public Policy*, vol. 10, no. 1, February 2003, pp. 140–58.

9   See Erik Jones, 'Four Things We Should Learn from Brexit', *Survival*, vol. 60, no. 6, December 2018–January 2019, pp. 35–44.

10 See Alasdair R. Young, *The New Politics of Trade: Lessons from TTIP* (London: Agenda Publishing, 2017).

11 See Adam Tooze, *Crashed: How a Decade of Financial Crises Changed the World* (New York: Viking, 2018).

12 See Philip H. Gordon and Jeremy Shapiro, *Allies at War: America, Europe and the Crisis over Iraq* (New York: McGraw Hill, 2004).

13 See Marieke de Goede, 'The SWIFT Affair and the Global Politics of European Security', *Journal of Common Market Studies*, vol. 50, no. 2, March 2012, pp. 214–30.

14 Henry Farrell and Abraham L. Newman, 'Weaponized Interdependence: How Global Economic Networks Shape State Coercion', *International Security*, vol. 44, no. 1, Summer 2019, pp. 42–79.

15 See Erik Jones and Andrew Whitworth, 'The Unintended Consequences of European Sanctions on Russia', *Survival*, vol. 56, no. 5,

October–November 2014, pp. 21–30.

16 See 'State of the Union Address
    by President von der Leyen at the
    European Parliament Plenary',
    European Commission, 16
    September 2020, https://ec.europa.eu/
    commission/presscorner/detail/en/

SPEECH_20_1655.

17 See Erik Jones, 'The US and the EU:
    Game Over?', in Mario Del Pero
    and Paolo Magri (eds), *Four Years of
    Trump: The US and the World* (Milan:
    Ledizione LediPublishing for ISPI,
    2020), pp. 161–79.

Copyright © 2021 The International Institute for Strategic Studies